MODERN LITTLE
MAHABHARAT

MODERN LITTLE MAHABHARAT

The GR8 Battle of National Election
and Politics of INDIA--before
and after May 26, 2014

Ashok K. Sinha

To order additional copies of this book, contact:
Xlibris
1-888-795-4274
www.Xlibris.com
Orders@Xlibris.com
549524

Books By Ashok Sinha

THE SUBLIME JOY OF THE GEETANJALIC PSALMODY (Translation of poems from the Collection "Geetanjali" by Nobel Laureate, Rabindra Nath Tagore)

THE NEXT LIFE (a Novel with glimpses of ancient and the present-day India)

REINCARNATION OF THE IRON-MAN (Socio-Political Fiction, with Pen-name: Ahnis Kosha)

A BIRD'S EYE-VIEW OF THE SANATAN DHARMA (Hinduism) (with Dr. Shardanand)

MODERN VIEWS AND MUSE ON HINDUISM (Editorials and Short Essays)

GLIMPSE OF SCRIPTURES OF RELIGIONS OF INDIAN ORIGIN: HINDUISM, BUDDHISM, JAINISM, SIKHISM

GLIMPSES OF THE SCRIPTURES OF MAJOR WORLD-RELIGIONS

THE HINDU AWAKENING (with Dr. Shardanand)

MODERN LITTLE MAHABHARAT (A Collection of over 1600 Verse-TWEETS

Mostly on Modern-day Indian Politics)

[Please visit https://www.twitter.com/aksinh]

IN HINDI

THE BHAGVAD-GEETA (Verse Translation of the Great Sanskrit Scripture)

PUNYADHANWA (Poetical Work Based on the Life of EKALAVYA, an Immortal Character of the Mahabharat)

BULBULON KE DARPAN ME (Collection of Poems)

INDRADHANUSH (Collection of Short Stories and One-Act Plays)

OMAR KHAYYAM KI RUBAIYAN (Translation of the 75 Well-Known Rubaya'ts of Omar Khayyam, in Hindi Rubaya'ts Format and Verse-Structure)

OMAR KHAYYAM KI NAI RUBAIYAN (Translation of the over 500 Lesser-Known Rubaya'ts of Omar Khayyam, in Hindi Rubaya'ts Format and Verse-Structure)

Also visit: www.ashoksinha.org for other works and details.

Introduction

About 5000 years ago (3000 BC), in India, there was a colossal war called the "MAHABHARAT" (Literally, the Great Indian War) in which all the kings of various kingdoms of India became involved on the side of one or the other warring parties. The root-cause of the Mahabharat War was disharmony between two royal families in the kingdom of Hastinapur (the present-day Delhi): the Kauravas with 100 brothers and the Pandavas with 5 brothers. The eldest Kaurava brother, Duryodhan, was most arrogant, selfish, tyrannical and unjust; while their cousins, the Pandavas -- Yudhisthir, Bheem, Arjun, Nakul, and Sahdev -- were truthful, humble, and peace-loving. Duryodhan wanted the entire kingdom of Hastinapur for himself, refusing to let the Pandavas have even 5 villages.Many attempts were made to persuade him to be at peace with the Pandavas, including Krishna -- a friend, philosopher, and guide for the Pandavas -- Himself carrying message for peace and harmonious coexistence, but all in vain.

Eventually the war broke out that lasted for 18 days, culminating in a crushing defeat and annihilation of the Kauravas as well as most of the kings of the day, and victory of the Pandavas.The battlefield, called Kurukshetra, is said to be soaked with blood to unfathomable depth.

The story of the Mahabharat War was written in Sanskrit by the great sage-poet "Vedvyas", the greatest epic in the world with 100,000 shlokas (verses). A portion consisting of 700 shlokas and containing a philosophical discourse given by Krishna to Arjuna in Kurukshetra just before the start of the war, became known as "Bhagvad-Geeta" (literally, the

Song of God), and forms an important part of the vast Hindu scriptures, revered by Hindus all over the world, and praised even by Western scholars and intellectuals for being a gist of universal guideposts for meaningful human living irrespective of faith and creed -- through adoption of one or more of the Paths of Knowledge (Jnan-Yoga), of Selfless Action or Duty (Karma-Yoga), or of Pure Devotion (Bhakti-Yoga). Yoga essentially means an identification of the Self (Aatma or Soul, Individual Consciousness) with the Supreme Being or the Ultimate Reality (Parmaatma or Supersoul, Universal Consciousness, God).

India is a country of a long history (10,000 years or more), cultural and literary traditions, and greatest diversity. Now, under the inspiration and initiative taken by the present Prime Minister, **Na**rendra **Mo**di, who is himself a great social media champion, there is a revolution sweeping the country: "Digital India." A desire on my part to chronicle some of the important political events and related personalities of India just prior, during, and after the democratic election of PM Modi (often also referred as NaMo) in May 2014, the leading opponents being the Congress Party (led by Ms Sonia Gandhi) and AAP (led by Arvind Kejriwal), among others, has led me to Tweet, off and on, mostly in the format of a loose verse of 4 lines and 140 maximum characters allowable. There are a small number of such verse-tweets commenting on some of the important world events -- NASA's milestone achievements, Pakistan's (ISI) and ISIS terror attacks, and so on. While these tweets already have made a place in the social media panorama, I thought it useful to collect these in book-form for interested readers to read about the sequence of events and snap-shots of people. In a sense, it is a new, small-scale Mahabharat, but referring to modern India, and expressed digitally.

So here it is, the "MODERN LITTLE MAHABHARAT," for your reading pleasure and for the posterity in this digital age.

Tweets of Ashok Sinha

Tweets sorted in reverse chronological order

{Chronicling Significant Political Events of India
before, during, and after the
National Election of 2014}

[Glimpses and Chronicles of a Brief Political History
of India for the Specified Period,
with Unabashed Bias and Personal Opinion]

Note:

A few Verses in Hindi Script
Written Well before the Election in 2014
Are Given at the Beginning of the Actual Tweets (in English)
Collected in this Book

🏠 Home	⚡ Moments	📢 Notifications	✉ Messages	🐦

Search Twitter 🔍

Ashok Sinha
@aksinh

@NaMo @arunjaitley @SushmaSwarajbjp
@RaviShankarBJP @M_Lekhi
@PrakashJavdekar @ShahnawazBJP
@naqvimukhtar-Pls.seeLink

6:37 AM - 3 Mar 2014

↩	🔁	📊	•••

Tweets of Mr. Ashok Sinha

Tweets sorted in reverse chronological order

❖ ('2009-10-14 15:02:14',
Celebrate Diwali on Oct 17'09; then to the FermiLab
(near Chicago, IL) for the weekend of 18-20 Oct (LINAC
Workshop)")

❖ ('2009-10-14 15:02:14',
Celebrate Diwali on Oct 17'09; then to the FermiLab
(near Chicago, IL) for the weekend of 18-20 Oct (LINAC
Workshop)")

❖ ('2009-10-14 15:04:56',
To submit Patent Applications for Forest Fire Control
and Optimal Antenna this week. Also sending 4 books
for publication.')

❖ ('2009-10-14 15:06:37',
Four books to go: Kurukshetra, Chandragupta,
Shakuntala, Geetanjali ready to be sent to publishers.')

❖ ('2009-10-14 15:08:08',
Must find a Literary Agent and also a Patent
Commercialization outfit. Need HELP to get things done
in time.')

❖ ('2009-10-14 15:10:40',
INVITING ALL TO JOINN GEETA, InC : see website www.
GeetaSinhaPhysicsEtAl.org (under development)')

❖ ('2009-10-14 15:12:58',
Correction re joining GEETA, InC (www.
GeetaSinhaPhysicsEtAl.org) - No fee to join for next 5
years. Circulate info.')

❖ ('2010-08-16 23:49:12',
A Meetup was scheduled for The Ann Arbor Poetry
Group. http://meetup.com/u/Cpx')

❖ ('2010-08-17 00:01:34',
I joined Freedom From Religion Foundation of
Washtenaw County on Meetup http://meetup.com/u/
BJg')

❖ ('2012-06-28 17:28:04',
World awaits latest in hunt for Higgs particle - Yahoo!
News http://t.co/Sodhaygd via @YahooNews')

❖ ('2012-06-28 17:38:54',
Twitter / Twitter buttons https://t.co/keHErb4r via
@aksinh Refer to Physics Link in website: http://t.
co/9LNywjwu for more.')

❖ ('2012-06-28 17:47:47',
Twitter / Twitter buttons https://t.co/
keHErb4r via @aksinh I proposed model:
UnifiedTheoryofElementaryParticlesandInetractions
(UTOEPI)2006')

❖ ('2012-07-17 17:20:53',
@PrabhuChawla Would like to send my new novel "THE
NEXT LIFE" on current political scene in India, with
your approval, & get your critique.')

❖ ('2013-06-18 13:13:11',
Airborne laser reveals city under Cambodian earth
- Yahoo! News http://t.co/1UXpJwTKYT via @
YahooNews')

❖ ('2013-09-23 21:07:02',
APS Physics | GSNP | Topical Group on Statistical & Nonlinear Physics http://t.co/26HPwuggL7')

❖ ('2013-09-30 04:00:31',
I've just updated my professional profile on LinkedIn. Connect with me and view my profile. http://t.co/WqThspRLXW #in")

❖ ('2013-11-11 13:51:55',
Enter to Win Shell V-Power\xae Premium Fuel for a Year for me and 5 Friends! If I win you might be one of my 5. http://t.co/wpkqMBapMy')

❖ ('2013-11-15 13:29:47',
@aksinh @PrabhuChawla')

❖ ('2013-11-15 13:40:17',
@PrabhuChawla Just noticed this Tweet. I'd be most interested in having my book "THE NEXT LIFE" critiqued and publicized by the media.Let's')

❖ ('2013-11-15 13:47:09',
@PrabhuChawla My book"NewDimensions inParticlePhysics andCosmology (2nd Ed.)" is just out --its simple model predicts 3 HiggsBosons,2CERN')

❖ ('2013-11-15 13:51:33',
@PrabhuChawla Must follow Tweets by A.NAMODIT- Great commentary on 2014 Election speeches by various 'Leaders'--send to BJP Leaders & media")

❖ ('2013-11-16 09:57:48',
Raj Babbar: "Modi is making Indian Capitalists or Public Rahul G.'s \'MAMA\'\'\'; while Modi meant Rahul\'s real MAMA (mothr's brother) in Italy.')

❖ ('2013-11-16 10:05:43',
One 'Khooni Panja' suffocates an innocent person's throat, while Sonia's Hand symbol has cruelly suffocated millions of Indians for 9 years.")

❖ ('2013-11-16 10:22:27',
S.Gandhi:"Some in BJP are DAY-DREAMING of Kursi."
How dare they even think of it? Congress KNOWS only
the Shahzada OWNS it when she retires.')

❖ ('2013-11-17 00:14:42',
@arorapulkit1 @devanghvyas @SushmaSwarajbjp We
thought he was a Sinh; but he turned out to be biggest
'Geedar' rubber-stamp PM of India.")

❖ ('2013-11-17 00:15:07',
RT @arorapulkit1: What a shameless liar Manmohan
Singh is. @SushmaSwarajbjp exposed him well...
http://t.co/54gzpa3mct')

❖ ('2013-11-17 00:17:03',
RT @cool_man85: manmohan singh \u092f\u0947 \
u091c\u0928\u0924\u093e \u0915\u094b \u0924\
u092f \u0915\u0930\u0928\u093e \u0939\u0948 \
u0915\u093f \u092a\u093f\u091b\u0932\u0947 9 \
u0935\u0930\u094d\u0937\u094b\u0902 \u092e\
u0947\u0902 \u0924\u0930\u0915\u094d\u0915\
u0940 \u0915\u0930\u092a\u094d\u0936\u0928 \
u092e\u0947\u0902 \u0939\u0941\u0908 \u0939\
u0948 \u092f\u093e \u0921\u0935\u0932\u0947\
u092a\u092e\u0947\u0902\u091f \u092e\u0947\
u0902,\u0915\u094d\u092f\u094b\u0902\u0915\
u093f.\u092f\u0947 \u091c\u094b \u092a\u092c\
u094d\u0932\u093f\u0915 \u0939\u2026')

❖ ('2013-11-17 00:23:51',
@timesnow @devanghvyas For reality check on many
of the Congress and anti-Modi speeches, follow Tweets
by @ANAMODIT. Let's campaign 4 MODI.")

❖ ('2013-11-17 00:28:52',
@PrakashJavdekar @devanghvyas Now NitishKumar
says MODI's Hunkaar ralley was successful because of
the Patna serial bomb-blasts.Shame!Shame!")

❖ ('2013-11-17 00:33:44',
@PrakashJavdekar @devanghvyas 4 great Tweets,
follow @ANAMODIT. That is A+NAMO+ MODI+IT--The
Tweets should be seen by SONIA+Rahul bunch too.')

❖ ('2013-11-17 00:46:08',
@Oneindia @devanghvyas @ANAMODIT Actually,
Congress has imported pure Fascism from ITALY
through you know who! India needs to throw this out')

❖ ('2013-11-17 00:49:21',
@Inquisitive_Ind @Oneindia Could it be that SG is, in
fact, a Fascist agent from Italy, trying to dominate or
virtually colonize India.')

❖ ('2013-11-17 00:57:27',
@devanghvyas @ANAMODIT @timesnow @
PrakashJavdekar And we thought NKumar was a
Development guy come to get Bihar out of Lal s clutches !")

❖ ('2013-11-17 01:05:45',
@arvind_joshi @MrsGandhi @narendramodi @
ANAMODIT Md Gori & Jayachand have happened to
India time and again, and this time it is SG & NK.')

❖ ('2013-11-17 01:08:20',
@arvind_joshi @MrsGandhi @narendramodi @
ANAMODIT Just like Guru GovindSingh and Shivaji,
today we have Narendra Modi to save the country !')

❖ ('2013-11-29 02:08:42',
KapilSibal proves the proverb 'CHOR KI DADHI ME
TINAKA' by his reaction to Sushma Swaraj's Tweet.
What newspaper does he read about Gujarat?")

❖ ('2013-11-29 02:12:08',
RahulGandhi and KapilSibal appear to be confused
about which Government ruled which State; and with
what track-record of development there.')

❖ ('2013-11-29 02:16:38',
The outrage in the media and in public against
TarunTejpal well sums up India's gradual coming of age
on attitude towards women, rape, sex.")

❖ ('2013-11-29 02:21:39',
The hypocrisy and fearful mention of TarunTejpal--as
Tehelka's Editor vs. a common criminal of rape--speaks
volumes about his true color.")

❖ ('2013-11-29 02:29:45',
The dirty hand of Congress at the bottom of Tehelka
now exposed by TarunTejpal-the-Terrible's scared face;
his wish to move Court(Goa2Delhi)")

❖ ('2013-11-29 02:33:20',
The cartoonist on NDTV doing the 'SoSSSorry' deserves
a gold medal for his/her good grasp of the ground-
realities with imagination's hands.")

❖ ('2013-11-29 02:45:49',
@narendramodi @YashwantSinha @SushmaSwarajbjp
@M_Lekhi @ndtv @justicearnab @timesnow @
prbhhuchawla @amitabh_bigb @IndiaToday @
timesofindia *')

❖ ('2013-11-29 02:46:59',
RT @ANAMODIT: Diggy Singh: "BJP-\'Muh me Ram,
bagal me chhuri\' " Wrong! But Diggy really has \'Muh
me Chhuri, bagal me Kursi; and sir pe Talw\u2026')

❖ ('2013-11-29 02:51:06',
@narendramodi @YashwantSinha @SushmaSwarajbjp
@M_Lekhi @ndtv @justicearnab @timesnow @
prbhhuchawla @amitabh_bigb @IndiaToday @
timesofindia')

❖ ('2013-12-02 19:09:59',
@Swamy39 Your heroic effort to oust corruption and to save the country and its majority would be proudly recorded in the history of India.')

❖ ('2013-12-02 19:16:43',
@Swamy39 The mountain-size questions of lack of progress in J&K (Art 370), Scams, corruption stand, now this EVM hacking...where's freedom!")

❖ ('2013-12-02 19:17:00',
RT @Swamy39: My friends in high places have informed me that TDK and Buddhu have set up a Rs. 5000 crore fund for hacking EVMs.I will appro\u2026')

❖ ('2013-12-13 11:00:42',
I've just updated my professional profile on LinkedIn. Connect with me and view my profile. http://t.co/VjjxVICD2Z #in")

❖ ('2013-12-30 09:45:40',
http://t.co/sDXIEPqbUs http://t.co/URYcV0yfUH')

❖ ('2013-12-30 16:35:22',
Pa. man lands 'corrected' 1918 stamps http://t.co/mv9yFxjf3D via @YahooNews')

❖ ('2013-12-30 19:08:20',
http://t.co/PG8gvrOHG6 http://t.co/PG8gvrOHG6')

❖ ('2013-12-31 20:08:52',
10 things not to buy in 2014 http://t.co/lE8ZaWGgKq via @YahooFinance')

❖ ('2014-01-13 15:50:05',
@jbsaran Hello Janki, Happy New Year! Good to know about http://t.co/dUWqV71Syg on Android for free phone calls and messages; I'd try it,too")

❖ ('2014-01-13 15:51:09',
Out of Jayanthi\u2019s office, house, over 350 files,
a couple from 2011 | The Indian Express http://t.
co/9WiVKs46PY via @sharethis')

❖ ('2014-01-13 16:18:32',
CONGRESS is the new AURANGZEB. He had ZAZIA TAX;
now we have JAYANTHI TAX. There may be also hidden
SONIA TAX & RAHUL TAX, one may guess!')

❖ ('2014-01-13 16:20:33',
Out of Jayanthi\u2019s office, house, over 350 files,
a couple from 2011 | The Indian Express http://t.co/
OV6jyL8yrY via @sharethis')

❖ ('2014-01-14 09:52:43',
@narendramodi"Kadam badhaye ja, na dar; Kadam
badhaye ja/ Panv-tale tere jamin jag pe chhaye ja,
Kadam badhaye ja."-All Eyes of India on U.')

❖ ('2014-01-14 09:57:26',
@narendramodi U R "REINCARNATION OF THE IRON-
MAN". A novel with this title has been just published
from UK. Can I send copy 2 U and others?')

❖ ('2014-01-14 10:01:53',
@narendramodi Piece of iron from
villagers&farmers is symbolic like the "ROTI
& KAMAL" of 1857 Revolution. Yours is equally
historic 4 UNITY')

❖ ('2014-01-14 10:09:12',
@narendramodi @JhaSanjay @M-@M_lekhi SanjayJha,
Learn 2 keep Ur mouth shut and ears open--it'd do U
good. But now it is too late 4 U anyway.")

❖ ('2014-01-14 10:13:39',
@narendramodi @JhaSanjay @justicearnab Rahul G.is
too immature to step out of 10 Janpath. He should go 2
school 2 learn politics/governance.')

❖ ('2014-01-14 10:17:55',
@ArvindKejriwal @AapYogendra AAP may b OK 4
JANLOKPAL; but U R acting like JAYACHAND against
NaMo, the only RIGHT CHOICE 2 save INDIA 2DAY..')

❖ ('2014-01-14 10:25:44',
@thekiranbedi @ArvindKejriwal @justicearnab
KBedi, U R like CHAND-BARDAI to NaMo; AAP is like
JAYACHAND 4 NaMo. History'll remember U both")

❖ ('2014-01-14 10:32:29',
@narendramodi @ArvindKejriwal @justicearnab Some
say,'NaMo/BJP is rattled by AAP.' A lion is never rattled
by a fox. May God save India.")

❖ ('2014-01-14 10:47:14',
@ArvindKejriwal @justicearnab @thekiranbedi India
has 2 choose: governance from atop a BUILDING or a
CAR vs.by NaMo's Gr8 'Statue of Unity.'")

❖ ('2014-01-14 10:50:42',
@narendramodi @ArvindKejriwal @justicearnab All
truly patriotic Indians (+ NRIs) R with NaMo 2day --
there is NO OTHER CHOICE 2 SAVE INDIA.')

❖ ('2014-01-14 10:57:34',
@narendramodi @justicearnab @thekiranbedi If U can,
pls.read the novel fromUK on India: "REINCARNATION
OF THE IRON-MAN"; U\'ll b glad U did.')

❖ ('2014-01-14 11:01:33',
@narendramodi @justicearnab @thekiranbedi NaMo
is the "REINCARNATION OF THE IRON-MAN"--SARDAR
PATEL. He is the ONLY HOPE 4 INDIA in MAY2014')

❖ ('2014-01-18 03:16:39',
Start 2 new Discussion Groups in Theoretical Physics:
(1) Are there more than 1 Higgs Bosons? (2) Relation
between Mass and Interaction?.')

❖ ('2014-01-18 03:20:21',
My book "NEW DIMENSIONS IN ELEM PARTICLE
PHYSICS AND COSMOLOGY" published in 2012 giving
model for Mass vs. Interaction Constant Relation.')

❖ ('2014-01-18 03:23:37',
The model in my book "NEW DIMENSIONS IN ELEM.
PARTICLE PHYSICS AND COSMOLOGY" predicts 3 Higgs
bosons (God Particles)Model proposed in 2006.')

❖ ('2014-01-18 03:27:13',
The model in my book "NEW DIMENSIONS IN ELEM.
PARTICLE PHYSICS AND COSMOLOGY" indicates that
Mass results from the four Basic Interactions.')

❖ ('2014-01-18 03:30:56',
My book "THEORY OF SATELLITE AND MOBILE
TELECOMMUNICATIONS" being published. I Invite
interest from satellite communications professionals.')

❖ ('2014-01-18 03:33:00',
My book "REINCARNATION OF THE IRON-MAN"
(Fiction-a political Novel about India) being republished
from UK -- to be available in India soon.')

❖ ('2014-01-18 03:40:15',
Politics--Rahul Gandhi's new vigor for election-
campaign is artificial. AAP is all confused. NaMo is the
only answer for India's future.")

❖ ('2014-01-20 17:42:03',
#AAPDrama Kejri\'s DHARANA NOT truly 4 Janata,
but just an ultra-rush-agenda for 2014-LOKSABHA
Election?The "Jhad may sweep-off AAP itself')

❖ ('2014-01-21 22:32:34',
#AAPDrama Irrespective of other factors (motives,
unholy marriage of Congress+AAP), AAP has made Jan
21'14 a Black Day in India's history.")

❖ ('2014-01-21 22:34:52',
#AAPDrama Many looked up to AAP and A.Kejriwal
for a better tomorrow; now they are let down and look
down upon AAP's true motive and methods")

❖ ('2014-01-22 00:05:47',
@anamodit @anamodit @narendraModi @timesnow
@thekiranbedi @rprasad @M-@M_Lekhi @BJP4India
@ndtv @ZeeNews @justicearnab @tnwtk @
rahulkanwal')

❖ ('2014-01-25 02:26:19',
RT @BJPDelhiState: Watch the beautiful speech of shri
@narendramodi on how technology helped Gujarat govt
eradicate corruption - http://t.\u2026')

❖ ('2014-01-25 02:32:28',
RT @samirvarier: What Shri Narendra Modi as PM will
deliver @swapan55 http://t.co/AroXnutDbG')

❖ ('2014-01-25 03:02:50',
RT @PathanAsmakhan: Join the movement to pay
a tribute to Sardar Vallabhbhai Patel: http://t.
co/0JTDglt9I6 @narendramodi http://t.co/QllbmO\
u2026')

❖ ('2014-01-25 03:08:45',
@PathanAsmakhan @narendramodi I\'m looking
for photos of Sardar Patel and NaMo for my book
"Reincarnation of the Iron-Man,\' Request ur help.')

❖ ('2014-01-25 03:25:29',
@yogrishiramdev @narendramodi @ndtv A world of
gr8 things'll surely happen--but only with #NaMo as
PM. BLACK-MONEY-BACK2INDIA is 1 of them.")

❖ ('2014-01-25 03:37:55',
@tajinderbagga @narendramodi Where canI get this
picture on #NaMo with 2014? I\'d like to use it in my
book "REINCARNATION OF THE IRON-MAN".')

❖ ('2014-01-25 03:40:07',
RT @tajinderbagga: This SRCC Pic of @narendramodi
giving One Message, 2014 Going to Become Election of
"YUVRAJ Vs YUVAraj" #NaMoIn2013 http\u2026')

❖ ('2014-01-25 03:43:46',
@tajinderbagga @narendramodi Could I get this
picture (&clearance) for my Novel called
"REINCARNATION OF THE IRON-MAN"(2be published
in UK).')

❖ ('2014-01-25 03:56:05',
@IndiaToday #NaMo272+ Would U believe @NaMo will
SWEEP India (#AAP may sweep Delhi-gali\'s with his
"Jhad). Read the writing on the wall.')

❖ ('2014-01-29 09:12:09',
@Via_Satellite Request that the magazine"Via
Satellite"be mailed regularly to: Ashok Sinha, 1375 Civic
Center Dr.(# 1),Santa Clara, CA 95050')

❖ ('2014-01-29 10:11:34',
Narendra Modi plans Statue of Unity, twice as high
as Statue of Liberty ~The Narendra Modi http://t.co/
BCh3Xsf5As via @TheNarendraModi')

❖ ('2014-01-29 10:21:18',
@narendramodi I humbly request your kind permission
to use the first image (with your photo) on Cover of my
Book "REINCARNATION OF IRON-MAN"')

❖ ('2014-01-29 10:43:02',
@thenarendramodi Just tweeted 2 get SriNaMo\'s kind
permission to use SardarVBPatel\'s & NaMo-FB
images in my book "ReincarnationOfTheIronMan"')

❖ ('2014-01-29 10:47:37',
@thenarendramodi Request your kind permission to
use Sardar Patel\'s and your images (from Goo.gl &
FB) on Cover of my Book "REINCARNATION...')

❖ ('2014-01-29 10:52:02',
@thenarendramodi My Socio-Political Novel
"REINCARNATION OF THE IRON-MAN" 2 b Published
from UK shortly. To get SriNaMo\'s permission 4 Cover')

❖ ('2014-02-01 06:11:42',
Signing with HARO. Sent them the draft material on
Higgs bosons and GEETA already a few days ago. Ashok
Sinha- #publicity')

❖ ('2014-02-21 05:00:11',
I'm attending Overseas Volunteer for a Better India
(OVBI) Event http://t.co/DbIcK22NAF #constantcontact
#@OverseasVBI .")

❖ ('2014-02-27 23:22:49',
@ModiTeam @ShahnawazBJP This is to request yr
permission to use the image of @Statueof_unity &
@NaMo in my novel("REINCARN.IRON-MAN")Cover')

❖ ('2014-02-27 23:30:20',
@NaMo I\'ve a Novel ("REINCARNATION OF IRON-
MAN") being published in UK. Seek yr permission to use
an image from @NaMo Google Photos on Cover')

❖ ('2014-02-27 23:41:13',
@PrakashJavdekar @NaMo Is it OK to use an image
from @NaMo Google Photos (@Statueof_unity) on
Cover-Design of my Novel ("Reincarn.IronMan")?')

❖ ('2014-02-27 23:46:08',
@ShahNawazBJP @ModiTeam @PrakashJavdekar Pls.
send yr Email addresses to aksinha1722@yahoo.com to
let me send a request to you and @NaMo4PM')

❖ ('2014-02-28 13:45:43',
aksinha1722@yahoo.comI'm attending Overseas
Volunteer for a Better India Event http://t.co/
DbIcK1LKyF #constantcontact #@OverseasVBI
-GEETA")

❖ ('2014-03-01 00:46:13',
@NaMo4PM #MISSION2014 All those who continue
blaming Modi about 2002 after CLEAN CHIT by SC
should be tried/jailed for contempt of Court.')

❖ ('2014-03-01 00:52:11',
@TheHindu Kamal Faruqui is Kamal indeed! He calls
Modi\'s speech on Bangladeshi refugees ("Send Muslims
back; shelter Hindus") Communal.')

❖ ('2014-03-01 01:06:02',
@NaMo SalmanKhurshid's sinking to a new Low; in
indecent speech & in Polls- -such Mud-slinging will
cost dearly to him and to @Congressorg.")

❖ ('2014-03-01 01:19:18',
@Congressorg ship sinking fast, after 10 years of
corrupt & incapable Govt. of @PMOIndia, @sonia .
@SALMANKHURSHID, What's yr word 4 'em?")

❖ ('2014-03-03 12:56:49',
@NaMo4PM @M_Lekhi I request yr kind permission to
use an image from yr Google/PHOTOS for COVER of my
new Novel "REINCARNATION OF IRON-MAN".')

❖ ('2014-03-03 13:31:09',
@ShahnawazBJP @M_Lekhi May I use @Statueof_unity
& @NaMo -image from Google for my novel
"REINCARNATION OF IRON-MAN"? Pls. reply to @
aksinh')

❖ ('2014-03-03 13:44:26',
@ShahnawazBJP @M_Lekhi Waiting for your reply to
use @Statueof_unity image (from Google)for my Novel
"REINCARNATION.IRON-MAN".Pls.- @aksinh')

❖ ('2014-03-03 14:01:31',
@NitishKumarJDU giving bad name to Bihar. History'll
remember his bigotry. He criticizes @NaMo: Takshshila
is in Pak because of Congress.")

❖ ('2014-03-03 14:08:31',
@laluprasadrjd @mulayamsingh @NitishKumarJDU
should go back to school (or follow @NaMo4PM)to learn
about Democracy, Secularity, Governance.')

❖ ('2014-03-03 14:14:29',
@NaMo4PM 's value-added definition for @NDA
(National Development Alliance) is inspiring, as is every
word he utters in every rally. Jai Ho!")

❖ ('2014-03-03 14:37:18',
@NaMo @arunjaitley @SushmaSwarajbjp @
RaviShankarBJP @M_Lekhi @PrakashJavdekar @
ShahnawazBJP @naqvimukhtar-Pls.seeLink http://t.co/
l4FEy060X8')

❖ ('2014-03-03 22:51:43',
@tnwtk #TorrentOfScams @ndtv @timesnow @
ZeeNews @IndiaToday @GenBakshi Pls.Consider filing
FIR,jointly,against Shinde/Anthony& @congressorg')

❖ ('2014-03-03 23:23:37',
RT @NaMo4PM: #RunForUnity Special: Is @
narendramodi the Sardar Patel of Modern India ? Join us
on G+ Hangout with @anirbanganguly http://t.\u2026')

❖ ('2014-03-04 00:24:09',
@aksinh wrote a novel 3 yrs ago,2 b republished
(2nd,UK, Ed."ReincarnationOf Iron-Man").Request Kind
Permission 2Put this pic.on Book-Cover')

❖ ('2014-03-04 00:33:15',
@NaMo4PM @narendramodi I wish to put the pic. here
4 my Novel "Reincarnation Of Iron-Man" to be published
shortly. SeekKindPermission 2DoSo.')

❖ ('2014-03-04 00:41:48',
@NaMo4PM I-@aksinh -wrote a Socio-Political Fiction-
cum-history Novel ("Reincarnation Of Iron-Man")years
ago. A new, 2nd Ed.is 2 b published')

❖ ('2014-03-04 00:56:30',
@NaMo4PM Kindly send permission to put the images of @StatueOfUnity & @NaMo onCoverOf my Book withText"REINCARNATION OF IRON- MAN"-BookTitle')

❖ ('2014-03-07 22:42:37',
RT @thekiranbedi: Can formation of AAM AURAT Morcha (AAM)by BJP be considered to respond PEACEFULLY guerrilla tactics of political outfit \ u2026')

❖ ('2014-03-07 22:43:03',
RT @thekiranbedi: I believe RSS has Durga Vahini? Can they not be present outside BJP Offices+cameras to respond to Guerrilla attack from p\u2026')

❖ ('2014-03-07 22:43:48',
RT @thenarendramodi: New Blog : Secularism for BJP is an Article of Faith, for us it means India First: Shri Modi http://t.co/MiHqNm10tB')

❖ ('2014-03-07 22:44:05',
RT @TheEconomist: The World Economic Forum recently published a list of the top ten emerging technologies for 2014 http://t.co/aHLFAJFMaC')

❖ ('2014-03-07 22:44:48',
RT @thekiranbedi: While we have a right to protest we have a responsibility to protect')

❖ ('2014-03-07 22:45:08',
RT @thenarendramodi: New Blog : We need to realize the Mahatma Gandhi\u2019s dream of Congress Mukt Bharat: Shri Modi http://t.co/YEwjDgNFZg')

❖ ('2014-03-07 22:46:44',
RT @thekiranbedi: When a particular political outfit goes to another political party office in anger,does it go it to 'defend' or provoke &\u2026")

❖ ('2014-03-07 22:47:03',
RT @thekiranbedi: Speed at which particular outfit is
getting in conflict with law,will it not need a special
court to try its case of riot\u2026')

❖ ('2014-03-07 22:48:53',
RT @thekiranbedi: Our democracy may slip into a
mobocracy if we do not bring in clear majority with
allies for @narendramodi to govern! Cha\u2026')

❖ ('2014-03-07 23:22:38',
RT @India272: Every vote matters. Reminding &
Persuading every voter to vote is equally important.
Volunteer for Mission272+ Today http://t\u2026')

❖ ('2014-03-07 23:22:48',
RT @narendramodi: I call upon the people of India
to bless us, give BJP-led NDA a majority & make
Mission272+ a grand reality for the prosp\u2026')

❖ ('2014-03-07 23:23:26',
RT @narendramodi: My special welcome to 10 crore
new voters! You have an important role to play in
strengthening & continuing democratic tr\u2026')

❖ ('2014-03-07 23:23:43',
RT @narendramodi: Poll bugle has been sounded! Best
wishes to EC in conducting polls & congrats to
people on commencement of biggest festiv\u2026')

❖ ('2014-03-07 23:25:05',
RT @narendramodi: Next "Chai Pe Charcha" with a
focus on women empowerment will be on 8th March,
which is International Women\'s Day.')

❖ ('2014-03-07 23:25:24',
RT @thenarendramodi: New Blog : Congress leaders
speak as though they have come from Mars: Shri Modi
http://t.co/pqtbRXScNZ')

❖ ('2014-03-07 23:34:15',
RT @thenarendramodi: New Blog : Prior to Election
a saffron storm is brewing, it will transform into a
Tsunami\u2026 http://t.co/8XFhcj7jCx')

❖ ('2014-03-07 23:52:14',
RT @rupasubramanya: Score!! Great line. "My priority
is to solve India\'s problems. Our rival\'s priority is to
solve the Modi problem: Naren\u2026')

❖ ('2014-03-07 23:57:47',
RT @narendramodi: \u092c\u0940\u091c\u0947\
u092a\u0940 \u0915\u0940 \u0906\u0901\u0927\
u0940 \u091a\u0932 \u0930\u0939\u0940 \u0939\
u0948 \u0914\u0930 \u092f\u0947 \u0938\u0941\
u0928\u093e\u092e\u0940 \u092c\u0928 \u091c\
u093e\u090f\u0917\u0940! '\u0938\u092c\u0915\
u093e' - '\u0938' \u092f\u093e\u0928\u0940 \u0938\
u092a\u093e, '\u092c' \u092f\u093e\u0928\u0940 \
u092c\u0938\u092a\u093e \u0914\u0930 '\u0915\
u093e' \u092f\u093e\u0928\u0940 \u0915\u093e\
u0902\u0917\u094d\u0930\u0947\u0938 \u0915\
u093e \u0938\u092b\u093e\u092f\u093e \u0939\
u094b \u091c\u093e\u2026")

❖ ('2014-03-07 23:59:07',
RT @narendramodi: Their secularism is about
votebank politics but for us it means India First. For
them its an empty slogan, for us its an \u2026')

❖ ('2014-03-07 23:59:47',
RT @narendramodi: Journey to developed India will
begin when we sow the seeds of a developed UP. Once
UP is developed, India's development \u2026")

❖ ('2014-03-08 00:06:20',
RT @narendramodi: Technology can increase
awareness about judicial system. Why can't we have
a TV channel devoted to legal awareness & info\
u2026")

❖ ('2014-03-08 00:11:04',
RT @Narendramodi_PM: Democracy has 4 enemies-
dynasty, casteism, communalism and opportunism
sadly Congress has all 4 in them')

❖ ('2014-03-08 00:12:50',
RT @narendramodi: Nation wants jobs, skill
development & prosperity. Since Congress can't
provide these, it is time to uproot Congress http\
u2026")

❖ ('2014-03-08 00:14:17',
RT @narendramodi: On National Science Day, greetings
to all science enthusiasts We salute the hardwork
& innovation of our scientists, who \u2026')

❖ ('2014-03-08 00:31:13',
@SrBachchan Yr support to @NaMo would b historic, if
U decide to do that. I\'d send a novel "REINCARNATION
OF THE IRON-MAN" 2 C it 4 Filming.')

❖ ('2014-03-08 00:40:01',
From 2day, A Doha per day from @ANAMODIT would be
Re-Tweeted. 65 days by May 16\'14, "65-DOHAWALI" for
65-year old @NaMo4PM. Check it out.')

❖ ('2014-03-08 03:59:02',
@NaMo @aksinh To Gujarat, Ex-Delhi-CM, Kejriwal--
Goes, No approval by EC at all; Then drives2Modi, like a
pal-- No apptmt.Just 16-'Sawal'")

❖ ('2014-03-08 04:04:29',
Arvind-- hard 2 define, indeed: Is he a stuntman of
mystery's creed? Or, a Gorilla-Chief, sowing seed Of
dissent, or blind from Kursi-Greed?")

❖ ('2014-03-08 04:17:53',
@NaMo @aksinh A new #AAPDRAMA each morn--
Won\'t charm Aam Aadami torn \'tween @congressorg
& oath sworn: "No-VIP-Car" vs rich jet airborne!')

❖ ('2014-03-08 04:27:32',
@NaMo @aksinh Medha P. defends Chief of @AAP-- His
duplicious Lies&"PAP": Riding Jets, favoring KHAP
-- An activist reduces to AK\'s staff !')

❖ ('2014-03-11 12:50:49',
@NaMo @justicearnab Simple-Living &
Hi-thinking Make a truly great life; but
#AAPDRAMA& #arvind got the Sting: Shun All
Action & Strife!')

❖ ('2014-03-11 13:09:59',
@rahulkanwal @ndtv In #RightToBeHeardTownHall,
Shouts the man from @ArvindKejriwal: "@NaMo is
Communal" Did @congressorg turn @AAP\'s Skull?')

❖ ('2014-03-11 13:24:58',
@ArvindKejriwal has no qualms In calling Living
ones dead! Is this the Blind-Spot from the chasms Of
desperately attracting the Media's Aid?")

❖ ('2014-03-11 15:50:36',
@NaMo4PM @Moditeam @PrakashJavdekar @
yogarishramdev @ShahnawazBJ I\'ve just Emailed request
2 put @Statueof_unity Photo on my Book "Reincarn.')

❖ ('2014-03-11 16:22:36',
@congressorg @rahulgandhi Shall never cease to
Conspire-- Blaming RSS,Waving ISI--but the Aandhi
(Modi-Wave)shall never cease 2 Inspire!')

❖ ('2014-03-13 10:26:24',
@namo @arunjaitley @RaviShankarBJP @M_Lekhi @
PrakashJavdekar @ShahnawazBJP @naqvimukhtar A
Magnified English Transliteration to follow soon.')

❖ ('2014-03-15 05:12:09',
@ndtv, #AAPDRAMA is an epitome Of arrogance &
plain stupidity; Why can\'t people see its "Dhong", And
its childish game -- that\'s a pity!')

❖ ('2014-03-15 08:27:52',
For @ArvindKejriwal, one should utter The naked truth
unadorned; And echo the little boy\'s whisper-- "Look,
the Emperor has no clothes on!'")

❖ ('2014-03-15 08:38:02',
"The media is all sold out; When our govt. comes, we\'ll
send Them all to jail" -- no doubt Only @ArvindKejriwal
could such #theatrics lend.')

❖ ('2014-03-15 09:07:38',
@AapYogendra & @PMOIndia, whom We all know
as incompetent, say @narendramodi'd b a prophet of
doom; @AAP & @Congressorg better relent.")

❖ ('2014-03-15 09:16:53',
@Congressorg is surely bankrupt: Chidambaram says
he won't run! This decision abrupt Reflects that @sonia
& @rahulgandhi2020 are all done!")

❖ ('2014-03-15 09:32:29',
India\'s VP & Foreign Minister Do NOT respect this
country, When they regard "\'Vande Mataram" sinister,
Or discredit in UK its EL.COMMITTEE')

❖ ('2014-03-15 09:44:10',
@kamalfaruqui can't understand That Bangladeshi
Hindus need shelter In @India, to save'em from tyranny,
and The Muslims're illegal invader")

❖ ('2014-03-15 09:53:19',
#IntolerantAAP & @ArvindKejriwal Create
strange waves to ride -- They bat hard, but there is no
ball at all. They attack and quickly hide')

❖ ('2014-03-16 06:56:50',
Wireless electricity may soon power cell phones, cars
and even heart pumps http://t.co/KT9tfRJJue via @
YahooNews')

❖ ('2014-03-17 04:54:04',
#YourVote2014 @congressorg & #AAPDRAMA
Suffer from the severe thirst For the Kursi & the
Media,O Rama! Only @NaMo cares for "INDIA FIRST."')

❖ ('2014-03-17 05:11:47',
@rahulmehra--puppet of @ArvindKejriwal; @
DRSinghvi1973 sings @Congressorg's dull song; They'll
fade and surely fall. Only @NaMo4PM is strong")

❖ ('2014-03-26 03:25:01',
@gauravcsawant @NaMo4PM @htTweets @
headlinesToday @IndiaReports For a set of Verse-
Tweets on @NaMo & #Mission, pls.see Tweets/day
by @aksinh')

❖ ('2014-03-26 03:30:48',
@gauravcsawant Could U pl.give me Contact Info 4
Andy Marino-I\'d like to request him to see my book
"REINCARNATION OF IRON-MAN" to film it.')

❖ ('2014-04-02 08:41:09',
@TimesNow and @varungandhi80 explain The good-
old #GandhisBonhomie The Mahabharat\'s brothers,
once again, have Arjun-Karna duel: "Show me!"')

❖ ('2014-04-02 08:50:59',
@TimesNow, @NaMo Mahabharat you can see unfold
before your eyes-- read "INCARNATION OF THE IRON-
MAN", A Novel by Ahnis Kosha in disguise!!')

❖ ('2014-04-02 08:58:30',
Let #AK49 & @AAP bite the bullet bitter And
ingest this @Twitter -- Say @NaMo Kamal @NaMo
Kamal And dedicate yr vote as 'phool' and 'phal'!")

❖ ('2014-04-02 09:06:10',
Didn't Mahadev rescue gods and get rid of many a
'Nishachar'? Vote 4 @thenarendramodi, to beat all odds,
Saying @timesnow @NaMo 'Har-Har'!!")

❖ ('2014-04-02 09:18:45',
To rise together & throw off The 'Panja' and
'Jhadoo' is @timesnow! @congressorg &
#aapdrama we scoff; To vote 4 @NaMo4PM &
'KAMAL', we VOW.")

❖ ('2014-04-02 09:25:04',
@AamAadmiParty'll be gone by itself! @congressorg
must be shown the door! Vote 4 @NaMo4PM as a Self-
help; To joyously dance @TimesNow more!")

❖ ('2014-04-02 09:34:57',
@timesnow every single VOTE Is IMPORTANT, as never
before; Get rid of @congressorg & #AAPDRAMA,
to Note: History'll Open Its Golden Door!")

❖ ('2014-04-02 09:44:19',
An ERA of @IndiaToday's DEVELOPMENT & PEACE
& A NEW INDEPENDENCE From @congressorg is
@timesnow, THIS MOMENT- Waste not a single VOTE,
hence")

❖ ('2014-04-02 09:53:19',
@narendramodi is the Answer @timesofindia, @
IndiaToday @timesnow yearn for; So VOTE 4 @
NaMo4PM & 4 'KAMAL' Flower, & win
VICTORY, for sure!")

❖ ('2014-04-02 10:15:17',
@timesofindia @timesnow @Swamy39 @
nytimes, @NaMo4PM, C http://t.co/HEBDVkw8kX
"REINCARNATION OF THE IRON-MAN" by \'Ahnis
Kosha\'-a PenCanon!')

❖ ('2014-04-04 18:37:50',
@ndtv @TimesofIndia @TimesNow @aajtak @
justicearnab WE'll VOW: END CORRUPTION &
CHAOS-- VOTE 4 @NaMo4PM & THROW @
AAPDrama & @congressorg.")

❖ ('2014-04-04 18:54:05',
VOTE 4 @Mission272 & ALL, @M_Lekhi @
Swamy39 @naqvimukhtar, DEFEAT @rahulgandhi2020
& @ArvindKejriwal MAKE @VisVp @rprasad_bjp
OUR Gr8 STAR')

❖ ('2014-04-04 18:54:05',
VOTE 4 @Mission272 & ALL, @M_Lekhi @
Swamy39 @naqvimukhtar, DEFEAT @rahulgandhi2020
& @ArvindKejriwal MAKE @VisVp @rprasad_bjp
OUR Gr8 STAR')

❖ ('2014-04-04 18:59:38',
@congressorg & @AAPDrama bring Issues of
Masjid & & Pseud0-Secularity-- They Know
NOT that the Vicious STING Shall Bite them 2 DEATH
& PITY')

❖ ('2014-04-04 19:06:54',
Rastra-Premi Kavi ki PUKAR Aati hai Baarmbaar --
@aajtak @NaMo4PM ko VOTE Daar, Phenko Ganda
'Jhadoo' & 'Panze' ka War, Jeeto Runn Aar-Paar!")

❖ ('2014-04-04 19:21:01',
Yuva-Varg, Dhyaan Rahe: BHARAT ka Maan Rahe! Aaj
@NaMo4PM ko JEET De, Bolo @satyamevjayate! Kaho
@M_Lekhi @naqvimukhtar se @mataram VANDE!!')

❖ ('2014-04-04 19:38:38',
Hindu, Sikh, Musalman, Isaai Naujawan, Briddh Traan-
Traan: Jaag Gao @VisVp @NaMo4PM Gaan, Rakhho @
bbgarg7 DESH ki SHAAN: BHARAT MERA MAHAAN!')

❖ ('2014-04-04 19:46:37',
@aajtak @congressorg @AAP's Trap Nahi Banenge
Rastra-Shraap! Dur Karo 'Jhadoo', 'Haath'; VOTE Deke
'KAMAL'-Chhap, Karo @Narendramodi_PM Jaap")

❖ ('2014-04-04 19:59:08',
Sankat ke ban Baadal- Ghirate hain @Aaj-Kal 'Panja'
& 'Jhadoo' Kar Chhal. Khile @NaMo4PM ka
'KAMAL'; Banaa BHARAT ko Saral Vishwa-Bal ATAL.")

❖ ('2014-04-04 20:15:21',
Aaj 'KAMAL' hai Sunaharaa- Khilataa hai Haraa-Bharaa!
'Jhadoo' phenk, 'Haath'-Mukta Bane Desh Aaj Jaraa!
Chhinn-Bhinn @congressorg-Kaaraa!")

❖ ('2014-04-04 20:28:57',
@congressorg #AAPDrama Saare Doob Gaye Bechaare!
Hain Bulanda Saare Jag me @BJP4India ke Taare! 'INDIA
FIRST' ke Hi Re Yahaan Goonjate NAARE")

❖ ('2014-04-04 20:38:52',
O Rahul G! O @ArvindKejriwal! Lad Gaye Tere Din!
Ab 'KAMAL' ka Kamaal Dekho to VOTE Gin-Gin! Desh
Naache @aajtak 'TakDhinTakTakDhinDhin!!!")

❖ ('2014-04-04 20:59:39',
@timesofindia @timesnow @nytimesworld, visit: @
amazon.com/REINCARNATION-OF-THE-IRON-MAN-
AHNIS-KOSHA/dp/149314197X/ --it Is @aajtak bst hit')

❖ ('2014-04-04 21:06:34',
Reincarnation of Saradar Patel U Can Tell- By Reading
@amazon.com's newest Novel w/ key-word 'Ahnis
Kosha' - an Author Best! B My Guest!!")

❖ ('2014-04-04 21:19:00',
@NaMo4PM @VisVp @congressorg @ArvindKejriwal @
nytindia @washingtonpost @nytimes C @amazon.com
Ahnis Kosha's NOVEL, & Rejoice Well & Tell !")

❖ ('2014-04-04 22:21:16',
@timesnow @justicearnab @htTweets @timesofindia
#Babaristing, Make INDIA yr god & yr Song 2 Sing!
Why keep Enmity, B Friends Gr8 Sweet!')

❖ ('2014-04-05 06:29:22',
@timesnow @justicearnab @ndtv & ALL, If it
stirs U 2've a bit of fun abt @congressorg #aapchaos @
ArvindKejriwal, C @aksinh's Verse-@twitters")

❖ ('2014-04-05 06:52:31',
My Collection of Verse-@twitters Is a Joy Neat &
Sweet! So, 2 Have these GR8 Treasures, View &
Follow Me--My TREAT! @Tweet as Sweetmeat')

❖ ('2014-04-05 07:25:23',
@VisVp @justicearnab @timesnow @ndtv @
timesofindia @aajtak @rahulkanwal, Follow @aksinh 2
See Verse @Tweets w/o Equal ! 4 Pure Fun Low-Cal.')

❖ ('2014-04-09 08:19:43',
RT @BJP4India: Congress is like a watermelon. It is
green from outside and red from inside and the Left
carries the red flag- http://t.co/I\u2026')

❖ ('2014-04-09 08:21:33',
RT @timesofindia: Global financial giants catch India
poll fever http://t.co/vC7Ldzuq2a')

❖ ('2014-04-09 08:22:17',
RT @thenarendramodi: New Blog : BJP Manifesto:
A vow to take India a leap forward http://t.co/
CvO8am2qli #narendramodivideo')

❖ ('2014-04-09 08:29:13',
@ndtv @TimesofIndia @TimesNow @HeadlinesToday
&All, @NarendraModi @M_Lekhi @justicearnab 4
a twist in twitter & Literature, Follow @aksinh')

❖ ('2014-04-09 08:40:41',
@AJAMKHAN b ashamed! #ArmyAbovePolitics is the
Norm-- B one Ram or Rahim named-- Even a child
knows this Form. An Ugly Dog must B Tamed of')

❖ ('2014-04-09 08:41:08',
RT @BJP4India: Statement of Azam Khan is an insult
to Indian soldiers: Dr. @SudhanshuTrived: http://t.co/
FPTCF47OAT')

❖ ('2014-04-20 08:50:48',
@ndtv @IndiaToday @timesnow @timesofindia @
Telegraph @ANI_news @justicearnab @rahulkanwal
Pls.Follow the Link below http://t.co/Pz2nRdIMzB')

❖ ('2014-04-20 09:06:47',
Mahabharat Rishi Vyas wrote, And 2day it seems @
aksinh pens 4 @BJPteam Funny Tweets on Vote- Bank
of @congressorg & #aapdrama 4 U 2 Quote.')

❖ ('2014-04-20 09:22:27',
@BJPRajnathSingh is Yudhisthir, @AmitShahOffice
Bheem, @NaMo is Arjun Veer, Janata-Janardan is
Krishna, @arunjaitley Nakul @Swamy39 Sahdev.')

❖ ('2014-04-20 09:41:01',
The Kauravas: @rahulgandhi2020 is Duyodhan @
SoniaGandhiG is Shakuni Ma-Ma @AapGhumaKeLeyLo
Dussashan & misguided people R Karna In this
Runn')

❖ ('2014-04-20 09:58:51',
'Satyamev Jayate'; and So, Victory'll Choose @NaMo.
The @BJP4India @Manifesto Shall become Tomorrow
The world'd GR8est SHOW 4 INDIA !")

❖ ('2014-04-20 10:09:40',
JAYACHAND had his day with GORI; & MIR KASIM
with EAST INDIA CO. So is @ArvindKejriwal's story:
Friend of 'KURSI', with INDIA as his FOE.")

❖ ('2014-04-20 10:31:46',
@ArvindKejriwal, Fighting against @ModiForVaranasi-
Is @congressorg's Team-B, @AK-49,who Is Back-Door
Congressi BlackJadoo & DirtyJhadoo!")

❖ ('2014-04-24 09:06:43',
@Time @Timesnow @IndiaToday @ZeeNews @
ndtv @timesofindia SAW AWED HISTORY, MUM--
MAHABHARAT'S GANGEY&PARTH WERE ONE-IN
@Narendramodi_PM.")

❖ ('2014-04-24 09:27:25',
@PTI_News @ArvindKejriwal @RahulG @
justicearnab @nitish ALL SAW AWED HISTORY, MUM
MAHABHARAT's GANGEY&PARTH WERE ONE--IN
@Narendramodi_PM")

❖ ('2014-04-24 09:31:48',
The Entire Family of Kaurav-DAL OF 1 HUNDRED
Brothers & ALL SAW AWED HISTORY, MUM
MAHABHARAT's GANGEY&PARTH WERE ONE--IN
@Narendramodi_PM")

❖ ('2014-04-24 09:42:11',
@justicearnab @rahulkanwal @M_Lekhi @
naqvimukhtar -- ALL SAW AWED HISTORY, MUM:
MAHABHARAT's GANGEY&PARTH WERE ONE--IN
@Narendramodi_PM.")

❖ ('2014-04-24 09:58:22',
@yogrishiramdev @thekiranbedi @the_hindu
@hindubharati -- SAW AWED HISTORY, MUM:
MAHABHARAT's GANGEY&PARTH WERE ONE--IN
@Narendramodi_PM.")

❖ ('2014-04-24 10:03:49',
@the_hindu @nytimesworld @nytindia @Gen_
VKSingh @Swamy39 SAW AWED HISTORY MUM
MAHABHARAT's GANGEY&PARTH WERE ONE--IN
@Narendramodi_PM.")

❖ ('2014-04-24 10:09:58',
@LKAdvaniBJP @SushmaSwarajbjp @arunjaitley
@Statueof_unity SAW AWED HISTORY, MUM
MAHABHARAT's GANGEY&PARTH WERE ONE--IN
@Narendramodi_PM")

❖ ('2014-04-24 10:16:43',
@BJP4India @BJPRajnathSingh @ShahnawazBJP
@naqvimukhtar SAW AWED HISTORY, MUM
MAHABHARAT's GANGEY&PARTH WERE ONE--IN
@Narendramodi_PM")

❖ ('2014-04-24 10:22:47',
#bigdebates @AMISHDEVGAN @amitabh_bigb
@aamir_khan SAW AWED HISTORY, MUM :
MAHABHARAT's GANGEY&PARTH WERE ONE--IN
@Narendramodi_PM.")

❖ ('2014-04-24 10:34:27',
#blackmoney @ANI_news #aapdrama #Torrentofscams
#bigdebates SAW AWED HISTORY, MUM
MAHABHARAT's GANGEY&PARTH WERE ONE-IN
@Narendramodi_PM")

❖ ('2014-04-24 10:44:34',
@PrakashJavdekar @rprasad_bjp @JhaSanjay @
rahulgandhi2020 SAW AWED HISTORY, MUM :
MAHABHARAT's GANGEY&PARTH WERE ONE--IN
@Narendramodi_PM.")

❖ ('2014-04-24 10:48:10',
@abdullah_omar @juniorbachchan @satyamevjayate
@aamir_khan SAW AWED HISTORY, MUM
MAHABHARAT's GANGEY&PARTH WERE ONE--IN
@Narendramodi_PM")

❖ ('2014-04-24 10:59:04',
@IndianExpress @JagranNews @aajtak @
gauravcsawant @YuvaiTV SAW AWED HISTORY, MUM
MAHABHARAT's GANGEY&PARTH WERE ONE--IN
@Narendramodi_PM")

❖ ('2014-04-24 11:03:47',
@ModiForVaranasi #MODIfiedKASHI @nytimes
@TIME @PTI_News SAW AWED HISTORY, MUM:
MAHABHARAT's GANGEY&PARTH WERE ONE--IN
@Narendramodi_PM.")

❖ ('2014-04-27 03:13:10',
@rahulgandhi2020 should first learn Pronouncing
words correctly ('Aatamhatya, Lokayuktaa,..?) before
showing concern About @narendramodi!")

❖ ('2014-04-27 03:24:09',
@PriyankVadra ought to find What @blackmoney14 her
husband plays To Grind Billions Out of Nothing, before
blames on @narendramodi she lays.')

❖ ('2014-04-27 03:28:54',
@SoniaGandhiG: God save the country from the @
GujratModel --- Ha! Ha! Surely She Means God save @
congressorg from @narendramodi, U can tell!')

❖ ('2014-04-27 03:35:26',
Now @congressorg is so desperate 2 save from
devastation its fate, That @SoniaGandhiG's @
DrAMSinghvi has 2 state: ANY Front is OK, To-Date!")

❖ ('2014-04-27 03:42:06',
@justicearnab's DirectTalk, @rahulkanwal's @
ElectionExpress's Runs & Walk, @AMISHDEVGAN's
#bigstorybigdebate, Are Saviors of India's Fate!")

❖ ('2014-04-27 03:46:12',
Some say the 3ʳᵈ Front will Decide the Country\'s
Winning Team-- This is like "Raja BHOJ vs. Bhojawa
Teli" Tale In FRONT of @Narendramodi_PM.')

❖ ('2014-04-27 03:49:22',
Just 19 days more For witnessing the History's biggest
turn-- When @congressorg'll be shown the door; And
India'll @Narendramodi_PM EARN !")

❖ ('2014-04-27 04:05:46',
@PMOIndia ManmohanSinghJi Is SAD:his Brother
joined @bjp_ 10 years of Servitude to @SoniaGandhiG-
He's lost all KEY http://t.co/BlbQYJWx3h")

❖ ('2014-04-27 04:27:23',
@BJP4India THANK YOU! A New Turn in India\'s History
is at hand! I also request help in publicizing the BOOK
"REINCARNATION OF THE IRON-MAN"')

❖ ('2014-04-27 04:32:42',
@BJP4India For FREE DOWNLOADing, Please visit
http://t.co/2Sr7Pc37jQ Also Please Follow TWEETS by
@aksinh Small Contributions for @NaMo4PM')

❖ ('2014-04-27 04:40:17',
The intellectual capital of India - let the change begin
from Varanasi #MODIfiedKashi http://t.co/6fgyYeFUJc
via @BJP4India Follow @aksinh')

❖ ('2014-04-27 09:34:15',
@Narendramodi_PM Yr Picture is on Cover of my New
socio-political Novel "REINCARNATION OF THE IRON-
MAN". Hope It\'s OK http://t.co/ocTYUpdv6h')

❖ ('2014-04-27 09:44:46',
Request @NaMo4PM to send to aksinha1722@yahoo.
com your Email Address and yr permission to send
NRI/USA views and VHPA publications to you.')

❖ ('2014-04-28 06:40:03',
Book Launch \u201cReincarnation of the Iron \u2013
Man\u201d by Ahnis Kosha | http://t.co/6TtBCe20dL
http://t.co/L5PjZ2oIvR')

❖ ('2014-04-30 18:37:10',
@NaMo4PM @NaMo Lo & Behold @timesnow
@nytimes @timesofindia @TIME #PakInterferes so
& Violates Ceasefire, Time & again,, &
must Pay a Fine.')

❖ ('2014-04-30 18:47:49',
@narendramodi @arunjaitley @India272 is so Happy,
Proud, Jubilant, 2 Be The Judge: The Verdict is In--
Victory Goes to BJP! Have SomeTea')

❖ ('2014-04-30 18:53:52',
@SoniaGandhiG @rahulgandhi2020 @PriyankaG
-- Haven't U Eyes To see @Modi-Lahar; So Bye-Bye @
congressorg must now Go--No More Tricks & Lies!")

❖ ('2014-04-30 19:00:26',
The @BJP272Plus Has surely Been A Saga Historic-- A
Modern Mahabharat-Like Is @NDTVElections-Epic. @
NaMo Has Itruly Been ARJUN+BHEESHMAin1')

❖ ('2014-04-30 19:09:40',
A Dawn Surely @IndiaToday Peaks up the Himalayas!
History Witnesses Victory of @BJP4India; A New Era 4
the @nytimesworld @worldteleport etc')

❖ ('2014-04-30 19:26:55',
@TIME @timesnow @timesofindia @nytimesworld @
TimesTodayNews @NaMo4PM @congressorg #AAP @
PTI_News 3 Cheers! ChaiWala is Here! GLORY2INDIA')

❖ ('2014-04-30 19:42:28',
Soon ll have Collector's Series of Tweets d like
to Save This Book of e-Verse on BHARATVARSH
#Elections2014Gave. http://t.co/ypMxxr4noE")

❖ ('2014-05-09 18:33:29',
#ModiSpeaksToArnab FLIES HIGH IN THE SOCIAL
MEDIA'S SKY. THE MEDIA SHALL FLY STILL HIGHER
ON MAY 16'14 WITH @NARENDRAMODI AS PRIME
MINISTER")

❖ ('2014-05-09 18:41:17',
#ModiSpeaksToArnabon ALL Issues: @NaMo Walks Tall
4 India 2 Choose, Even as EC sets #VaranasiBlock! @
congressorg & @AAP are In 4 Gr8 Shock.')

❖ ('2014-05-09 18:48:46',
Did 'DIDI' Forget Her Goal O'Lifting W.Bengal Up; And,
Like @congressorg & @AAP Sell Her Soul For Vote-
Bank Politics...Rub...Dub...Dub...!")

❖ ('2014-05-09 18:52:53',
Janata-Janardan has made a choice As soon the world'll
see: 'Ek Bharat, Shreshtha Bharat' -- One Voice-- @
NaMo4PM is the Mantra for Victory!")

❖ ('2014-05-09 19:00:59',
@congressorg @SoniaGandhiG @rahulgandhi2020
-- The Whole Family-- Are Blind out of Ego to See The
Simple Truth: The Next PM is @NarendraModi')

❖ ('2014-05-09 19:13:54',
@congressorg's @SoniaGandhiG Is a Fascist, Contriving
#VaranasiBlock, for Gaddi, And All Kinds of National
Tragedy; Surpassing Mossoulini")

❖ ('2014-05-09 19:18:20',
In India, the Roman Empire, & Italian-Mafia Style
Govt. Must Retire. The Dawn is Neigh, the Innate Fire Of
the East Rises, All to Inspire.')

❖ ('2014-05-09 19:22:40',
In Modern India's History-Line There is a New
Jayachand Whose New Name is #AAPDrama's Evil Hero:
AK-49, Who Runs On, and For, Foreign Fund.")

❖ ('2014-05-09 19:32:20',
In Modern India's History-Line, We've New RanaPratap + SwamyVivekanand, With Words Eloquent, Fine! Let this Tweet be New ChandbarDai-Chhand!")

❖ ('2014-05-11 07:49:50',
Rahul Gandhi – Dual Name and Dual passport http://t.co/HQ1PZGHDxp Qn-Is this legal?(Italy does NOT allowDualCitizenship:as 4 @ SoniaG.)')

❖ ('2014-05-11 07:55:12',
Rahul Gandhi \u2013 Dual Name and Dual passport | RTI Anonymous http://t.co/212NwsMI62 via @ rtianonymous Can he w/-Italian Passport b an MP/PM?')

❖ ('2014-05-11 07:59:22',
Twitter Buttons | About https://t.co/ZgyQ1S0HeZ via @ aksinh')

❖ ('2014-05-11 08:04:26',
Rahul Gandhi \u2013 Dual Name and Dual passport | RTI Anonymous http://t.co/212NwsMI62 via @ rtianonymous Legally, he CAN'T B MP or PM in INDIA?")

❖ ('2014-05-12 21:33:53',
I've just updated my professional profile on LinkedIn. Connect with me and view my profile. http://t.co/ KPghgJy6D1 #in")

❖ ('2014-05-12 22:54:52',
Anti-Hindu Congress Govt bans Hindu Janjagruti Samiti\ u2019s website once again | http://t.co/6TtBCe20dL http://t.co/j2r8Z8wCcL We Protest this')

❖ ('2014-05-13 12:10:32',
@Nitish4Bihar @mulayamsingh married & Many Others Added Much Odd Quantity Sans Quality, Equality or Even Unity -- So they lost: What a Pity!')

❖ ('2014-05-13 12:16:56',
Three Jeers 4 the 3rd Front -- All their Mutual Politeness
& Polity Was merely a Circus Stunt ! It was just a
Facade, a Parody O'Treaty !")

❖ ('2014-05-13 12:31:02',
@NaMo @NaMo...O Har-Har Modi! Three Cheers 4 Ghar-
Ghar Modi! @Narendramodi_PM is now Prime O'@
Kashi The Son now Shines in GangaMata'd Godi.")

❖ ('2014-05-13 15:06:09',
Read (FREE DOWNLOAD) a socio-political Novel
featuring @NarendraModi_PM : "REINCARNATION OF
THE IRON-MAN" by Ahni.. https://t.co/tOmLUyM2dp')

❖ ('2014-05-13 15:11:03',
Read Verse TWEETS of (& FOLLOW http://t.co/
PdtoHcIbhW) @aksinh with @India2014 described as
the New MAHABHARAT https://t.co/tOmLUyM2dp')

❖ ('2014-05-14 19:48:56',
A Full Victory of NDA on May 16, 2014 is only a
beginning of a new great chapter in the history of Free
INDIA, aft.. https://t.co/eJ2iqaBQnQ')

❖ ('2014-05-15 01:56:31',
#AAPDRAMA #AAPWave Come 2 a big Naught, and @
congressorg Gave Way 2 @Narendramodi_PM, rather 2
Pave Way of their own demise, like a Knave.')

❖ ('2014-05-15 02:07:26',
May 16'14,a New Morn'll Dawn, @Narendramodi_PM'll
B Sworn In with the Crown. History'll Wake-up; Idly Sit
Down No More, But March On&ON&ON.")

❖ ('2014-05-15 09:40:07',
Inviting ALL Members of 'LocalCircles': Please Follow @
aksinh for Collection of Verse-Tweets. Please pass this
on. https://t.co/Xy6K74GXB0")

❖ ('2014-05-16 05:41:44',
At 9:36AM, #16May2014 @timesnow BJP's Victory
was on the Screen of India's every News-Channel. @
congressorg!Heed History's Grand Show&Tell!")

❖ ('2014-05-16 05:45:44',
A New Torch has been Ignited and Lit Brightly on
#16may2014, And the Nation of Bharat Whole Salutes @
Narendramodi_PM with Heart and Soul !')

❖ ('2014-05-16 05:49:09',
A New Era has Just Dawned In the Country at this
Momentous Moment. The Great son of Gujarat has again
been crowned As the Samraat Effulgent.')

❖ ('2014-05-18 20:20:31',
Book Launch \u201cReincarnation of the Iron \
u2013 Man\u201d by Ahnis Kosha | http://t.
co/6TtBCe20dL http://t.co/L5PjZ2oIvR Follow @aksinh
4 Verse-Tweets')

❖ ('2014-05-18 20:25:00',
Book Launch \u201cReincarnation of the Iron \u2013
Man\u201d by Ahnis Kosha | http://t.co/6TtBCe20dL
http://t.co/L5PjZ2oIvR')

❖ ('2014-05-19 08:36:03',
I'm aksinha1722@yahoo.com @bjpsamvad @
LocalCircles @Narendramodi_PM I'd keep sending Verse-
Tweets, To convey ThoughtsWordsMusicHeart-beats.")

❖ ('2014-05-19 08:55:34',
I'm aksinha1722@yahoo.com @bjpsamvad @
LocalCircles @Narendramodi_PM I invite U 2 visit URL/
Link http://t.co/lARHfNYcoT To READ/SHARE/THINK")

❖ ('2014-05-19 09:02:51',
I'm aksinha1722@yahoo.com @bjpsamvad @
LocalCircles @Narendramodi_PM To see a predicted set
of Task & Time-Line, Please Open Novel, Page 339")

❖ ('2014-05-19 09:12:03',
The Novel "REINCARNATION OF THE IRON-MAN"
Suggests TASKS only @Narendramodi_PM CAN!
aksinha1722@yahoo Wrote: Let @PTI_News @
IndiaToday Note.')

❖ ('2014-05-19 09:21:57',
@timesofindia @IndianExpress @nytindia @bjpsamvad
@ZoomIndianMedia ALL pls.Look up p.339 Well Of
"REINCARNATION OF IRON-MAN"-A New NOVEL.')

❖ ('2014-05-19 09:31:26',
@bjpsamvad @LocalCircles @Narendramodi_PM Let
@RSSorg & Other Volunteers Streem Out to Each
Village and City &Collect Iron 4 @StatueOfUnity')

❖ ('2014-05-19 09:39:57',
@bjpsamvad @LocalCircles We Need To Strengthen
Dept.of Tourism For the World to Get the Deed Of India's
Spirit:Hinduism/Buddhism--Humanism.")

❖ ('2014-05-19 09:51:17',
Any Violation of CeaseFire, & Pak Must know It's
Playing with Fire- @Narendramodi_PM @bjpsamvad @
LocalCircles India MUST Show ItsTrueMetal")

❖ ('2014-06-02 23:20:01',
Mark my words @abdullah_omar #Article370 SHALL
be Tackled as a Prime Concern to @VisVp For, Kashmir
isn't Estate owned by Your GrandFather")

❖ ('2014-06-02 23:26:32',
If Kashmir, an Integral Part of India, is lagging behind
Then shouldn't we Indians debate on #370, as @bjp_
Suggests, and the culprit find?")

❖ ('2014-06-02 23:37:03',
An SIT with the sharp eyes of Justice And blessings of @
babaramdev4, Shall get back this Lost Treasure to India,
Satyamev Jayate for sure.')

❖ ('2014-06-02 23:40:42',
@ajaymaken says @smritiirani, Being only a High
School Graduate, Is unfit for Heading the Hindustani
Dept.of Education, dictate men's fate.")

❖ ('2014-06-02 23:58:49',
Has @ajaymaken & the likes of him Ever asked @
SoniaGandhiG's schooling-- She, a sly leader prim, Is @
congressorg's President, freely Ruling.")

❖ ('2014-06-03 00:04:00',
Those who sacrificed At the Nation's Altar-- If their
#SacrificeForgotten, and unjust Turn meted to their
families, that's a national scar!")

❖ ('2014-06-03 00:11:58',
Uttar Pradesh is NOT a State, But a pure
#HorrorPradesh, Where Women's Honor, Life, Fate Are
Trifles -- Shame Mulayam! #WakeUpAkhilesh!!")

❖ ('2014-06-03 00:17:22',
In a State where rapists Are excused as "Boys who
make mistakes" By the Governing Chief, and by CM\'s
jest- Doomsday is neigh for that State.')

❖ ('2014-06-03 00:37:06',
@narendramodi I (@aksinh) have mailed to you a
book "REINCARNATION OF THE IRON-MAN" with your
story--I humbly invite yr comments on p.339.')

❖ ('2014-06-03 00:40:06',
@narendramodi I know you won't have time to read it,
but a staff could do that. Still I wonder what you would
say on the content of p.339.")

❖ ('2014-06-03 00:45:16',
@narendramodi Many of us (NRIs in USA) prayed to
God for your supreme victory, and are so jubilant now
no words can describe our happiness.')

❖ ('2014-06-03 00:49:06',
@narendramodi We regard and felicitate you like
Chandragupta who saved the country. We know now
that achhe din aa gaye and glory to Bharat')

❖ ('2014-06-06 02:11:19',
4 ten years @congressorg & @SoniaGandhiG Did
nothing but fill their pockets With #Coal, #CWG2014,
#2G Now @VisVp's Acts & they lose rest.")

❖ ('2014-06-06 02:17:18',
PM @VisVp talks to beaurocrats And @congressorg
protest like crazy! Clearly they're rats Jumping off the
sinking ship, when not plain lazy!")

❖ ('2014-06-06 02:33:48',
@congressorg's Spokespersons-- Are blind from loyalty
to the Top, Protesting @VisVp to stop more scam-
skeletons From becoming a new crop.")

❖ ('2014-06-07 19:43:23',
The #BlueStarBattle is a bad sign: Of the spark of
Khalistan to be alive. It's is a danger clandestine -- Not
to quench it would be naive.")

❖ ('2014-06-07 19:47:08',
Now is the time to take to task @SoniaGandhiG in
earnest. India now must firmly ask: Why she destroyed
the house where she came as a guest?')

❖ ('2014-06-07 19:52:26',
A fitting rigorous punishment Must be meted to @
congressorg & @SoniaGandhiG And all those who
were hell-bent To loot this Grand country.')

❖ ('2014-06-07 19:56:20',
@AAP & @ArvindKejriwal, With their insignia of
a broom, Were so flimsy, whimsical, and artificial That
their very start spelled their doom.')

❖ ('2014-06-07 20:02:36',
#AAPBrekingUp so badly Because @AAP was quilted by
@ArvindKejriwal 4 "Seats" san a "Stand"; sadly, With no
"Seat" 2 sit, it\'s bound 2 Fall')

❖ ('2014-06-07 20:06:01',
Not surprising that AK49, Adept in the hit-and-run
game, Misfired, and became an accident, And hit himself
- proving the worth of his name.')

❖ ('2014-06-07 20:12:11',
@Narendramodi_PM carries on his shoulders The
aspirations of 1.2 Billion Indians--his every step &
word matters; The sage has just begun !')

❖ ('2014-06-07 20:19:48',
Now @Narendramodi_PM is invited by President
Obama: USA is as a land of opportunity cited; Denying 2
turn a page,US now wants full Modinama.')

❖ ('2014-06-07 20:26:36',
The 21st century surely belongs To India -- even
Nostradamus did bestow @narendramodi and India's
glorious songs As early as 450 years ago.")

❖ ('2014-06-09 08:19:37',
Started Study Group in Fed. of Hindu Religious Studies
(FHRS), viz."Theory of Eternal Elements of Rational
Truth and Humanism (TEERTH)".')

❖ ('2014-06-09 08:23:59',
Watched President's Addr in Parl.-- so gratifying that
NaMo's vision (as also captured/predicted in my book
ReincarnationIronMan) reflected.")

❖ ('2014-06-13 05:07:40',
@Narendramodi_PM An article written by @tavleen_
singh on the political culture of Lutyens' Delhi is worth
-reading by the PM&BJPTopLeaders.")

❖ ('2014-06-13 05:15:17',
As a member of LocalCircles, I'd like to send @
tavleen_singh's Article to @Narendramodi_PM / @
rajendraPratapGuptaJi, if I had the EmailAddrs")

❖ ('2014-06-17 06:29:39',
#article370 is a dark shadow Upon #Kashmir's fate; It's
time to shun it; much ado Is made of it, of late ! This,the
Paradise Must realize.")

❖ ('2014-06-17 06:39:02',
#karachisiege, a mean Sign of the Homegrown
terrorists Of Pak -- that country should've foreseen This
as coming-- Terror's terrible twists!")

❖ ('2014-06-17 06:45:13',
Terrorists attacked Consulate of India In Kabul,
#Afghanistan, May 26,'14: The work of #ISI &
#Lashkar-e-Tiaba-- A not too uncommon scene !")

❖ ('2014-06-17 06:56:51',
India's largest state Has become Center of
#SerialOffender,crimes- 3 #BJP leaders killed, and the
rate Of gangrapes horrifying these times")

❖ ('2014-06-17 07:04:28',
How souls're sold in blind loyalty, and headless tongues
rant-- This, in @congressorg's @JhaSanjay U see, And in
SP's @gaubhatia--arrogant!")

❖ ('2014-06-17 07:18:25',
An intellectual like @ShashiTharoor Has sold to @
congressorg his head; Why'd he take a detour O'@
rahulgandhi2020, of being himself instead?")

❖ ('2014-06-17 07:28:21',
@NaMo's inviting the Heads Of the SARC countries is
GR8! In his crown he should add jades By opening 4
Panchsheel Nations India's Gate !")

❖ ('2014-06-17 07:37:54',
Now @NitishKumarJDU is woing @laluprasadrjd
notorious: 'Politics makes strange bedfellows'--This
saying Is true 4 sure,as proven again just")

❖ ('2014-06-17 07:47:34',
India's Chanakya tied His shikha after ending the Nand-
Vansh; Today we've Baba Ramdev who tried And helped
India to get rid o'@congressorg.")

❖ ('2014-06-17 08:04:42',
Chanakya made Chandragupta Maurya The New
Emperor; Baba Ramdev helped make @Narendramodi_
PM o'India, Helping 2 Uproot corrupt @congressorg")

❖ ('2014-06-17 08:13:20',
After giving @congressorg a crushing defeat, @
patanjali_yog goes back to @Haridwar retreat, Much
like Chanakya the GR8, Resuming his trait')

❖ ('2014-06-17 08:19:31',
Who's a saint here, and who's a cheat? @
rahulgandhi2020 is a schoolboy, and @ArvindKejriwal a
parakeet! Cold feat, They should just retreat!")

❖ ('2014-06-17 08:26:25',
Why does the media even bother To quote what @
ArvindKejriwal says-- He has no experience, no posture,
No principle,no head or tail or ways')

❖ ('2014-06-17 08:31:31',
More than a minute is more than enough: @
ArvindKejriwal is a spoiled child Of politics, made of
artificial stuff-- Now acting silly,now wild')

❖ ('2014-06-17 08:41:50',
Seeing @medhadefend & @AAP, Rationalizing
erroneous "Paap" Of riding luxury-jets, sheltering the
KHAAP, U turn from an activist in2 a staff')

❖ ('2014-06-17 08:48:21',
Marial Ik Bhade ka Tattoo Kahe 'Napunsak' Lauh-
Purush Ko! Neem Hakeem Wah, Ultaa Lattoo-- Are
Haakimo, Pakado Usako.")

❖ ('2014-06-17 08:52:58',
Manmohan Singh: Goonge, Bahare, Aur Sonia ki Nakel
Me -- Kala Sona, CWG Khel, aur Sane Kaale Coal Se;
Unakaa Jeena Bhalaa Jail Me!')

❖ ('2014-06-20 09:25:10',
Can an Indian modify Einstein..?-Ajay Sharma.. Indians
have done many such things.See "New Dimensions in..
Particle Physics.."by Ashok Sinha')

❖ ('2014-06-20 19:15:35',
See http://t.co/n51RkYB0yz? via @YahooNews.
Connection: 380,000 years of Big-Bang Inflation vs.
340,000 years of Cosmic Hindu Calendar(Yug?)')

❖ ('2014-06-20 20:59:23',
Obama\u2019s war on ISIS could reach beyond Iraq
into Syria http://t.co/Ioavdmy5NF If the ISIS/ISIL war
is not stopped now, it'd be bad 4 world.")

❖ ('2014-06-21 02:01:14',
RT @cleanh2oaction: RT @NRDCWater: Congress
shouldn't muddy the waters on the EPA's Clean Water
Act rule http://t.co/bRSZqDFmpu #ProtectCle\u2026")

❖ ('2014-06-21 02:01:44',
RT @cleanh2oaction: Thanks to @SenatorBarb @
SenatorBoxer @SenFeinstein for their fight to
#ProtectCleanWater this week!')

❖ ('2014-06-21 02:06:02',
@cleanh2oaction This is a universal problem and
should be treated as such. #ProtectCleanWater should
be a mission 4all 4Life, in every Land.')

❖ ('2014-06-21 02:07:51',
RT @cleanh2oaction: Americans want @EPA to #ProtectCleanWater & NOT #DitchTheRule. So why is the #Senate trying so hard to silence us? http\u2026')

❖ ('2014-06-21 02:09:16',
RT @cleanh2oaction: The Senate needs to let @EPA #ProtectCleanWater. Spread the word http://t.co/QKPOidjLef http://t.co/pyjretqBq1')

❖ ('2014-06-21 02:11:34',
RT @cleanh2oaction: .@repgaramendi @EPA science panel found streams & wetlands vital to health of all waterways. #ProtectCleanWater')

❖ ('2014-06-21 02:13:43',
RT @EPAwater: Streams matter! Check out this infographic by @EarthGauge for all the reasons streams are important. #water #USwaters http://\u2026')

❖ ('2014-06-21 02:14:24',
RT @cleanh2oaction: "We can innovate our way to a better future. That\'s what America does best" - @GinaEPA announcing new #Carbon rules')

❖ ('2014-06-21 02:17:22',
RT @cleanh2oaction: RT @ltcwa: Drinking water depends on smart water policy & so do so many business TY@EPAwater http://t.co/U5O9gphTLq #Pr\u2026')

❖ ('2014-06-21 02:18:33',
RT @cleanh2oaction: New @EPA, @EPAwater rule would protect 2m miles of streams not clearly covered by #CleanWaterAct. #USWaters http://t.co\u2026')

❖ ('2014-06-21 02:19:34',
RT @cleanh2oaction: #CleanWaterAct loopholes threaten waterways for future generations. Our kids deserve clean water too #watercantwait')

❖ ('2014-06-21 02:21:18',
RT @cleanh2oaction: Want to #ProtectCleanWater?
Then join our team - http://t.co/YyYky4bkee')

❖ ('2014-06-21 02:21:55',
RT @cleanh2oaction: . @EPA, @WhiteHouse - We're in
it for the long haul to #ProtectCleanWater: http://t.co/
lvXexfo4W4")

❖ ('2014-06-21 02:22:44',
RT @cleanh2oaction: It's about time to
#ProtectCleanWater - http://t.co/KZHeYMG9ZL")

❖ ('2014-06-21 02:23:56',
RT @cleanh2oaction: We applaud @EPA 's action
because diesel use in hydraulic fracturing poses a public
health risk http://t.co/qSP0eqB5CK")

❖ ('2014-06-21 02:24:50',
RT @cleanh2oaction: Spills are bad but the everyday
stuff might be worse. Big Coal has been dumping
#coalash into our water for decades: ht\u2026')

❖ ('2014-06-21 02:33:02',
All over the world, industrial and public waste are
dumped into rivers. Clean water in rivers, lakes, and
streams are universal requirements')

❖ ('2014-06-21 04:12:53',
How to get started with Drive - https://t.
co/0l4ImVKKxK Starting to use Google Drive (15 GB) on
06/20/2014 for archiving my BOOKS &Files etc')

❖ ('2014-06-21 04:21:55',
To resume my verse tweets for the Modern Little
Mahabharat: PressRelease-- http://t.co/2Sr7Pc37jQ
Marketing by Xlibris disappointing. Late.')

❖ ('2014-06-27 20:45:32',
Sonia and terrorism http://t.co/YA9okWI1Fz via @
SlideShare Articles like this should come in light NOW
(also ref. to S. Swamy's 420 charge!)")

❖ ('2014-06-27 20:55:46',
Twitter Buttons https://t.co/ZgyQ1S0HeZ via @twitter
Let the messenger bird fly to spread the word on
Atlantic's either side, far & wide!!")

❖ ('2014-06-29 18:21:51',
RT @BJP4India: @aksinh The intellectual capital of
India - let the change begin from Varanasi. http://t.co/
R7TUMwrJcE')

❖ ('2014-06-29 18:32:42',
@rahulg Sorry I'm replying so late; I just saw yr Tweet;
so very sweet Of U 2 ask: Now India's Fate Is under no
less than an Epic feat.")

❖ ('2014-06-29 18:37:37',
@rahulg It's a Modern Mahabharat, In which @
narendramodi is like Parth- (Arjun), the Hero Greatest;
but At Nomination, he gave a new arth.")

❖ ('2014-06-29 18:52:09',
@rahulg 2 his role in this Gr8 War, who Said:"Ma Ganga
NeMujheBulayaHai." So he is Gangaputra(Gangey/
Bheeshma),too! Fighting 4 Dharma\'s JAI.')

❖ ('2014-06-29 19:04:30',
@rahulg Thus, @NarendraModi Ji Is both (like) Parth
and Gangey! I'm writing in Verse-Tweets-'The Modern
Mahabharat'-Satyamev Jayate,I C")

❖ ('2014-06-29 20:24:37',
@Narendramodi_PM @BJPlndia @ndtv @timesofindia
@timesnow @nytimesworld @PTI_News @
HeadlinesToday @SoniaGandhiG C India's 1 Month
Unfurled")

- ❖ ('2014-06-29 20:35:43',
In this 1 Month, we had SARC Countries Meet in
Hindusthan; @Narendramodi_PM Visited to Bhutan; @
SushmaSwaraj 2 Bangladesh--and All're Glad")

- ❖ ('2014-06-29 20:46:06',
Some Say:Talks+Terror is Bad Policy with Pak; &
Inflation is still Up; But 59 Months are yet 2 go, 2 Add,
& It is a Gr8 Start 2ward the Top.')

- ❖ ('2014-06-29 20:53:16',
@Congessorg is still analyzing Just What went Wrong
with them. Don't they have eyes 2 C Anything: Dozens
of Ghotales that brought such Shame")

- ❖ ('2014-06-29 21:11:24',
@digvijaya_28 @ManishTewari @JhaSanjay Still singing
4 @SoniaGandhiG Silly Loyal Bunch 2 the Dynasty; It's
@BJP4India one needs 2 Go See.")

- ❖ ('2014-06-29 21:16:07',
@Narendramodi_PM Going 2 Kedarnath-- How
Inspirational is our Prime- Minister! May He Live Long
4 Bharat! And Let Dharma Rule the Land&Time')

- ❖ ('2014-06-30 23:28:50',
Reminding China of 'Panchsheel' Is like asking Pak to
arrest LeT's Head -- both of them feel That lying is their
birthright,beyond any test!")

- ❖ ('2014-06-30 23:39:25',
@NaMoPM' presence At #ModiInSriharikota is a shot in
arm Of ISRO's #space Program, and hence, Testament of
India's gr8 #Development Dharma!!")

- ❖ ('2014-06-30 23:43:06',
The day isn't very far when France, Germany, Canada,
and Singapore And All'd India's praise sing and dance,
& Shake China's & America's core")

❖ ('2014-06-30 23:48:24',
@SwamySwaroopananda's declaration That India
should #article370 abrogate Is one step closer to the
solution For resolving #kashmir's Fate!!")

❖ ('2014-06-30 23:58:11',
@congressorg's Rai questions @NaMo4PM's Election
and the Premiership of India's! It's time @sonia_gandhi
comes To Apologize for such Jazz!!")

❖ ('2014-07-01 00:06:31',
@congressorg's ugly mouthpieces are blaring such
shameless speaks! Do they realize that the Polar Star
Gains its cognizance in more weeks!!")

❖ ('2014-07-01 00:11:14',
Give @Narendramodi_PM at least Ten weeks to mend
the fatal wounds That @congressorg created o'er ten
years Of scandals--like ghostly sounds!")

❖ ('2014-07-01 00:15:48',
What's this--the rising price Of onions? Isn't there a
better index To measure the Govt's efficacy &
choice Of how 2 keep balances & checks?")

❖ ('2014-07-01 00:23:16',
A mud-slinging, mad #tmcongres man is on Tape
Threatening Opposition all: #MPThreatensRape --an
ape Of the Jungle-Raj's animal--Tapas Pal!")

❖ ('2014-07-02 18:40:21',
@ShashiTharoor. Seems too sharp for @congressorg,
And even for the Juror! Is @SoniaGandhiG's visit to the
morgue The secret of his detour?")

❖ ('2014-07-02 18:50:37',
#PriceRise and #inflation'a string Raise its head! @
NaMo_PM has to bring The web of thread Under a wand
magical and saintly Persistently.")

* ('2014-07-02 18:55:51',
@Baghdadi is now close To seize the #Khaliphat. It's time the world chose To to make him stay put- 'fore he tramples Churches and Temples.")

* ('2014-07-02 19:06:48',
@Baghdadi is now close to seize the Khilaphate; It's time the world chose To make him stay put, Before he tramples Any Churches and Temples")

* ('2014-07-02 19:17:43',
@ShashiTharoor Too good for @congressorg, And for the Juror! Is @SoniaGandhiG's visit to the morgue The askance Of this Unholy Alliance?")

* ('2014-07-03 17:56:18',
#Kashmir-heaven on earth; Haven for Pundits & Sufi Saints- Was betrayed by #Article370's birth! Where now #KashmiriPandits Mantra-chants!")

* ('2014-07-03 18:03:13',
@justicearnab said today "INTEGRATION Shall Happen Soon"--Ghee-Shakkar Uske Munh Me!For this The NATION Will be so Grateful to Modi-Sarkar!')

* ('2014-07-03 18:13:43',
Such a controversy abt Sai Baba And Shankaracharya' statement: Granted either Kashi or Kaba Is fine, still their locations so different!")

* ('2014-07-03 18:25:12',
This is not to mean Exclusivity-- Hinduism Is Inclusive supremely; Yet each tradition has a sagacity Of its own, much dear to its family.')

* ('2014-07-03 18:25:12',
This is not to mean Exclusivity-- Hinduism Is Inclusive supremely; Yet each tradition has a sagacity Of its own, much dear to its family.')

❖ ('2014-07-03 18:33:40',
@Shankaracharya_is right in that Thousands of Saints,
Yogis, Rishis have graced this land--then at This
juncture why Sai Baba so unique is?')

❖ ('2014-07-03 18:54:30',
If \'Manokamana Poorna Karana" Is the Test, &
miracles Make one Gr8, then Banana & Apple are
more Worshipables- As is each stir Of Nature')

❖ ('2014-07-03 19:04:54',
@ShashiTharoor, is there something Fishy in @
sptvrock death-- Murder? Suicide? Poisoning? A Love-
Triangle's Aftermath? Come-on, Ex-UN man!")

❖ ('2014-07-03 19:13:32',
@SoniaGandhiG of @congressorg Tried saving @
ShashiTharoor, Visiting at the morgue Of Sunanda poor.
Is Sonia's stance- An unholy alliance?")

❖ ('2014-07-04 02:52:02',
#SunandaDeathMystery is a sad Comment On @
ShashiTharoor such A genius, but sold to @congressorg;
too bad! He could...and still can do much!')

❖ ('2014-07-04 02:58:21',
When'd our Government get it right? It's not just ISI and
LeT Who are anti-Indian; it's the whole might Of Islam,
including Pak Government.")

❖ ('2014-07-04 03:15:06',
Our leaders keep hoping That Pak would mend Her
ways, but Pak'd keep hurting India, and then pretend All
is Normal Biz- B it Nawaz or Hafiz.")

❖ ('2014-07-04 03:28:14',
Many Muslims feel they've done No wrong, if, to serve
Islam, they kill or lie or rape (no pun); @allah sees all
and would reward their verve")

❖ ('2014-07-04 03:37:54',
Lying for the sake of Islam is no moral crime, nor
looting, Burning, Massacre--in the name Of religion,
tyranny&terror is BestGr8est thing!')

❖ ('2014-07-09 19:45:03',
Only One Strong and Sane Voice, & Radiant,
Leading Face! @NaMo_PM is the Beacon of Hope;
Rejoice-- Look at the Wall of Memory of the Race!')

❖ ('2014-07-09 19:49:45',
@timesofindia @ndtv @timesnow @aajtak @htTweets
We Must Vow Never to let Corruption & Chaos
Creep Back In the Nation,Politics thru a crack.')

❖ ('2014-07-09 19:55:12',
Didn't @ArvindKejriwal say the media is paid by @
NaMo--What a Childish Mindset! He should be jailed,
laid Bare on Ice-Slab for such rubbish!")

❖ ('2014-07-09 20:02:27',
Raja should've taken a bold chance: The unwritten
testimony,unsigned Note! @congressorg's sick
Governance-- How this Party dared ask 4 vote?")

❖ ('2014-07-09 20:05:56',
@aamir_khan and his #SatyamevJayate Should be
written in Golden Letters-- Let's pay homage, &
say: He symbolized the concience of all of us!")

❖ ('2014-07-10 19:11:00',
http://t.co/mGHjXQsaN6 4 Civilization 2 Rise &
Make Progress, Nations Must Set Their Eyes 2 End
Terrorism with Finesse Every nation')

❖ ('2014-07-10 19:33:08',
@arunjaitley's #SuperBudget in the #parliament-- All
ears! ? on #infrastructure #infrastructure 2 B Spent, As
@bjp_ its Magic Wand Steers?")

❖ ('2014-07-10 19:39:48',
Rupees 60,000 crores for the Novel Bullet-Train
Between Ahmedabad and Mumbai This Budget'd
Entertain, And 200crores for the Statue of Unity!")

❖ ('2014-07-10 19:50:23',
Lot of fuss @congressorg made! Their frustration from
losing the Election Simmering from Top down to each
aide Without any true reflection.')

❖ ('2014-07-10 19:59:58',
It was fun to watch @SoniaGandhiG- & her
spent force of @DrAMSinghvi, @JhaSanjay & @
ManishTewari Fish for fault with #SuperBudget of @
bjp_.')

❖ ('2014-07-10 20:08:10',
@bjp_'s @smritiirani summed this sense Of
Hopelessness Desperate State Of @congressorg, living
in the past tense, & Not Repenting, Todate.")

❖ ('2014-07-10 20:18:21',
When'd @congressorg see The Light and Introspect
upon its Grave Sins of Abject Corruption and Policy-
Paralysis that drove it to the Grave?")

❖ ('2014-07-10 20:21:41',
Now @SoniaGandhiG arrogantly blames @bjp_ for
vindictive politics As @Swamy39 simply claims That
she & @rahulgandhi2020 played dirty tricks.')

❖ ('2014-07-10 20:36:03',
Let now the Great River Ganga flow Like the 'Anchal'
and 'Cummerband' Of BharatMata, in Full Glow And
Glory, from Gangotri to Uttarakhand!!")

❖ ('2014-07-10 20:42:54',
Let Grand Ships sail up and down, From Varanasi to the
Bay Of Bengal, Gracing many a Gram and Town, Gifting
Life, in every ripple and sway!!')

❖ ('2014-07-10 20:54:37',
Now, the famed Diamond-Interconnect Of the Indian
Railway speedy Will decorate the entire set Of
Metropolis:Delhi, Kolkata, Chennai, Mumbai!')

❖ ('2014-07-10 20:57:21',
From Rishikesh to VaishnoDevi, From Dwarka to
Jagannathpuri-- From Kashmir to Kanyakumari, All
destinations would invite every Teerthyatri.')

❖ ('2014-07-24 19:45:54',
@Narendramodi_PM is focusing on #SARC And @
brics2014 2 consolidate Friendship with countries that
mark @PMOIndia's Foreign Policy truly GR8.")

❖ ('2014-07-24 19:54:07',
Yet Onions make people cry, & Tomatoes turn their
cheeks red. When'd #prices b no longer sky-high; &
#Markets full of veges& butter & bread?")

❖ ('2014-07-24 20:01:42',
@congressorg is making Herculean effort 2 B the
#Leader Of Opposition: With just 44 Seats, &
#CongUnrest In Assam,J&K & Maha in
Rebellion.')

❖ ('2014-07-24 20:10:42',
@Narendramodi_PM is focusing on @SARC And the
#BRICS2014 to consolidate Friendship with countries to
mark @PMOIndia's Foreign Policy as GR8")

❖ ('2014-07-24 20:16:37',
@congressorg is in Herculean effort To B the @Leader
Of Opposition With just 44 Seats; #CongUnrest Reigning
in Assam,J&K,Maha-in Rebellion.')

❖ ('2014-07-24 20:26:54',
Swamy Swaroopanand, The Shankaracharya of Dwarka,
Says Sai Baba's worshipping and Treatment as God is
misguided Puja, as per Sanatan Dharma.")

❖ ('2014-07-24 20:41:07',
The Sai-Bhaktas are Adamant to worship him as their
God Just 'cause they've their heart's content Fulfilled by
him--then that's rather odd!")

❖ ('2014-07-24 20:49:21',
Devotees of Sat-Sai Baba shower Gold and silver and
cash at his feet To get their wishes--then whose power
Makes Sai Baba perform such feat?')

❖ ('2014-07-24 20:59:10',
Devotion to God and wanting One's wishes fulfilled in
exchange Is rather like a bargain, granting God your
trust as a quid-pro-quo arranged.")

❖ ('2014-07-24 21:03:07',
True devotion to God asks for nothing At all--Rather,
it's shear admiration Of the Nature, of the Universe and
Everything Of His Creation.")

❖ ('2014-07-27 06:17:48',
@justicearnab's mightily upset about Gujarati school
text-books; in his eyes Feeding the cow is a cause to
shout: Warning-#DesignToPolarise!")

❖ ('2014-07-27 06:27:06',
"India wants Peace," says @justicearnab, "What
difference a loudspeaker @Eid Atop a temple make?"
Did he snub An Azaan-Caller atop a Masjid?')

❖ ('2014-07-27 06:30:10',
The slave-mentality & the legacy Of colonial rule
for 400 years Have so blunted the sensibility of Desi
Hearts, they respond only to Fears.')

❖ ('2014-07-27 06:33:48',
Why should a student learn To perform Havan; 2 feed
the cow; To recite the Gayatri Mantra, and 2 yearn For
the country's past glory, to vow?")

❖ ('2014-07-27 06:38:03',
@SudhanshuTrived needed to point That it wasn't the
political map of 2014; But the Cultural-Spiritual Impact
Of Bharat that the world'd seen")

❖ ('2014-07-27 06:41:46',
Blowing candles on Birthday Is so fashionable, singing
"Happy B\'Day 2 U!" But isn\'t it indeed true 2 say That
we take pride in aping in zoo?')

❖ ('2014-07-27 06:45:26',
Who's @justicearnab to tell That the Golden Period of
Bharat didn't exist When the Cultural-Spiritual Spell Of
Bharat covered West and East?")

❖ ('2014-07-27 06:55:11',
Does @justicearnab \'Go\'swamy Feel that "Go" in his
name doesn\'t mean "Cow" Rather, it means Tan\'Go\' of
RSS-BJP? Would he feed the cow, Now?')

❖ ('2014-07-27 07:03:35',
I'd such admiration for @justicearnab, 4 his journalistic
acumen; (Visit http://t.co/lARHfNYcoT For my praise of
him in Political Fiction!)")

❖ ('2014-07-27 07:11:18',
But he rather disappointed me-- Like other soul-sold,
Hindu-bashing English-fashioned Pseudo-Secularist; he
Hardly does in a new tune sing!')

❖ ('2014-07-27 07:17:48',
Now people like @AtulAnjaan Belonging to the
UnIndian-Dharmaless CPI Preach what Secular
Hindusthan Should B, Finger-pointing, big-big eyes!')

❖ ('2014-07-27 07:24:10',
Congrats 2 @shivshaktijnu and @NalinKohli, Who
Show unflinching support To @Narendramodi_PM
convincingly; Facing those who the Truth distort')

❖ ('2014-07-27 07:36:40',
Barely 2 months in @Narendramodi_PM\'s regime; And
some keep hollering, "Achchhe Din?" They forget 60
years of @congressorg\'s crime, The sin.')

❖ ('2014-07-28 20:03:02',
@SoniaGandhiG @Rahugan & Top @congressorg
are doing 'Manthan' Introspection why they lost--Now
STOP This Drama-see the elephant:Corruption")

❖ ('2014-08-03 00:03:04',
This COMPLETES THIS EPISODE OF NATWAR SINGH\'S
BOOK: "ONE LIFE IS NOT ENOUGH." Hope U enjoyed it.
Pls Reply to @aksinh ****THE END****')

❖ ('2014-08-03 00:07:43',
Now, it's Wait & See What the Future and Fate
Bring: @congressorg's many many Scandals &
Scams Ugly Are quietly waiting in the Wing to Ring")

❖ ('2014-08-03 00:11:20',
Now the reign of terror and Control as Dictator had
gone: @congressorg has lost beyond A recovery, and @
narendramodi as India's PM is sworn.")

❖ ('2014-08-03 00:15:53',
Any remedy for the great loss Of her face & dignity
has gone--everyone Is asking why the Big Boss Had
stooped that low, lowering her big gun')

❖ ('2014-08-03 00:21:30',
The Truth that All now know Is that she and @
priyankagandh12, her daughter, Had gone to meet him,
though This dubious step could not buy her')

❖ ('2014-08-03 00:28:49',
Was @SoniaGandhiG frustrated, put down, &
Humiliated by this turn? Hardly--in fact, she does
proclaim That she'd write her own book, 2 churn")

❖ ('2014-08-03 00:34:53',
"NO, there is no motive behind This book," said @
Natwars01732549 in reply Of queries of every kind By
top anchors, scaling the earth and sky')

❖ ('2014-08-03 00:37:50',
Such an uproar quickly came to be From this sensitive
revelation! Interviews after interviews, in TV Channels
and newspapers in the nation.')

❖ ('2014-08-03 00:40:50',
So, basically, this #NatwarBookRow Had brought down
the image Of @SoniaGandhiG, to bestow A scandalous
downfall, like a transparent mirage!')

❖ ('2014-08-03 00:44:06',
The string, and make people Do her vested bids, with no
risks Or responsibility on paper, casting spell Of power
and charm (?) and kicks (?)')

❖ ('2014-08-03 00:49:27',
Her and kill her in a riot Of emotional outburst vengeful.
Better to be behind a tight Door or curtain, and
surreptitiously & remotely pull')

❖ ('2014-08-03 00:52:57',
So, it was just for mundane safety And security of her
life, to ward Off any potential incident untoward, and
nutty Enemy who might discard')

❖ ('2014-08-03 01:01:27',
Fatal risk to her life. He had lost his Grandmother @
IndiraGandi1722, and Father, @RajivGandhi, in strife--
Getting hit by bullets & terror.')

❖ ('2014-08-03 01:04:12',
Of fear, forbade his mother From accepting the
prestigious post, Saying that this made his mother
Vulnerable 2 inadvertently invite and host')

❖ ('2014-08-03 01:09:07',
The only reason @SoniaGandhiG Didn't grab India's
Premiership Was thitimid son of hers, for he Simply and
obstinately, in a fearsome grip")

❖ ('2014-08-03 01:12:23',
"It wasn\'t an act noble Of fathomless sacrifice great;
But, rather, the whole drama, with null Touch of
greatness -- just a twist of Fate!')

❖ ('2014-08-03 01:19:03',
And now, after some 9 years or so, This notorious
#NatwarBookRow Has become an embarrassing expo
Of the Truth, announcing unambiguously,"NO,')

❖ ('2014-08-03 01:26:20',
@SoniaGandhiG's son, @rahulgandhi2020 Was
appointed the Vice-President Of @congressorg; and the
Mother-&-Son, Pity! Team became a target!")

❖ ('2014-08-03 01:31:52',
Because the QueenO' Hearts In the GameO' CardsO'
Indian Politics Now the President of @congressorg, and
the Parts And the Party, All tricks")

❖ ('2014-08-03 01:36:18',
"No one could throw away The Power, Prestige, and
Fortune Of being the PM of India," so did say The man
on street; & thus @SoniaGandhiG soon')

❖ ('2014-08-03 01:42:05',
"What a Supreme Sacrifice!" -- Shouted the whole of
India, "Just like their great tradition!" the dice Was cast
by @congressorg, for @Sonia.')

❖ ('2014-08-03 01:52:35',
In 2004, our Sonia sweet Declined the Prime-Minister-
Ship, gave it to Manmohan @Plaid_Singh, a Treat,
Attributing this to her Voice Inner!')

❖ ('2014-08-03 01:56:19',
A book, "One Life Is Not Enough," And it sparks a huge controversy: It contains a bit of volatile stuff, Hardly hiding the rhyming nursery!')

❖ ('2014-08-03 02:00:41',
@Natwars01732549, the Ex-Foreign- Minister O'India, under Rajiv &@SoniaGandhiG Writes a book; then Publishes it, yielding a bit of History.")

❖ ('2014-08-03 02:16:55',
@aksinh offers the following @Verse-Tweets A revealing episode of #NatwarBookRow: A measure of @SoniaGandhiG's Heart-Beats! So, Here we GO!")

❖ ('2014-08-13 08:22:36',
@congressorg's ally in J&K-- @abdullah_omar-- looking so meek, Sitting by @Narendramodi_PM today: He must join @BJP4India by the Kargil Peak!")

❖ ('2014-08-13 08:27:31',
@rahulgandhi2020 & @SoniaGandhiG-- Watch how the man on the street Shows you once again that he Is wiser than U, & gives U both little treat')

❖ ('2014-08-13 08:30:51',
@SoniaGandhiG is just like Pak-- Truth for her is of no value. Resorting to Untruth they balk Not; in her dealings, Truth has nothing to do.')

❖ ('2014-08-13 08:34:22',
For her gossipy piece ridiculous, Since Communism gives a hoot In religion or faith in God, and thus Numbers--God's gift--for them is moot")

❖ ('2014-08-13 08:40:22',
Granted,Communism cares little For religious bent- so,communal Riot-news as voiced by the Master (Mistress?)of VoteBankPolitics runs faster!')

❖ ('2014-08-13 08:44:34',
@SoniaGandhiG chooses Kerala To announce her piece
of mathematical Wizardry--Are Communists more
prone To fall for her numbers & the throne?')

❖ ('2014-08-13 08:55:27',
Hasn't she learned by introspection (That @
BJP4India holds @congressorg'd do) That it's
'Arrogance'&'Corruption' That felled her
CongressZoo")

❖ ('2014-08-13 09:02:56',
And that\'s in UP alone, mind you! @SoniaGandhiG
says with grace: "Some 600 riots in Maharastra, too." 2
States where she faces the Vote-Race')

❖ ('2014-08-13 09:06:42',
600 riots in, say, 80 days Means 7.5 riots/day, on the
average. The math here stretches in queer ways,
Involving Real & Imaginary Stages.')

❖ ('2014-08-13 09:11:58',
A new wave not of @NarendraModi4PM But of
communal riots in UP! 600 riots, she says, in 3 months
Of @Narendramodi_PM and @BJP4India victory.')

❖ ('2014-08-13 09:15:31',
@SoniaGandhiG still arrogantly Pursues
#VoteBankPolitics that gave Her such a crushing defeat.
now patently And falsely says: "The\'s a wave-')

❖ ('2014-08-13 09:20:13',
#rahulwakesup when @SoniaGandhiG Pushed him up.
Lo and behold! Now he's attacking @bjp_ From the Well
of Parliament--Typhoon in a tea-cup!")

❖ ('2014-08-13 10:03:49',
@BJP_Team, I, @aksinh (full name: Ashok K. Sinha)
hereby pray And apply to be a Member with the aim Of
serving my country (India) each day.')

❖ ('2014-08-13 10:09:34',
I pen verse-tweets to portray Significant happenings
in India --My beloved country--though in USA I live and
have 2 b a citizen of America!')

❖ ('2014-08-13 10:13:06',
Follow @aksinh to enjoy Verse-Tweets singing @
NaMo4PM's praise; & see my Novel for the joy Of
reading on India's cultural-historical phases.")

❖ ('2014-08-13 10:18:46',
@TeamBJP, would U give a tip For how I could join U and
serve India: Could you grant me Membership Despite
my having a passport of America?')

❖ ('2014-08-15 10:23:58',
Book Launch \u201cReincarnation of the Iron \u2013
Man\u201d by Ahnis Kosha | World Hindu News http://t.
co/L5PjZ2oIvR Lt(2ⁿᵈ)Link: http://t.co/lARHfNYcoT')

❖ ('2014-08-15 11:13:33',
@aksinh:I JUST DISCOVERED THAT MY BOOK
"REINCARNATION OF THE IRON-MAN" IS LISTED
IN http://t.co/JJhZoIZbqm & most major book
webstes. BAH!')

❖ ('2014-08-15 11:19:37',
@aksinh I'm interested in info re publishing/marketing
my (22) books all over; I'd appreciate info from Book
Distributors & others in reply.")

❖ ('2014-08-15 11:34:50',
My BOOK with 500 Verse-Tweets on India's 2014
Election,Poltcs @Narendramodi_PM @BJP4India Ready.
Pl Contact @aksinh or Kosha.Ahnis@gmail.com")

❖ ('2014-08-15 12:39:04',
@shivshaktijnu I wonder if U were able to send to
PMO or @Narendramodi_PM @VisVp the book I
sent("Reincarnation.."),now on @google -Ashok')

❖ ('2014-09-21 05:40:53',
AshokSinha asking @xlibrispub: I authored 12+ books
published by U- Listed in many a website & book-
club, Please make'em 'Returnable,' too?")

❖ ('2014-09-21 05:46:26',
@xlibrispub'd get a manuscript For Publishing soon:
A Collection Of 500 Verse-Tweets on India's politics- A
First in History of Publication!")

❖ ('2014-09-21 05:51:49',
@FareedZakaria Congrats on your recent Interview
with @Narendramodi_PM! I invite U to Visit Urgent- Ly
http://t.co/nB7ZwtWhZp on the same!')

❖ ('2014-09-21 06:09:08',
@FareedZakaria Congrats 2 U on your visit 2 India to
C @Narendramodi_PM, 4 sure! Pls. also visit a Bit 4 @
TIME @CNN http://t.co/VutbG8roti')

❖ ('2014-09-21 06:18:06',
@FareedZakaria & @BillGates, may I add: @
washingtonpost too- Pls. visit http://t.co/nB7ZwtWhZp
ll B glad 2 C Reincarnation's wonderful hue")

❖ ('2014-09-21 06:26:21',
@BillGates & @FareedZakaria, I wish 2 send 2 you
a small gift; May I ask 4 yr favor as an India- N: Pls. send
me your Email Addr as a lift!')

❖ ('2014-09-21 06:34:19',
@Richardvermaas Congrats 2 U as @BarackObama
Names U 2 B U.S.Ambassador 2 India: d witness the
panorama Depicted in http://t.co/nB7ZwtWhZp")

❖ ('2014-09-21 06:52:01',
@shivshaktijnuji,Thanks-Hope U gave 2 @PMOIndia on
my behalf Reincarnation of the Iron-Man: @ModiWave
Makes @congressorg cry & @bjp_ laugh')

❖ ('2014-09-21 07:01:23',
@shivshaktijnu U could pls. also distribute The Link:
http://t.co/nB7ZwtWhZp 2 Media and All 2 bear fruit!
Could U send me some Emails more?')

❖ ('2014-09-21 07:17:14',
@shivshaktijnuji I'm preparing A Book of 500 Verse-
Tweets On @narendramodi @SoniaGandhiG, 2 sing A
New Mahabharat:of @congressorg's defeats.")

❖ ('2014-09-21 07:33:24',
I've gathered many a name Of Media & Senior
Journalists But need Email addresses 2 Email it with
the aim Of spreading the word:story's gist.")

❖ ('2014-09-21 07:54:42',
@Narendramodi_PM to @FareedZakaria, "4 India\'ll
live & die the Muslims of India. Terrorists\'re
delusional 2 feel they\'d be anti-national.')

❖ ('2014-09-21 08:05:25',
"We believe in Development.. I\'ve felt since childhood
That Muslims\'re born with talent, Even in a poorest
family--it should B understood!')

❖ ('2014-09-21 08:14:09',
"But @congressorg & @samajvadiparty1 Playing
Vote-Bank politics Gave the Muslims no opportunity-
none. @bjp_ & @Narendramodi_PM want 2 fix')

❖ ('2014-09-21 08:24:39',
"This problem: give them Opportunity. We need 2 reach
out 2 Muslims and Other sections of the society, In
Gujarat and in rest of this land.')

❖ ('2014-09-21 08:34:29',
Said @narendramodi to @CNN,"Islamic Terrorists are
no champions of Muslims(or of Islam; their dirty trick
Earns them only bad name, scoff.)"')

❖ ('2014-09-21 08:43:20',
@ShahnawazBJP said,"@Narendramodi_PM-Ji Has said
the right thing:The Muslims in India love the country
And will do anything 4 the country.'")

❖ ('2014-09-21 08:54:38',
Said @NajmaHeptullah,"Thrilled that @
Narendramodi_PM has endorsed Patriotism of Indian
Muslims(\'Death\'s Merchant\' Him @SoniaGandhiG
called).')

❖ ('2014-09-21 09:13:18',
"(@NarendraModi\'s saying so) Will prevent
Muslim boys from falling in ISIS-AlQaeda trap.It\'s
laughable(Ho!Ho!) He\'s called anti-Muslim-')

❖ ('2014-09-21 09:24:30',
"By the Opposition."(@SoniaGandhiG & Pseudo-
Secularists in the country Who know not ABC of
\'Secularism,\' Only Vote-banking with Muslims)')

❖ ('2014-09-21 09:30:09',
And look what @SALMANKHURSHID gay (The Ex-
ForeignMinister)had to say: "@Narendramodi_PM is
saying this, may Be,because he has to go to USA.'")

❖ ('2014-09-21 09:39:46',
@shahiimam1 said, "If from heart Comes such (@
Narendramodi_PM\'s) statement, It can be seen as a
fresh start (In the Minority\'s interest.)'")

❖ ('2014-09-21 09:54:17',
@FareedZakaria (& @aksinh) say, @
Narendramodi_PM'd be seen at World's Stage As a Great
Statesman;the Day Is neigh 4 India's New Golden Age.")

❖ ('2014-09-21 16:05:41',
Today @FareedZakaria @ibnlive #TheModiInterview Is
being rebroadcast by @CNN-IBN again; So I, @aksinh,
must continue My Verse-Twitter Train')

❖ ('2014-09-21 16:13:16',
This Modern Mahabharat of a sort Is worth-penning in
some detail; For the posterity to exhort And to learn
from @NewBJP, and to @NaMo Hail!')

❖ ('2014-09-21 16:25:29',
So, here we've some more words Echoing great
promises, averting danger; And watch as our Captain
girds To sail to become a new sea-changer.")

❖ ('2014-09-21 16:33:36',
"India & China both grew Together, rapidly," said @
narendramodi Ji To @FareedZakaria in his 1ˢᵗ Interview
After becoming PM of the Country.')

❖ ('2014-09-21 16:43:23',
"China cannot live in isolation: Its neighbors it must
engage! In this era of Partnership, our Nation Must trust
China to obey Global Laws.')

❖ ('2014-09-21 16:48:48',
(Then comes the news-50 Chinese Troupes're trying 2
infiltrate Into India in Chunar Sector of Assam State:
Won't they such activities cease?")

❖ ('2014-09-21 16:54:12',
Some 200 Terrorists-ISI's stooges- Are also trying into
India to infiltrate, Taking advantage of the deluges
That've visited the J&K State.")

❖ ('2014-09-21 17:01:49',
@alqaeda is trying to infiltrate In the Indian State
Of Assam-they're truly delusional To think Indian
Muslims'll dance to their tune dull.")

❖ ('2014-09-21 17:11:43',
.@Narendramodi_PM said abt USA He\'s to visit shortly,
"Both our countries Have common history &
culture: our ties Are in Upswing, so to say.')

❖ ('2014-09-21 17:18:13',
"There has been a big change In Indo-US Relations this
century! Ups &Downs there have been strange In
the century past,that we must now bury')

❖ ('2014-09-21 17:26:18',
"Both our great Democracies Can have new Strategic
Alliance. Democracy is in India\'s DNA: It\'s Indian
legacy; We\'ve 2 gain our old instance.')

❖ ('2014-09-21 17:36:34',
"We don\'t need 2 become anything else Or emulate
China:India must remain India:We fell from a high place,
But now have chance 2 rise again.')

❖ ('2014-09-21 17:44:09',
"This is an era in which Asian Powers\'ll play key role.
Our Relations\'ll be more than a sandwich Between
Delhi&Washington;but see the whole')

❖ ('2014-09-21 17:58:17',
"World-a new global strategy, 2 fight Terrorism, for
instance,which is a crisis Against Humanity-AlQaeda
& ISIS- We must finish their might')

❖ ('2014-09-21 18:08:45',
"There are many similarities between
India&USA;and new Strategic Alliance is possible!
I\'m confident such alliance genuine We\'ll now Will.')

❖ ('2014-09-21 18:15:46',
"A word about Women\'s Empoerment- It can follow
only by ensuring Education For girls (and hence girls\'
toilet In every school is my mission.')

❖ ('2014-09-21 18:20:01',
"Dignity of Women is the collective Responsibility of
ALL Indians; And central for our plans and activity For
a \'Clean\' society and Nation.')

❖ ('2014-09-21 18:30:57',
"Work is my true Relaxation; And Books are my
Companions. I never feel lonely. And my concentration-
Level increases through Yoga-Aasans.')

❖ ('2014-09-21 18:43:45',
"I started doing Yoga at an early age. People\'ve faith
in me Always. It\'s my Duty not to break This Trust
they\'ve in me,for Country\'s sake."')

❖ ('2014-09-21 18:51:03',
Here're some other facets of the ongoing New
Mahabharat: New caveats-- UddhavThakare of the Shiv-
Sena Wing Has asked for at least 151 Seats")

❖ ('2014-09-21 18:59:16',
For the 25-year Alliance to survive. It may be that @
bjp_ refuses this Demand And severs the Alliance; and
strives 2 have Pawar's MNS-Band.")

❖ ('2014-09-21 19:06:53',
Another great: Expose: @praful_patel,UPA's Ex-Civil
Aviation Minister, Ordered 50 Air-India aircraft instead
of 28-- Does a scam lurk there?")

❖ ('2014-09-25 02:04:47',
@ISRO-SCIENTISTS! @ISRO-PLANNERS! O ISRO!
#MANGALYAN ! SALUTE 2 U ALL; LO AND BEHOLD!
WHAT INDIA CAN ! THIS TWEET @ YOUR FEET @
YOUR FEAT.')

❖ ('2014-09-25 02:29:04',
#MANGALYAN WITH A COST< THAN 4 MAKING A
HOLLYWOOD FILM (450 CR. RS.) ONLY INDIA SUCH
MAGIC CAN MAKE GOOD! JUST(<1/9=)11% OF WHAT
@NASA SPENT')

❖ ('2014-09-25 02:42:17',
@TIMESofINDIA @TIMESNOW @HEADLINETODAY @
ZEENEWS @ARNABGOSWAMI PLEASE FORGET NOT
TO SAY ON TV: ONLY 450 RUPEES!! TO PLANET RED IF
INDIA-MADE!')

❖ ('2014-09-25 02:49:08',
INDIA IS 1ST COUNTRY IN ASIA TO ACHIEVE THIS LOFTY
ASCENT! 1ST IN THE WORLD -INDIA TO REACH THIS
GOAL IN THE VERY 1ST ATTEMPT JUST 1ST&1ST !')

❖ ('2014-09-25 02:57:41',
LITMUS TEST FOR #MISSIONMARS & SUCCESS
100% #MANGALYAN IS NOW AMONG STARS
THAT WILL SHINE IN HISTORY MOST EFFULGENT
CELEBRATE & CONGRATULATE')

❖ ('2014-09-25 03:02:31',
23 SEPT.2014 #MOM MEETS MARS; 30 SEPT.@NaMo
MEETS OBAMA-- THESE TWO DATES SHALL SHINE AS
STARS IN INTERPLANETARY AND INTERNATIONAL
PANORAMA')

❖ ('2014-09-25 03:08:02',
#MOM(MARS ORBITAL MISSION) COULD'NT
DISAPPOINT(WITH SO AUSPICIOUS A NAME), AS
SAID @Narendramodi_PM SPECIALLY AS JUST B4
NAVARATR IT CAME!")

❖ ('2014-09-25 03:24:44',
"THE HUNGER O\' EXPLORATION & THE THRILL
O\' DISCOVERY AREN\'T 4 FAINT-HEARTED," NATION
HEARS FROM PM @NARENDRAMODI \'WORDS 2
PONDER & WONDER!')

❖ ('2014-09-25 03:34:56',
ONLY 3 OTHERS:@NASA @ESA & RUSSIA WERE
ABLE TO PERFORM THIS MISSION;& IN ASIA
ONLY INDIA HAS MADE INTO REALITY THIS FABLE.
SO, JAI HO!')

❖ ('2014-09-25 03:41:51',
@Narendramodi_PM GOES ON 2 SAY HEARTFELT
CONGRATULATIONS 2 ALL FELLOW INDIANS, AND 2
THOSE WHO GIFTED #MANGALYAN 2 THE NATION SO,
JAI-JAIHO!')

❖ ('2014-09-25 03:53:17',
ISRO! OF INDIA, TERI JAI-HO !! THIS LITTLE TWEET
2 MARK YOUR GREAT-SWEET- WONDERFUL
VICTORY, WITHOUT ECONOMY PARAMOUNT OF
CHARACTER-COUNT.')

❖ ('2014-09-25 04:12:32',
2day I Mailed 4 @Narendramodi_PM (c/o. President @
BarackObama in D.C.) 5 Books 2 gift on my behalf;Hope
this @Mission Of mine works-Let's C")

❖ ('2014-09-27 14:07:05',
RT @skumarcool008: \u092e\u094b\u0926\u0940\
u091c\u0940 \u0928\u0947 \u091a\u093e\u092f \
u092a\u0940\u0924\u0947 \u092a\u0940\u0924\
u0947 \u0915\u093e\u0902\u0917\u094d\u0930\
u0947\u0938 \u0915\u0940 \u0938\u0930\u0915\
u093e\u0930 \u0917\u093f\u0930\u093e \u0926\
u0940 \u0905\u092c \u092a\u0924\u093e \u0928\
u0939\u0940 \u0905\u092e\u0947\u0930\u093f\
u0915\u093e \u092e\u0947\u0902 \u092e\u094b\
u0926\u0940\u091c\u0940 5 \u0926\u093f\u0928 \
u0928\u093f\u092e\u094d\u092c\u0942 \u092a\
u093e\u0928\u0940 \u092a\u0940\u0915\u0930 \
u0915\u094d\u092f\u093e \u0915\u094d\u092f\
u093e \u0917\u093f\u0930\u093e\u090f\u0902\
u0917\u2026')

❖ ('2014-09-27 14:42:04',
2 @PresidentObarna(@WhiteHouse DC) I mailed 5
Books(Reinc..,etc) 4 @PMOIndia @narendramodi-little
gift,short Notice- HopeTheyDon'tMindThis!")

❖ ('2014-09-27 15:10:28',
@Narendramodi_PM is in NewYork: Paid Homage 2
9/11 Victims, Met NY-Mayor, He'll Address @UNGA;His
Work & Words'll Thrill WholeWorld on Spur.")

❖ ('2014-09-27 15:23:51',
JayaLalita, @tamilnadu CM,is convicted: Lost Chair
& 4-Years 2B Jailed-- Making 63 from 3 (Cr.Rs.) She
succeeded; A Moral Leader,she failed.')

❖ ('2014-09-27 15:33:11',
Corrupt Leaders, specially 8 High Places, There's Gr8
Lesson in HC Verdict: In shrt Trm, U might get Aces; But
in long, Law'll get U Strict.")

❖ ('2014-09-27 15:40:02',
@satyamevjayate Always Applies. Even 2Day,Dharma is
the only True Way! @congressorg's Corrupt Rule Dies;
And @BJP4India Ushers New Hope-Ray.")

❖ ('2014-09-27 15:48:20',
Thanks 2 @Swamy39 & @swamy_sena, 4 bringing
Charge on JayaLalita Ji! Now @BehenMayawati @
mamatabanarjee @rahulgandhi2020 & @
SoniaGandhiG??')

❖ ('2014-09-29 01:28:10',
@WhiteHouse I've mailed 5 books of mine 2 U,from
Santa Clara, CA, (To make a small gift from me shine
Million-fold)if presented 2 PMofINDIA.")

❖ ('2014-09-29 01:35:06',
@WhiteHouse I've followed the Indian Election And
his epic-Journey sweet Frm this lil corner of the
Planet,writing Fiction And Verse-Tweets.")

❖ ('2014-09-29 01:43:04',
@WhiteHouse I hope this humble offering Doesn't
offend any1 in any way; 4, unable 4 gifting In person,
I''ve tried to save 4 myself the Day!")

❖ ('2014-09-29 01:57:26',
@SrBachchanJi,I\'d sent a NOVEL called
"TheNextLife"& now take liberty Of sending a new
Link 2 reignite stalled Contact 4 your gr8 charity.')

❖ ('2014-09-29 02:03:30',
@SrBachchanJi, Pls.visit the Link: http://t.co/
nB7ZwtWhZp The New NOVEL there'll ink India's
& NaMo's ongoing story 2 a new level, new shore")

❖ ('2014-09-29 02:13:32',
@SrBachchanJi I earnestly hope, 4 a Nu Paradigm In
Story-telling & Movie-making, Kindly eye this
NOVEL, in time, Even if a lil painstaking.')

❖ ('2014-09-29 02:24:14',
@SrBachchan @aamir_khan @rohitshettyfilm, and
many Gr8 celebrities & Personalities,keen 2 Show
& Tell India's & NaMo's story GR8, Uncanny.")

❖ ('2014-09-29 02:43:32',
@SrBachchan Let @Time @nytimesworld @
BollywoodTimes @younghollywood @TheEconomist
get uncurled 2 Know @PMOIndia @satyamevjayate 2
include.')

❖ ('2014-09-29 02:50:21',
@SrBachchan Ji Once Again I request U 2 visit the
LINK http://t.co/nB7ZwtWhZp & @train All
involved,& RETWEET these lil verses 2 C &
Think.')

❖ ('2014-09-29 03:29:07',
@shivshaktijnu I\'ve sent info to @SrBachchan abt
Book"REINCARN.." Thru LINK http://t.co/nB7ZwtWhZp
Pls Retweet this 2 @PMOIndia & others')

❖ ('2014-09-29 12:47:02',
@SrBachchan @rohitshettyfilm PLS. C LINK http://t.
co/nB7ZwtWhZp ISBN 9781493141968 ON INDIA MODI
GR8 PUBLISH YOUR VIEW TELL ME ? U THINK.')

❖ ('2014-09-29 12:54:03',
@RashtrapatiBhvn I INVITE U PLS. see LINK http://t.
co/nB7ZwtWhZp ISBN 9781493141968 ON INDIA MODI
GR8 PUBLISH YOUR VIEW TELL ME ? U THINK.')

❖ ('2014-09-29 12:55:46',
@PresidentObarna I INVITE U PLS. see LINK http://t.
co/nB7ZwtWhZp ISBN 9781493141968 ON INDIA MODI
GR8 PUBLISH YOUR VIEW TELL ME ? U THINK.')

❖ ('2014-09-29 13:06:02',
@billclinton @VP I INVITE U PLS. see LINK http://t.co/
nB7ZwtWhZp ISBN 9781493141968 ON INDIA MODI
GR8 PUBLISH YOUR VIEW TELL ME ? U THINK.')

❖ ('2014-09-29 13:24:02',
@HillaryClinton I INVITE U PLS. see LINK http://t.co/
nB7ZwtWhZp ISBN 9781493141968 ON INDIA MODI
GR8 PUBLISH YOUR VIEW TELL ME ? U THINK.')

❖ ('2014-09-29 13:25:02',
@Narendramodi_PM I INVITE U PLS. see LINK http://t.
co/nB7ZwtWhZp ISBN 9781493141968 ON INDIA MODI
GR8 PUBLISH YOUR VIEW TELL ME ? U THINK.')

❖ ('2014-09-29 13:30:29',
@SushmaSwarajMP I INVITE U PLS. see LINK http://t.
co/nB7ZwtWhZp ISBN 9781493141968 ON INDIA MODI
GR8 PUBLISH YOUR VIEW TELL ME ? U THINK.')

❖ ('2014-09-29 13:33:21',
@MEAIndia @PMOIndia I INVITE U PLS. C LINK
http://t.co/nB7ZwtWhZp ISBN 9781493141968 ON
INDIA MODI GR8 PUBLISH YOUR VIEW TELL ME ? U
THINK')

- ❖ ('2014-09-29 13:36:15', @PrakashJavdekar I INVITE U PLS. see LINK http://t.co/nB7ZwtWhZp ISBN 9781493141968 ON INDIA MODI GR8 PUBLISH YOUR VIEW TELL ME ? U THINK.')

- ❖ ('2014-09-29 13:41:44', @XlibrisUK I INVITE U PLS. see LINK http://t.co/nB7ZwtWhZp ISBN 9781493141968 ON INDIA MODI GR8 PUBLISH YOUR VIEW TELL ME ? U THINK.')

- ❖ ('2014-09-29 13:42:28', @xlibrispub I INVITE U PLS. see LINK http://t.co/nB7ZwtWhZp ISBN 9781493141968 ON INDIA MODI GR8 PUBLISH YOUR VIEW TELL ME ? U THINK.')

- ❖ ('2014-09-29 13:46:18', @WorldHinduNews I INVITE U PLS. see LINK http://t.co/nB7ZwtWhZp ISBN 9781493141968 ON INDIA MODI GR8 PUBLISH YOUR VIEW TELL ME ? U THINK.')

- ❖ ('2014-09-29 13:49:43', @WSJ @nytimes I INVITE U PLS. see LINK http://t.co/nB7ZwtWhZp ISBN 9781493141968 ON INDIA MODI GR8 PUBLISH YOUR VIEW TELL ME ? U THINK.')

- ❖ ('2014-09-29 13:50:45', @nytimesworld I INVITE U PLS. see LINK http://t.co/nB7ZwtWhZp ISBN 9781493141968 ON INDIA MODI GR8 PUBLISH YOUR VIEW TELL ME ? U THINK.')

- ❖ ('2014-09-29 13:51:46', @washingtonpost I INVITE U PLS. see LINK http://t.co/nB7ZwtWhZp ISBN 9781493141968 ON INDIA MODI GR8 PUBLISH YOUR VIEW TELL ME ? U THINK.')

- ❖ ('2014-09-29 13:53:41', @HoustonChron I INVITE U PLS. see LINK http://t.co/nB7ZwtWhZp ISBN 9781493141968 ON INDIA MODI GR8 PUBLISH YOUR VIEW TELL ME ? U THINK.')

❖ ('2014-09-29 13:54:44',
@BostonGlobe I INVITE U PLS. see LINK http://t.co/
nB7ZwtWhZp ISBN 9781493141968 ON INDIA MODI
GR8 PUBLISH YOUR VIEW TELL ME ? U THINK.')

❖ ('2014-09-29 13:57:11',
@sfchronicle I INVITE U PLS. see LINK http://t.co/
nB7ZwtWhZp ISBN 9781493141968 ON INDIA MODI
GR8 PUBLISH YOUR VIEW TELL ME ? U THINK.')

❖ ('2014-09-29 13:58:46',
@timesofindia I INVITE U PLS. see LINK http://t.co/
nB7ZwtWhZp ISBN 9781493141968 ON INDIA MODI
GR8 PUBLISH YOUR VIEW TELL ME ? U THINK.')

❖ ('2014-09-29 14:00:19',
@PioneerPress I INVITE U PLS. see LINK http://t.co/
nB7ZwtWhZp ISBN 9781493141968 ON INDIA MODI
GR8 PUBLISH YOUR VIEW TELL ME ? U THINK.')

❖ ('2014-09-29 14:02:29',
@PTI_News @timesnow I INVITE U PLS. C LINK http://t.
co/nB7ZwtWhZp ISBN 9781493141968 ON INDIA MODI
GR8 PUBLISH YOUR VIEW TELL ME ? U THINK.')

❖ ('2014-09-29 14:05:50',
@TIME @TheEconomist I INVITE U PLS. C LINK http://t.
co/nB7ZwtWhZp ISBN 9781493141968 ON INDIA MODI
GR8 PUBLISH YOUR VIEW TELL ME ? U THINK.')

❖ ('2014-09-29 14:08:35',
@BillGates I INVITE U PLS. see LINK http://t.co/
nB7ZwtWhZp ISBN 9781493141968 ON INDIA MODI
GR8 PUBLISH YOUR VIEW TELL ME ? U THINK.')

❖ ('2014-09-29 14:10:36',
@google @YahooNews I INVITE U PLS. see LINK
http://t.co/nB7ZwtWhZp ISBN 9781493141968 ON
INDIA MODI GR8 PUBLISH YOUR VIEW TELL ME ? U
THINK')

❖ ('2014-09-29 14:12:43',
@Gen_VKSingh I INVITE U PLS. see LINK http://t.co/
nB7ZwtWhZp ISBN 9781493141968 ON INDIA MODI
GR8 PUBLISH YOUR VIEW TELL ME ? U THINK.')

❖ ('2014-09-29 14:14:22',
@ARNABGOSWAMl I INVITE U PLS. see LINK http://t.
co/nB7ZwtWhZp ISBN 9781493141968 ON INDIA MODI
GR8 PUBLISH YOUR VIEW TELL ME ? U THINK.')

❖ ('2014-09-29 14:16:03',
@bhupendrachaube I INVITE U PLS. see LINK http://t.
co/nB7ZwtWhZp ISBN 9781493141968 ON INDIA MODI
GR8 PUBLISH YOUR VIEW TELL ME ? U THINK.')

❖ ('2014-09-29 14:17:13',
@thekiranbedi I INVITE U PLS. see LINK http://t.co/
nB7ZwtWhZp ISBN 9781493141968 ON INDIA MODI
GR8 PUBLISH YOUR VIEW TELL ME ? U THINK.')

❖ ('2014-09-29 14:21:10',
@Swamy39 @ShahnawazBJP I INVITE U PLS. C LINK
http://t.co/nB7ZwtWhZp ISBN 9781493141968 ON
MODI GR8 PUBLISH YOUR VIEW TELL ME ? U THINK')

❖ ('2014-09-29 14:21:10',
@Swamy39 @ShahnawazBJP I INVITE U PLS. C LINK
http://t.co/nB7ZwtWhZp ISBN 9781493141968 ON
MODI GR8 PUBLISH YOUR VIEW TELL ME ? U THINK')

❖ ('2014-09-29 14:27:52',
@rahulkanwal @gauravcsawant @NavbharatTimes I
INVITE U PLS. see LINK http://t.co/nB7ZwtWhZp ON
MODI GR8 PUBLISH YOUR VIEW TELL ME ? U THINK')

❖ ('2014-09-29 14:29:25',
@navikakumar I INVITE U PLS. see LINK http://t.co/
nB7ZwtWhZp ISBN 9781493141968 ON INDIA MODI
GR8 PUBLISH YOUR VIEW TELL ME ? U THINK.')

❖ ('2014-09-29 14:34:37',
@TheHindu @aajtak I INVITE U PLS. see LINK http://t.
co/nB7ZwtWhZp ISBN 9781493141968 ON INDIA MODI
GR8 PUBLISH YOUR VIEW TELL ME ? U THINK.')

❖ ('2014-09-29 14:36:39',
@HeadlinesToday I INVITE U PLS. see LINK http://t.co/
nB7ZwtWhZp ISBN 9781493141968 ON INDIA MODI
GR8 PUBLISH YOUR VIEW TELL ME ? U THINK.')

❖ ('2014-09-29 14:39:01',
@generalelectric I INVITE U PLS. see LINK http://t.co/
nB7ZwtWhZp ISBN 9781493141968 ON INDIA MODI
GR8 PUBLISH YOUR VIEW TELL ME ? U THINK.')

❖ ('2014-09-29 14:42:54',
@OverseasVBI I INVITE U PLS. see LINK http://t.co/
nB7ZwtWhZp ISBN 9781493141968 ON INDIA MODI
GR8 PUBLISH YOUR VIEW TELL ME ? U THINK.')

❖ ('2014-09-29 14:46:34',
@BharatBarai Ji, I INVITE U PLS. see LINK http://t.co/
nB7ZwtWhZp ISBN 9781493141968 ON INDIA MODI
GR8 PUBLISH YOUR VIEW TELL ME ? U THINK.')

❖ ('2014-09-29 14:49:12',
@KaranThapar_TTP I INVITE U PLS. see LINK http://t.
co/nB7ZwtWhZp ISBN 9781493141968 ON INDIA MODI
GR8 PUBLISH YOUR VIEW TELL ME ? U THINK.')

❖ ('2014-09-29 14:51:51',
@awasthis @BDUTT I INVITE U PLS. see LINK http://t.
co/nB7ZwtWhZp ISBN 9781493141968 ON INDIA MODI
GR8 PUBLISH YOUR VIEW TELL ME ? U THINK.')

❖ ('2014-09-29 14:54:30',
@sambitswaraj I INVITE U PLS. see LINK http://t.co/
nB7ZwtWhZp ISBN 9781493141968 ON INDIA MODI
GR8 PUBLISH YOUR VIEW TELL ME ? U THINK.')

❖ ('2014-09-29 14:58:39',
@HinduAmerican I INVITE U PLS. see LINK http://t.co/
nB7ZwtWhZp ISBN 9781493141968 ON INDIA MODI
GR8 PUBLISH YOUR VIEW TELL ME ? U THINK.')

❖ ('2014-09-29 15:00:55',
@AmitShahOffice I INVITE U PLS. see LINK http://t.co/
nB7ZwtWhZp ISBN 9781493141968 ON INDIA MODI
GR8 PUBLISH YOUR VIEW TELL ME ? U THINK.')

❖ ('2014-09-29 15:02:55',
@AMISHDEVGAN I INVITE U PLS. see LINK http://t.co/
nB7ZwtWhZp ISBN 9781493141968 ON INDIA MODI
GR8 PUBLISH YOUR VIEW TELL ME ? U THINK.')

❖ ('2014-09-29 15:04:57',
@thenewshour I INVITE U PLS. see LINK http://t.co/
nB7ZwtWhZp ISBN 9781493141968 ON INDIA MODI
GR8 PUBLISH YOUR VIEW TELL ME ? U THINK.')

❖ ('2014-09-29 15:08:07',
@justicearnab I INVITE U PLS. see LINK http://t.co/
nB7ZwtWhZp ISBN 9781493141968 ON INDIA MODI
GR8 PUBLISH YOUR VIEW TELL ME ? U THINK.')

❖ ('2014-09-29 15:11:29',
@YahooNews @gmail I INVITE U PLS. see LINK http://t.
co/nB7ZwtWhZp ISBN 9781493141968 ON INDIA MODI
GR8 PUBLISH YOUR VIEW TELL ME ? U THINK.')

❖ ('2014-09-29 15:13:20',
@baltimoresun I INVITE U PLS. see LINK http://t.co/
nB7ZwtWhZp ISBN 9781493141968 ON INDIA MODI
GR8 PUBLISH YOUR VIEW TELL ME ? U THINK.')

❖ ('2014-09-29 15:18:32',
@Boeing @IBM I INVITE U PLS. see LINK http://t.co/
nB7ZwtWhZp ISBN 9781493141968 ON INDIA MODI
GR8 PUBLISH YOUR VIEW TELL ME ? U THINK.')

❖ ('2014-09-29 15:19:43',
@FortuneMagazine I INVITE U PLS. see LINK http://t.
co/nB7ZwtWhZp ISBN 9781493141968 ON INDIA MODI
GR8 PUBLISH YOUR VIEW TELL ME ? U THINK.')

❖ ('2014-09-29 15:22:37',
@Forbes @WashTimes I INVITE U PLS. see LINK
http://t.co/nB7ZwtWhZp ISBN 9781493141968 ON
INDIA MODI GR8 PUBLISH YOUR VIEW TELL ME ? U
THINK')

❖ ('2014-09-29 15:26:39',
@librarycongress I INVITE U PLS. see LINK http://t.co/
nB7ZwtWhZp ISBN 9781493141968 ON INDIA MODI
GR8 PUBLISH YOUR VIEW TELL ME ? U THINK.')

❖ ('2014-09-29 15:27:57',
@britishlibrary I INVITE U PLS. see LINK http://t.co/
nB7ZwtWhZp ISBN 9781493141968 ON INDIA MODI
GR8 PUBLISH YOUR VIEW TELL ME ? U THINK.')

❖ ('2014-09-29 15:29:23',
@ndtv @ndtvfeed I INVITE U PLS. see LINK http://t.
co/nB7ZwtWhZp ISBN 9781493141968 ON INDIA MODI
GR8 PUBLISH YOUR VIEW TELL ME ? U THINK.')

❖ ('2014-09-29 15:31:51',
@ETVBIHARJHAR I INVITE U PLS. see LINK http://t.
co/nB7ZwtWhZp ISBN 9781493141968 ON INDIA MODI
GR8 PUBLISH YOUR VIEW TELL ME ? U THINK.')

❖ ('2014-09-29 15:34:22',
@SenTedCruz I INVITE U PLS. see LINK http://t.co/
nB7ZwtWhZp ISBN 9781493141968 ON INDIA MODI
GR8 PUBLISH YOUR VIEW TELL ME ? U THINK.')

❖ ('2014-09-29 15:35:52',
@SenatorReid I INVITE U PLS. see LINK http://t.co/
nB7ZwtWhZp ISBN 9781493141968 ON INDIA MODI
GR8 PUBLISH YOUR VIEW TELL ME ? U THINK.')

❖   ('2014-09-29 15:37:43',
@SenJohnMcCain I INVITE U PLS. see LINK http://t.co/
nB7ZwtWhZp ISBN 9781493141968 ON INDIA's MODI
GR8 PUBLISH YOUR VIEW TELL ME ? U THINK.")

❖   ('2014-09-29 15:38:38',
@TulsiGabbard I INVITE U PLS. see LINK http://t.co/
nB7ZwtWhZp ISBN 9781493141968 ON INDIA MODI
GR8 PUBLISH YOUR VIEW TELL ME ? U THINK.')

❖   ('2014-09-29 15:40:06',
@congressdotgov I INVITE U PLS. see LINK http://t.co/
nB7ZwtWhZp ISBN 9781493141968 ON INDIA MODI
GR8 PUBLISH YOUR VIEW TELL ME ? U THINK.')

❖   ('2014-09-29 15:42:46',
@BobbyJindal I INVITE U PLS. see LINK http://t.co/
nB7ZwtWhZp ISBN 9781493141968 ON INDIA MODI
GR8 PUBLISH YOUR VIEW TELL ME ? U THINK.')

❖   ('2014-09-29 15:47:52',
@VHPAP @VHPsampark I INVITE U PLS. see LINK
http://t.co/nB7ZwtWhZp ISBN 9781493141968 ON
INDIA MODI GR8 PUBLISH YOUR VIEW TELL ME ? U
THINK')

❖   ('2014-09-29 15:52:03',
@BJPRajnathSingh I INVITE U PLS. see LINK http://t.
co/nB7ZwtWhZp ISBN 9781493141968 ON INDIA MODI
GR8 PUBLISH YOUR VIEW TELL ME ? U THINK.')

❖   ('2014-09-29 15:53:22',
@rammadhavbjp I INVITE U PLS. see LINK http://t.co/
nB7ZwtWhZp ISBN 9781493141968 ON INDIA MODI
GR8 PUBLISH YOUR VIEW TELL ME ? U THINK.')

❖   ('2014-09-29 15:55:18',
@RNTata2000 I INVITE U PLS. see LINK http://t.co/
nB7ZwtWhZp ISBN 9781493141968 ON INDIA MODI
GR8 PUBLISH YOUR VIEW TELL ME ? U THINK.')

❖　('2014-09-29 15:57:13',
@RajivPratapRudy I INVITE U PLS. see LINK http://t.
co/nB7ZwtWhZp ISBN 9781493141968 ON INDIA MODI
GR8 PUBLISH YOUR VIEW TELL ME ? U THINK.')

❖　('2014-09-29 15:59:28',
@SudhanshuTrived I INVITE U PLS. see LINK http://t.
co/nB7ZwtWhZp ISBN 9781493141968 ON INDIA MODI
GR8 PUBLISH YOUR VIEW TELL ME ? U THINK.')

❖　('2014-09-29 16:01:56',
@naqvimukhtar I INVITE U PLS. see LINK http://t.co/
nB7ZwtWhZp ISBN 9781493141968 ON INDIA MODI
GR8 PUBLISH YOUR VIEW TELL ME ? U THINK.')

❖　('2014-09-29 16:04:47',
@mangeshkarlata I INVITE U PLS. see LINK http://t.
co/nB7ZwtWhZp ISBN 9781493141968 ON INDIA MODI
GR8 PUBLISH YOUR VIEW TELL ME ? U THINK.')

❖　('2014-09-29 16:06:34',
@satyamevjayate I INVITE U PLS. see LINK http://t.co/
nB7ZwtWhZp ISBN 9781493141968 ON INDIA MODI
GR8 PUBLISH YOUR VIEW TELL ME ? U THINK.')

❖　('2014-09-29 16:08:23',
@BollywoodTimes I INVITE U PLS. see LINK http://t.
co/nB7ZwtWhZp ISBN 9781493141968 ON INDIA MODI
GR8 PUBLISH YOUR VIEW TELL ME ? U THINK.')

❖　('2014-09-29 16:09:50',
@juniorbachchan I INVITE U PLS. see LINK http://t.co/
nB7ZwtWhZp ISBN 9781493141968 ON INDIA MODI
GR8 PUBLISH YOUR VIEW TELL ME ? U THINK.')

❖　('2014-09-29 16:12:48',
@PenguinUKBooks I INVITE U PLS. see LINK http://t.
co/nB7ZwtWhZp ISBN 9781493141968 ON INDIA MODI
GR8 PUBLISH YOUR VIEW TELL ME ? U THINK.')

❖ ('2014-09-29 16:14:24',
@penguinusa I humbly INVITE U PLS. see LINK http://t.
co/nB7ZwtWhZp ISBN 9781493141968 ON INDIA MODI
GR8 PUBLISH YOUR VIEW TELL ME ? U THINK')

❖ ('2014-09-29 16:15:40',
@penguinrandom I INVITE U PLS. see LINK http://t.co/
nB7ZwtWhZp ISBN 9781493141968 ON INDIA MODI
GR8 PUBLISH YOUR VIEW TELL ME ? U THINK.')

❖ ('2014-09-29 16:19:23',
@cnnbrk @ibnlive I INVITE U PLS. see LINK http://t.
co/nB7ZwtWhZp ISBN 9781493141968 ON INDIA MODI
GR8 PUBLISH YOUR VIEW TELL ME ? U THINK.')

❖ ('2014-09-29 16:22:36',
@CNN @anubhabhonsle I INVITE U PLS. C LINK
http://t.co/nB7ZwtWhZp ISBN 9781493141968 ON
INDIA MODI GR8 PUBLISH YOUR VIEW TELL ME ? U
THINK.')

❖ ('2014-09-29 16:25:26',
@AuthorDanBrown I INVITE U PLS. see LINK http://t.
co/nB7ZwtWhZp ISBN 9781493141968 ON INDIA MODI
GR8 PUBLISH YOUR VIEW TELL ME ? U THINK.')

❖ ('2014-09-29 16:27:06',
@aauthorsmusic I INVITE U PLS. see LINK http://t.co/
nB7ZwtWhZp ISBN 9781493141968 ON INDIA MODI
GR8 PUBLISH YOUR VIEW TELL ME ? U THINK.')

❖ ('2014-09-29 16:36:15',
@AuthorMarketing I INVITE U PLS. see LINK http://t.
co/nB7ZwtWhZp ISBN 9781493141968 ON INDIA MODI
GR8 PUBLISH YOUR VIEW TELL ME ? U THINK.')

❖ ('2014-09-29 16:45:00',
@amazon @GuardianBooks @nybooks @Book_Fair I
INVITE U PLS. C LINK ISBN 9781493141968 ON INDIA
MODI GR8 PUBLISH YOUR VIEW TELL ME ? U THINK')

❖ ('2014-09-29 16:47:39',
@UnivPressClub I INVITE U PLS. see LINK http://t.co/
nB7ZwtWhZp ISBN 9781493141968 ON INDIA MODI
GR8 PUBLISH YOUR VIEW TELL ME ? U THINK.')

❖ ('2014-09-29 16:49:50',
@floridapress I INVITE U PLS. see LINK http://t.co/
nB7ZwtWhZp ISBN 9781493141968 ON INDIA MODI
GR8 PUBLISH YOUR VIEW TELL ME ? U THINK.')

❖ ('2014-09-29 16:53:41',
@drharshvardhan I INVITE U PLS. see LINK http://t.
co/nB7ZwtWhZp ISBN 9781493141968 ON INDIA MODI
GR8 PUBLISH YOUR VIEW TELL ME ? U THINK.')

❖ ('2014-09-30 09:15:07',
@aksinh @NarendraModi_PM INTERSTING Kurzweil:
Solar Energy Will Be Unlimited And Free In 20 Years
http://t.co/pg6Zz3WWTz via @BI_Science')

❖ ('2014-09-30 10:19:48',
@BNBuzz PLS. see LINK http://t.co/0pBQCWDh0s ISBN
9781493141968 ON INDIA/ NARENDRA MODI GR8 I
would like to have this book on BN-bookshelf')

❖ ('2014-10-01 02:17:55',
@timesofindia The choice of gifts From @
Narendramodi_PM To @PreObama simply reflects The
great convergence of thoughts and 2 gr8 minds.')

❖ ('2014-10-01 02:28:39',
@timesofindia Even to a layman It is by now Clear that
@Narendramodi_PM Talks with conviction and how He
backs his Word by Action.')

❖ ('2014-10-01 02:42:50',
@timesofindia The first such state Under ISI already
existed before; So ISIS is the second one, of late,
Knocking aloud @ the world's door.")

❖ ('2014-10-01 02:55:30',
@timesofindia This is a good news; & @
babaramdev4's Tapasya Would surely release Other
sufferers of evil rule in India. @satyamevjayate")

❖ ('2014-10-01 03:13:51',
@indian1997 @timesofindia Please See my Tweet
(Release...) @babaramdev4 is truly a Rishi-Muni Today's
India owes much to this Yogi unique.")

❖ ('2014-10-01 03:29:52',
@timesofindia That's a good start.. Now, from this iron-
ore- Scam to the #CoalGate apart! Much compensation
to the Exchequer in store!!")

❖ ('2014-10-01 04:05:06',
@naqvimukhtar "Cleanliness Is Next to
Godliness","Work Is Worship" "SATYA-AHIMSA-PREM"
R Mantras of @Narendramodi_PM- Captain of our Ship')

❖ ('2014-10-01 04:15:42',
@BillGates @smart_sparrow @acrobatiq Could the
software work like AI-based solution to Medical
Diagnostics, but even more Intelligently?')

❖ ('2014-10-01 04:45:02',
@MEAIndia @timesofindia @Narendramodi_PM @
PresidentObarna A Visitor's Comment That's a historic
event: Constitution Of Continental Vision!")

❖ ('2014-10-01 04:57:39',
@ndtv No, of course not! But a Terrorist State crossing
all limits of humanity? That may be a different story, If
at all caught By history!')

❖ ('2014-10-01 05:27:08',
@NASA Does this mean that the mini-star Had far-
stronger magnetic field reconfiguration Than in the
sun: A dwarf flexing muscle from far?')

❖ ('2014-10-01 06:55:33',
@FrankWilczek @PioneerWorks_ @NanotronicsImag
What do you think abt cyclic/evolutionary uni/
multiverse and/or 3-Dim.time (6-D spacetime)?')

❖ ('2014-10-01 06:59:38',
@FrankWilczek @PioneerWorks_ @NanotronicsImag @
tegmark With your permission I'd like to submit a book
(ISBN 978-1-4836-1731-2) for comments")

❖ ('2014-10-01 07:04:53',
@FrankWilczek @PioneerWorks_ @NanotronicsImag @
tegmark The book presents a simple model for Higgs in
the Standard Model,among other results.')

❖ ('2014-10-07 11:06:53',
RT @FrankWilczek: A bright idea is one thing, one that
works is another. Or, sometimes, not. Bravo Aksaki,
Amano, Nakamura! @NobelPrize htt\u2026')

❖ ('2014-10-07 11:21:47',
@FrankWilczek @NobelPrize What abt a bright idea
that also "works"! Incidentally, I\'d like 2 send 2 you
book for your comments, if that\'s OK')

❖ ('2014-10-07 11:28:42',
@FrankWilczek @NobelPrize The book,"New
Dimensions in Elementary Particle Physics &
Cosmology (2nd Edition),"predicts masses including
Higgs')

❖ ('2014-10-07 11:38:22',
@FrankWilczek @NobelPrize I've submitted on Oct 6 a
paper 2 Phys.Rev.-D, taking the liberty of naming you as
a Referee. Hope you don't mind.")

❖   ('2014-10-07 11:46:14',
RT @BJP4India: \u092d\u094d\u0930\u0937\u094d\
u091f\u093e\u091a\u093e\u0930 \u0915\u0940 \
u0939\u094b\u0917\u0940 \u0939\u093e\u0930, \
u091a\u0932\u094b \u091a\u0932\u0947\u0902 \
u092e\u094b\u0926\u0940 \u0915\u0947 \u0938\
u093e\u0925\u0964 #BJP4Haryana http://t.co/
S0japC3iMB')

❖   ('2014-10-07 11:53:30',
@BJP4India To see @Narendramodi_PM's role in
India of today and of tomorrow, pls visit http://t.co/
nB7ZwtWhZp Pls. send your comments to me.")

❖   ('2014-10-07 12:05:05',
@BJP4IndiaI Pls.Do me a favour:Pls.send
info abt this book& link to the media
(NewsPapers,Magazins,TV) for their book-reviews
& publicity.')

❖   ('2014-10-07 12:15:50',
@globaltelesatuk @WorldSpaceWeek Indian @ISRO
:#MOM (Mars OrbitalMission):MANGALYAN-100%
success in 1ST.attempt, with 11% of @NASA budget!.')

❖   ('2014-10-07 12:30:06',
@timesofindia I\'d appreciate if you pls.print book-
review of "New Dimensions in Elementary Particle
Physics and Cosmology" (from amazon.in)')

❖   ('2014-10-07 12:49:14',
@ndtv @timesnow I\'d be thankful if you
pls.book-review of "NewDimensions in
ElementaryParticlePhysics & Cosmology(2nd Ed.)"
& publicize it.')

❖   ('2014-10-07 12:59:34',
@NobelPrize @timesofindia Wonderful. May I also
request to review the book "New Dimensions in
El.Particle Physics & Cosmology(2nd Edition)".')

❖ ('2014-10-07 13:11:12',
@sahibdadkhan Yes, Pakistan should get it--for being lead.state for inventing and nurturing terror: Anti-Peace Ashanti-@NobelPrize, that is!')

❖ ('2014-10-07 13:13:04',
RT @timesofindia: #Nobelprize for Physics awarded to Isamu Akasaki, Hiroshi Amano @NagoyaUniv_info Shuji Nakamura @ucsantabarbara http://t.\u2026')

❖ ('2014-10-07 13:23:36',
@SES_Satellites @AnantSahai This should be useful. Does connectivity mean for communication (only)?If not, then in what other ways it is?')

❖ ('2014-10-07 13:38:24',
@BJP4India @narendramodi @MahaBJP A @Modiwave sweeping victory in @Maharashtra (and @Hariyana) would complete @congressorg-Mukta Bharat.')

❖ ('2014-10-07 14:03:22',
@timesofindia Exterminating @ISIS is essential, but NOT enough for @WorldPeace. @Pakistan's terror factory (Madrassas)must be abolished,too.")

❖ ('2014-10-07 14:07:04',
@timesofindia Pakistan has recruited a large contingent from Vazirestan for terrorism in Afghanistan and India and other places in the world')

❖ ('2014-10-07 14:21:14',
@timesofindia There goes another battalion of terrorists. Eventually Pakistan'll pay for it, perhaps by getting exterminated by the UN & USA")

❖ ('2014-10-07 15:16:17',
@timesofindia Nehru Era is over; Let the era of @ Narendramodi_PM begin and let @congressorg go to rest 4 good. India now needs @narendramodi')

❖ ('2014-10-07 15:33:41',
@HinduDefense Is this a picture of people doing Namaz with their heads toward Mecca(burying their heads in sand, literally) What a devotion!')

❖ ('2014-10-07 15:38:34',
RT @BillGates: .@narendramodi has India talking about toilets\u2014and that\u2019s a great thing. http://t.co/WWK0HyN1Pd http://t.co/RI0rxyxDUY')

❖ ('2014-10-07 15:55:40',
@BillGates Only a visionary&courageous leader like @Narendramodi could give clarion call to clean-up country from every house to @RiverGanga')

❖ ('2014-10-07 16:06:37',
@thekiranbedi @newsflickshindi Maybe @Amma could share her secrets with @TheEconomist.She sowed 1 Rupee and grew the Money-Tree of Rupees .')

❖ ('2014-10-07 16:08:16',
RT @Swamy39: Illiterates call opinion change inconsistency. Scholars call it course correction.First we thought world was flat. Then we hel\u2026')

❖ ('2014-10-07 16:22:38',
@Swamy39 The foolish call a GR8 new idea 'absurd',

then they resist it, and finally, as they get succumbed, they say it was truly their idea")

❖ ('2014-10-07 16:33:02',
@Swamy39 There r some who still believe that the earth is flat,& God made the world in 7 days(Course Correction:6 days,He took rest on 7th)')

❖ ('2014-10-07 16:41:09',
@AnitaChawala @Swamy39 Tab to ISI ko khatam karane se Black netaon ko bhi mukti milegi aur Black $ ko bhi--Ek panth do kaj (2 kill 2 birds..')

❖ ('2014-10-07 16:48:04',
@Swamy39 U are doing a GR8 service to @India
by charging @SoniaGandhiG & company for
corruption; but why is her arrest getting postponed?')

❖ ('2014-10-07 16:55:32',
@Swamy39 It'd be good to keep @Amma (Jayalalita), @
Didi (Mamata) & @SoniaGandhiG together, in jail,
so they can cook their khichari together")

❖ ('2014-10-07 16:59:06',
RT @YahooNews: Nobel Prize in medicine awarded
to three scientists for brain's 'GPS' discovery: http://t.
co/0iv3Ub0sfP http://t.co/NXji3jQG\u2026")

❖ ('2014-10-07 17:07:26',
@YahooNews Now we know why fools lose their place
in the world so quickly. The GPS satel. (GOD) send signal
OK, but the receiver is no good.')

❖ ('2014-10-07 17:13:26',
@YahooNews By the way, what r their names?
Alzheime's connection?")

❖ ('2014-10-07 17:17:15',
@YahooNews @billclinton You mean, boycotting the
election?!')

❖ ('2014-10-07 17:23:29',
@timesofindia Khisiyani billi khambha noche! Pak
giving more reasons 2 b isolated.They'll end up as total
non-entity in the world-community.")

❖ ('2014-10-07 17:29:15',
@NASASolarSystem @NASA Good interaction between
NASA & the public should give GR8er visibility of
its achievements and also widen knowledge.')

❖ ('2014-10-07 17:36:02',
@rishikarwi @HinduDefense File cases against @ SoniaGandhiG & @ArvindKejriwal and all LEADERS OF CORRUPTION; A Better place for them is Jail.')

❖ ('2014-10-07 17:41:33',
@YahooNews The world must end terrorism in all its manifestations. ISIS & ISI and all such outfits must be uprooted completely to gain peace')

❖ ('2014-10-07 17:47:16',
@YahooNews If the world still looks the other way 4 fighting terrorism, there'd be no way left to look at all. No longer 1 country's problem")

❖ ('2014-10-07 20:17:02',
@CmJayalalitha posed as an honest Leader, taking only 1 Rs for pay. Now she\'s been convicted 4 graft "It\'s a defining moment,"BJP should say')

❖ ('2014-10-07 20:29:06',
@timesofindia This goes to show That "Ghar ki Murgi Daal Barabar" is true Not only in India, but also In many other countries, & orgs too')

❖ ('2014-10-07 20:30:42',
RT @timesofindia: Nobel winner got $180 for inventing blue LED http://t.co/WjcfEagE92')

❖ ('2014-10-07 20:39:06',
@timesofindia @arnabtheheel this invention Must go 2 @Narendramodi_PM @PiyushGoyal 4 help in lighting the nation Where grid is unavailable.')

❖ ('2014-10-07 21:05:33',
#JayaStaysInJail and some in TN R upset when they should really celebrate, @ARNABGOSWAMl, without much ado, Showed shades of Love and Hate.')

❖ ('2014-10-09 02:35:13',
Bees are facing massive die-offs from neonic pesticides.
Join the call for a ban to save the honey bees: https://t.
co/vrd7D17Vtm B a bee 2 C')

❖ ('2014-10-10 08:50:38',
@ARNABGOSWAMl, #ComeTogetherIndia Exhortation
Exhibits lil minds like Ami Yajnik @congressorg's
politicization Of Vital Interest National.")

❖ ('2014-10-10 09:00:25',
It's an act of terrorism: At a Time for Patriotism When
#PakBorderDare & #IndiaRetaliates, There r
some,in Big Debates, Unabashedly Quibble")

❖ ('2014-10-10 09:15:31',
140 CeasefireViolations in 1 Year A @GWR in @
HISTORY! Congrats 2 @PMLN1 Dear. @Narendramodi_
PM, Theory Abt 'Laat Ke Mahajan,' Fits Pakistan")

❖ ('2014-10-10 09:27:33',
#ComeTogetherIndia, Celebrate #Pakistanprovokes
& #IndiaRetaliates! But @congressorg calculates
How @Narendramodi_PM Turns Fate Bleak 2 GR8.')

❖ ('2014-10-10 09:42:57',
@ManishTewari @salmankhurshid3 @amiyagnik
@Rashidalvi8 @SalmanSoz- Such Loyals 2 @
SoniaGandhiG: Forging @congressorg even as Off it
goes')

❖ ('2014-10-10 09:57:59',
The stooges of @SoniaGandhiG Spare no chance 2
Malign @Narendramodi_PM & @BJP4India Even
When GR8 Glory @timesnow Seeks INDIA's Welcome !")

❖ ('2014-10-10 10:14:03',
Pakistani Army Gen.(Retd. or active) & politicians
alike- R they blind 2 C true perspective? #PakistanDare
& dreaming 2 get J&K in a strike!')

❖ ('2014-10-10 10:24:44',
MayB nostalgia Of the Mughal-Empire in India Drives
@ISI 2 woo 2 recreate, & ISIS sees mirage of
#Ottoman GR8. Such Illusions & Confusions!')

❖ ('2014-10-10 10:36:55',
Kailash Satyarthi won Nobel #peaceprize, It's a
recognition in world's eyes Of @Narendramodi_PM's
Vision of Paradise Of India on a New Rise.")

❖ ('2014-10-10 10:43:37',
There're Indians in Physics, Literature & Medicine..
4 whom #NobelPrize & highest yardsticks R long
overdue..& now we'll C more recognition")

❖ ('2014-10-10 10:54:36',
#ZuckerbergInIndia The Facebook CEO, Says it well:
"Connectivity Is a Human Right"-An Echo Of "Vasudhaiv
Kutumbakam," 4 New Village Global.')

❖ ('2014-10-11 03:02:00',
RT @TheEconomist: This year's Nobel peace prize:
a joint award for fighting to promote the interests of
children http://t.co/Bz8v33U5dH htt\u2026")

❖ ('2014-10-11 03:14:08',
@timesnow What a beautiful picture! @k_satyarthi
& @Malala Sharing the @World's Stage together
the Globe's grandest honor @NobelPrize Gala!")

❖ ('2014-10-11 03:18:53',
A humble true worker for welfare, The bravest girl in
the world-- One from India, other from #PakistanDare,
Two neighbors' victory unfurled!")

❖ ('2014-10-11 03:32:23',
Instead o'Daggers drawn, Let @Pakistan Join with @
India to improve the fate Of children by rescue-plan:
End child labor & Taliban; Educate!")

❖   ('2014-10-11 03:41:57',
Such a GR8 symbolic gesture By @NobelPrize
Committee-in face Of irony of border-conflict &
War- Like States, Let Peace &Progress Gain Pace.')

❖   ('2014-10-11 03:49:13',
As @Malala said, Let @PMLN1 And @Narendramodi_
PM and the 2 Nations, Not B foes, become One, &B
Friends, and Cheer their daughters & Sons.')

❖   ('2014-10-11 04:00:06',
Thanks 2 @ndtv @timesnow @HeadlinesToday, @GEO..
All Media! Aim your Camera, Lime-light & Ray
O'Hope on Pak's @Malala & @k_satyarthi o'India.")

❖   ('2014-10-11 04:07:20',
People-2-People Contacts Btwn the 2 countries can
usher miracle; Even to rewind history, and burying
facts Of Wars of the Past and shackle.')

❖   ('2014-10-11 04:18:48',
Let History B writ by @Narendramodi_PM & Pak-
Head, & Announce: "No War, Enmity, Ill-Will of any
kind; Only Friendship Given Fullest chance!"')

❖   ('2014-10-11 04:30:26',
Terrorism-Scourge O'Humanity- B it from @LeT, @
Lashkar, @ISI, @ISIS Or Any Variation O'Name,Theme
or Fraternity- All Must Death's Feet Kiss.")

❖   ('2014-10-11 04:41:00',
Little minds like the Pak Brigadier, Colonel, Interlocutor,
or @congressorg O'India, Arrogant,Dense,Boorish--
Let's stay clear Of their Idea.")

❖   ('2014-10-11 04:48:00',
Models Like @MALALA & @k_satyarthi &
Leaders Like @Narendramodi_PM, With @Media Like
@timesnow @NDTV @HeadlinesToday,should lead the
@TIME')

❖ ('2014-10-11 14:04:34',
@k_satyarthi saved >80,000 Children from bonds,
labor, as part Of his "Bachapan Bachao" Aandolan, Since
1990: Celebrating @LIFE @soul, Heart')

❖ ('2014-10-11 14:18:16',
On Oct.9,2012, by Taliban, @Malala was shot in her
head- Just 'cause this Brave Girl in Pakistan Defied a
Deadly Order, even if Shot Dead")

❖ ('2014-10-11 14:23:36',
Taliban in Pakistan'd issued An order on the radio
that no girl Should go to school 2 B educated; Such
barbarism was beyond @MALALA's world.")

❖ ('2014-10-11 14:32:16',
Why should 1 b deprived Of education, privileges,
opportunities, Just 4 being born a female?-she cried.
Islamic fanaticism she'd not appease")

❖ ('2014-10-11 14:37:36',
A child's wisdom & courage & an NGO's
resolve to rescue Children from bonds of labor in early
age-- The combination- the passion 2 B & Do")

❖ ('2014-10-11 14:45:16',
Let Congrats be showered upon both Of above GR8
souls from Pak And India, and let us take the Oath 4
education;& on the path of Peace, Walk.')

❖ ('2014-10-11 14:57:21',
It's a Day of Jubilation, But 4 the story O'@
SunandaTharoor: She's killed--many an indication:
Polonium-210 & all (but who's the evil-doer?)")

❖ ('2014-10-11 15:04:46',
Sunanda was @ShashiTharoor's sweet Wife--A
dignitary @UNO he was, & now he's a man @ the
feet Of @congressorg, with @SoniaGandhiG in-charge.")

❖ ('2014-10-11 15:09:27',
? a strange coincidence: Sunanda was found dead in Room 345 Of Hotel Leela, New Delhi, while thence She was to have a Press-Conference live.')

❖ ('2014-10-11 15:24:44',
Was @SunandaPushkar Injected A lethal Drug & forced 2 digest other drugs, case projected That she died of drug-overdose-depressed, divorced?')

❖ ('2014-10-11 15:35:28',
Why did @ShashiTharoor send to @AIIMSNewDelhi Email that she'd Lupus, when she'd none? Of the Rx ALPRAX, what's the key? ? an #InjuryNo10!")

❖ ('2014-10-11 15:41:49',
@Swamy39 filed FIR to investigate Such questions and matters mysterious, Saying '@ShashiTharoor was a suspect Because he said so many lies.'")

❖ ('2014-10-11 15:56:04',
@ShashiTharoor's Lawyer, Tulasi, & @Poonawala, @congressorg spokesperson, Shielded him nervously, desperately. & @ARNABGOSWAMI asked a Qn:")

❖ ('2014-10-11 16:07:24',
"Was there some1 very powerful Who could\'ve been seriously blamed, If @Sunanda revealed something in the scheduled Press-Conference at 3:pm?')

❖ ('2014-10-11 16:18:23',
In this tragic horrid drama, Apparently the guilt directly goes To @SoniaGandhiG, presiding UPA Of @ congressorg 2 which @ShashiTharoor owes.')

❖ ('2014-10-11 16:25:15',
Was some key issue compromised By UPA Govt.,@ SoniaGandhiG, That involved @ShashiTharoor's hand, eyes, & @Sunanda threatened their security?")

❖ ('2014-10-11 16:33:17',
We trust @ARNABGOSWAMI'll go Relentlessly, with GR8 intelligence, To solve this mystery, so He proves 2 be a fit &GR8 Journalist that he is.")

❖ ('2014-10-11 16:42:24',
Patriotic @K_Satyarthi, recited A beautiful couplet: "Vatan ki rait, mujhe ediyan ragadane de; Mujhe yakeen hai ki pani yahin se nikalega."')

❖ ('2014-10-11 16:48:25',
@Narendramodi_PM meets @k_satyarthi-- Two Self-Committed GR8 Souls Devoted to Development of the country & Girls' Education & similar Goals.")

❖ ('2014-10-13 07:02:12',
RT @thekiranbedi: Well depicted. Toon in @the_hindu concerning child labour. NOBEL provides a new hope... http://t.co/0XOhY0w9mS')

❖ ('2014-10-13 07:22:05',
@Malala-1Brave Girl of Pak Did > 4 her country & humanity Than 10000s of coward @ISI & @ PMLN1-talk; They live in vain;she in GR8 posterity.')

❖ ('2014-10-13 07:39:27',
Pak's dirty tricks never end. Behind border-fires, they conspire 2 infiltrate in2 India: pretension of friend-Ship'd drown &set'em afire.")

❖ ('2014-10-13 07:55:09',
Islamists' sick depravity, treachery Lie in their belief by the book That 4 Islam, sinking in lies, debauchery Is fine, by hook or crook.")

❖ ('2014-10-13 08:10:53',
1000000s of lies, rapes &killing Millions of innocent women & Children, Jehadists say, Is virtually a rewarding Act 2 get a pass in2 heaven.')

❖ ('2014-10-13 08:34:25',
They say,'Islam prescribes 2 rule Barbarically,
with bars &war Muslim-majority land as tool:
Convert,subvert,conspire 2 become world-power.")

❖ ('2014-10-13 08:48:56',
Byzantium turned in2 Ottoman Empire. Cathedral in
Constantinople in2 the spire Of GR8 Mosque of Sophia
Hagia; & Hindukush led 2 Mughal India')

❖ ('2014-10-13 08:57:37',
@timesnow @timesofindia @TIME Have marched
ahead & @TheEconomists R all different now; yet
the crime Of Islamization relentlessly persists.')

❖ ('2014-10-13 09:02:05',
Sooner the world O'Islam realizes That to March with
@TIME is the Call Of the Day, and to languish in bygone
days Is folly supreme suicidal,")

❖ ('2014-10-13 09:29:56',
The better it'd B 4 them, their law, The world and the
human race: To emerge from cacoon of burqa, And to fly
as @Malala's butterfly-face.")

❖ ('2014-10-13 09:31:22',
RT @Via_Satellite: .@GDC4Systems Completes Four-Day
#MUOS Airborne Satcom Demonstration http://t.co/
dGfnFx4Qf2 #satellite http://t.co/5Zy02\u2026')

❖ ('2014-10-13 09:35:25',
RT @timesofindia: Heart to heart: How we can help
to rebuild Kashmir http://t.co/GZgmGiX0Cz http://t.
co/19Zs9oypI)

❖ ('2014-10-13 09:46:21',
@timesofindia @timesnow all, Rebuilding Kashmir
Must Surmise Open-doors 2 all Indian;so the wall
O'Article370 must yield 2 Door of Paradise.")

❖ ('2014-10-13 10:04:12',
@BJP4India What's This Childish cry of @ShivSena and
@raj_s_thakare--one to kiss Goodbye to @MahaBJP, the
other to beat @Marathi-Manus-Band!")

❖ ('2014-10-13 13:24:12',
#pakdares again, after a lil lull, This fox of a country
posing as a bull, One'd have caught by the horn, But that
without one it was born.")

❖ ('2014-10-13 13:31:16',
One brave soldier of @Indian Army Became the
latest martyr in this last Ceasefire-Violation, #Pak's
treachery-- Over 150 in 1 year past.")

❖ ('2014-10-13 13:34:47',
How long should @India tolerate When @Pakistan
never learns Its lesson: Firing indiscriminately to
infiltrate In the smoke-screen it churns')

❖ ('2014-10-13 13:42:19',
@pak is truly fast descending In a hell it's creating 4
itself-- A failed State, a nuisance, a sting Operation upon
itself, losing US help.")

❖ ('2014-10-13 13:59:21',
Unfortunately @Pak is our neighbor! So hard @
ArnabGoswami @timesnow @maroofraza @
SheshadriChari Dissuaded it from pursuing its course
anew!')

❖ ('2014-10-13 14:09:16',
@Pak thinks no one can see Its Foul, Foolish,
Treacherous Game! Yelling #kashmir to divert country's
fancy, In False Freedom's & UN's name!")

❖ ('2014-10-13 14:18:18',
@Pak's @ISI & Govt has amassed Such bad name,
earned Isolation In world-community, & masked,
Unsuccessfully, Mounting Economic depression.")

❖   ('2014-10-13 14:24:45',
May @Pakistan's people be saved From its @ISI's own
home-grown terrorism, & not succumb in its
depraved Ways, giving way to harmful schism.")

❖   ('2014-10-13 14:32:08',
'Sarve Bhawantu Sukhinah,' we pray For welfare of one
and all. Yet @Pak has continued from Day 1 2 have ill-
will 4 India and 2 freely fall.")

❖   ('2014-10-13 14:40:36',
3 times it has fought wars With us--this neighbor
of ours-- Losing each time, bearing scars, Yet it
misbehaves, remains unworthy of trust.')

❖   ('2014-10-13 14:42:18',
RT @PeshmergaGo: The Kurds need your support in
their fight against the tyranny that is "Islamic State".
Please Retweet #TwitterKurds https\u2026')

❖   ('2014-10-13 14:56:36',
@ISIS in the Middle East And the likes of @ISI of
Pakistan R curse 2 Humanity & @peace, And must
be demolished 2 usher @HISTORY's New @dawn!")

❖   ('2014-10-15 15:42:10',
@timesnow @ARNABGOSWAMI:Debate On @
OmarAbdulla's attitude dangerous-zigzag On 3
incidents in #Kashmir to-date of display of @
ISIS-flag...")

❖   ('2014-10-15 15:49:55',
@OmarAbdullah said today-- That @ISIS-flag-hoisting
after some prayer- Meeting, in #Kashmir deserves pay-
-ing no attention since the tailor')

❖   ('2014-10-15 16:00:08',
"The person who sewed the @ISIS-flag Had been
arrested, so he did redeem His duty; there was no
presence or tag Of #ISIS," said #Kashmir-CM.')

❖ ('2014-10-15 16:06:38',
Just some TV channels Made noise abt #ISIS Flag-
hoisting By some foolish chap In #Kashmir (where else);
To worry about, there was nothing!')

❖ ('2014-10-15 16:13:04',
@OmarAbdullah_JK, Chief Minister Of #Kashmir, thus
spake reassuringly: Is he the CM of the State, or a care-
taker Of #ISIS-Press PR kingly?')

❖ ('2014-10-15 16:22:34',
A great ominous threat Posed by #Lashker -e-Toiba
of #Pakistan, With #borderbetrayal; and to get
Complacent with #ISIS-sign should be taken')

❖ ('2014-10-15 16:35:28',
It's treason-some, unbelievable That son of @
FarooqAbdullah_, Grandson of @SheikAbdullah, able To
rule thru #NationalConf. like a #Mullah")

❖ ('2014-10-15 16:40:13',
Muslim clerical ruling a congregation, The Tri-son,
without enough regard For the Tricolor, have black-
mailed the nation Of India,off-guard')

❖ ('2014-10-15 16:45:22',
Compromising National security, National Honor,
National interest, As @ARNABGOSWAMl @timesnow
pointedly Pointed out to the #Kashmiri-guest-')

❖ ('2014-10-15 16:51:22',
Patriotic proper anchor of @timesnow, @
ARNABGOSWAMl, keep up the good Work of taking to
task, U know best how To boldly tackle, as U should')

❖ ('2014-10-15 17:01:52',
Dubious, ambiguous, ineffective, Obviously @
ObliviousOmar, CM fickle Of #Kashmir, Only @
congressdotgov @congressorg could tolerate #Article')

❖ ('2014-10-15 17:10:21',
#Article370 of #Kashmir somehow Must B abrogated
4 good, 4 good and Prosperous State of #India, @
timesnow, Free this Country, people &Land')

❖ ('2014-10-15 17:19:27',
@HeadlinesToday @timesnow @timesofindia @ndtv,
all Indians and the media Wonder If @ShashiTharoor
was axed By @SoniaGandhiG, utterly vexed')

❖ ('2014-10-15 17:24:49',
@SoniaGandhiG clearly thinks That #PRAISING @
Narendramodi_PM Is a sin,and @ShashiTharoor sinks
From being a @congressorg valued spokeperson')

❖ ('2014-10-15 17:29:09',
All the bright and straightforward Poor @
ShashiTharoor did was to #praise @Narendramodi_
PM's and the reward He reaped was to lose his days")

❖ ('2014-10-15 17:34:09',
As a @congressorg spokesman smart, @ShashiTharoor
must learn the art A little more 2 lick the boots Of his
boss, & 2 share her scams & loots')

❖ ('2014-10-15 17:44:03',
@ShashiTharoor is being a good And loyal @
congressorg-man, despite his Intelligence, to preclude A
word to @SoniaGandhiG to mind her own biz')

❖ ('2014-10-15 17:50:38',
Does poor @ShashiTharoor Have any self-respect, or
is he complicit In @Sunanda's murder, sure Not 2 go
against @congressorg even a lil bit?")

❖ ('2014-10-15 17:50:38',
Does poor @ShashiTharoor Have any self-respect, or
is he complicit In @Sunanda's murder, sure Not 2 go
against @congressorg even a lil bit?")

❖ ('2014-10-15 17:57:55',
There lies a GR8 deal of mystery: @sptvrock @
SunandaPushkar killed By a lethal poison injection, in a
hurry; Is he being to some1 a shield?')

❖ ('2014-10-15 18:05:43',
At 3 pm @SunandaTharoor was Scheduled to have a
press-conference; And hours before--mayB because She
was 2 reveal something--she is silenced')

❖ ('2014-10-15 18:12:16',
It's not fair to presume guilt Against someone
without a trial. But, then, why a defense is built For @
ManmohanSingh's lost coalgate files?")

❖ ('2014-10-15 18:17:05',
@timesnow will hopefullly reveal What scams were
committed, what deals Were carried out Bhind the veil;
Who's guilty-who buys, who sells!")

❖ ('2014-10-15 18:31:26',
@TheEconomist @nytimes @timesofindia
Have news--a novel by @RichardFlan Won
#bookerprize; & I've a ? & an idea:
REINCARNATION-of-IRON-MAN?")

❖ ('2014-10-15 18:44:33',
@ARNABGOSWAMl @timesnow In Today's debate,on @
Pakistan's stand, Ask @MissAbidHussain & @Abidrao
how It's that 2 @UN & @USA runs @Pakistan")

❖ ('2014-10-15 18:48:46',
@Pak begging attention and favor To intervene in @
INDIA-Pak Interelation On #Kashmir, forever &
ever, Rapidly becoming an irrelevant nation')

❖ ('2014-10-15 18:55:42',
@Pak plays again its N-Card silly; & @
MissAbidHussain says nily-willy, "@ARNABGOSWAMl, U R
the most Presumptuous Anchor &Television-host."')

❖ ('2014-10-15 19:00:27',
With an air of utmost superiority, The @Pak-lady tells
@ARNABGOSWAMl, On air, @India is a no-good country
Practicing a custom called Satee-')

❖ ('2014-10-15 19:16:26',
The prim lady grimly pronounces: #Shimla-Agreement
let @Pakistan Seek outside help in #Kashmir, she says.
@ARNABGOSWAMl corrects her then.')

❖ ('2014-10-15 19:29:20',
'Only with strict,explicit mutual consent Of @India
& @Pakistan could, in fact, A non-bilateral avenue
be entertained,' Says the #ShimlaPact")

❖ ('2014-10-15 19:34:29',
The @Pak-lady's face fell, yet she Kept calling @
HafizSaeedJUD A social-worker who did GR8 deed Of
rescuing #KashmirFloods victims in need.")

❖ ('2014-10-15 19:43:34',
@ARNABGOSWAMl then invited The @Pak-lady @
AbidHussain 2 include @DowdIbrahim, who fled India;
& @GenBakshi said,"Also add Osama-bin-Laden."')

❖ ('2014-10-15 19:47:32',
It is pitiable that @Pakistan Refuses to C the light,
the stark Reality, that it is writing the plan Of its own
demise, continuing to bark.')

❖ ('2014-10-16 01:44:34',
To fully narrate this Grand Modern Mahabharat, an
Observer must view Maha-Mahabharat, its twists
&turn, In Maharashtra, occurring now just.')

❖ ('2014-10-16 01:53:56',
So 2 observe & report properly The Fate of each
#Assembly #Seat, there are From @india360_m, @ndtv
@timesnow & @HeadlinesToday 100s O'Star")

❖ ('2014-10-16 01:58:18',
Media Reporters & Editors & Sen- -Ior
Journalists, from wide and far Witnessing it, and many
a TV-Screen R ablaze, and resonating the Radar')

❖ ('2014-10-16 02:05:18',
They're witnessing 2 the Nation 2 provide Such a
Revolution taking place: @MahaBJP's momentous
stride; History unfolding right in our face.")

❖ ('2014-10-16 02:13:48',
@congressorg's @ManiShankarIyer, & @
SoniaGandhiG, @rahulgandhi2020's #Hand-sign
(Panja), Eat your Heart out & watch @ModiWave
sweep, tease!")

❖ ('2014-10-16 02:19:28',
@congressorg's stalwarts had Their Hour when they
were bad Enough 2 challenge @narendramodi The
'Chaiwala' 2 open a Tea-stall in #NewDelhi")

❖ ('2014-10-16 02:29:01',
@SoniaGandhiG & all @congressorg men Failed
to C the Tsunami, and arrogance Paved their way 2 go
down the drain; Now they are past instance.')

❖ ('2014-10-16 13:48:42',
Hello @gotowebinar, I'm interested. Please count me in
and let me know how to join & learn a bit more the
power of the Power-Point. Thanks.")

❖ ('2014-10-16 14:05:48',
@ndtv It's sad that #HudHud, Its GR8 devastation
notwithstanding, Should cause something Like
shortage of food, essential commodities&goods")

❖ ('2014-10-16 14:13:26',
@ndtv How did a smart CM like @ncbn (@
ChandraBabuNaidu) Fail to anticipate the crisis and strike
A good solution &avoid,4 Nothing Much Adoo!')

❖ ('2014-10-16 14:19:45',
@ndtv @timesnow One can Only Hope that
#KashmirFloods & #HudHudCyclone Are followed by
Smart Reconstruction Of the #Valley & #Vizag Zone.')

❖ ('2014-10-16 14:28:49',
@ndtv Let the #Kashmir Valley, Free of #Article370,
as Popular Choice, Be Rebuilt as a Paradise Anew:
#KashmirFloods'd B A Boon in disguise!")

❖ ('2014-10-16 14:37:37',
Here the Words of @Narendramodi_PM Would Bring
New Fruit--to @makeinindia_ A #Kashmir 2 B proud of,
Once Again, And the world would rely.')

❖ ('2014-10-16 14:42:35',
Come, One and All, Answer the Clarion Call Of the
Day, #MakeInIndia & Manufacture A State Called
#Kashmir-New Pinnacle of Beauty of Nature!')

❖ ('2014-10-16 14:49:27',
Only a Visionary and Tall @Narendramodi_PM could
defeat obstacles all, & Dream Promise of @
satyamevjayate In Conjunction of @SHRAMEVJAYATE.')

❖ ('2014-10-16 14:55:03',
Building a New India with Smart Cities, With
#DEVELOPMENT Mantra GR8... May U LIVE LONG 2
Usher Promises these & a NEW Society, too, Create!')

❖ ('2014-10-16 14:56:08',
RT @NASA: Did you miss the @PBS @MAKERSwomen
special about women in space? Watch it here: http://t.
co/p8DswCqBgl @WomenNASA http://t.co/aet\u2026')

❖ ('2014-10-16 15:05:51',
@NASA @PBS @MAKERSwomen @WomenNASA The
Place of Women is in the Senate, & #SPACE &
#ISLAMIC #MADERSA, Thru @Malala's Face,&
HEADS OF STATE!")

❖ ('2014-10-16 15:07:03',
RT @timesofindia: Azam Khan questioned at
Delhi airport for carrying live bullets http://t.co/
wPrqojeZKI')

❖ ('2014-10-16 15:16:52',
@timesofindia 4 heaven's sake, Why @AzamKhan
carries Bullets In Handbag, and @abdullah_omar issues
Fake Assurance abt @ISIS, & away he gets.")

❖ ('2014-10-16 15:28:46',
@YahooNews Putin's #RussiainvadedUkraine &
@Pakistan_Army Threat that it's #N-Power country
would not B in vain If the World Opens its Eyes.")

❖ ('2014-10-16 15:59:20',
The High Time threats of Abject #Communism and
#Terrorism & #Conversions Religious the @World
Totally Rejects, And #FreedomSpeaks san Guns.')

❖ ('2014-10-16 16:07:48',
Fanatic Islamic @Terror Must B Shunned Off the Stage
of the World, & It's FREED Of #EVANGELIONs; and
the @UN Must Abolish Such Many a Creed.")

❖ ('2014-10-17 06:31:02',
@BJP4India 4 Serving INDIA, With Humility &
Labor, & 2 B able 2 communicate, thru Media, &
Directly with @Narendramodi_PM, I ask this favor.')

❖ ('2014-10-17 06:38:50',
@BJP4India It's a Critical Epoch, like a New Modern
Mahabharat; & I'm proud 2 Dedicate 2 National
& Internatnal Readers My Verse-Twitters @")

❖ ('2014-10-17 06:45:15',
@BJP4India Let the World Stand in Awe: We
'TRANSFORM INDIA WITH @NARENDRAMODI' An
INDIA, JAGADGURU 1S Again, that Saw New Pinnacle
O'Glory.")

❖ ('2014-10-17 06:50:47',
@timesofindia @NDTV @timesnow @TIME. Ye all
Witness @Pakistan's folly- Indulging in Perpetration of
its Crime Of Ceasefire Violation, Unholy")

❖ ('2014-10-17 07:01:11',
@timesofindia Alliance with Terrorism And Arrogantly
Disturbing Peace In its Neighborhood, causing Schism
Using Repeatedly such Practice...')

❖ ('2014-10-17 07:07:08',
@timesofindia @Pakistan is Writing Its Own Obituary,
Beating War-Drums, Inviting Such Drama Dangerous
Leading to a Catastrophic Panorama..')

❖ ('2014-10-17 07:12:15',
@timesofindia @Pak Boasting of Being A Nuclear-
Capable State; Unfortunately not Even Realizing This
Phrase Could Drown Permanently Its Fate')

❖ ('2014-10-17 07:16:54',
@timesofindia We all pray that @Pak Comes 2 Its
Senses & Refrains From Unnecessary Antagonism,
Idle Talk, & Stability, Prosperity It Gains.')

❖ ('2014-10-17 07:24:37',
@timesofindia Now Parvez Musharraf Who Betrayed
@lNawazSharifl, Let Alone India, Is Bragging abt @Pak
Military Might & Stuff Prone 2 Drone.')

❖ ('2014-10-17 07:33:41',
@timesofindia If @Pakistan Ventures Militarily,
Imposing War Over India, @Narendramodi_PM'd surely
crush For good, this bumbling fake spar.")

❖ ('2014-10-17 07:39:31',
@Narendramodi_PM Is Having Urgent Meeting with the
Heads Of the 3 Military Services: Army, Navy, &
Wing, 2 Discuss @Pak & @Chinese Threats..')

❖ ('2014-10-21 03:40:56',
@arunjaitley announced the #Ordinance To e-auction
the #coal-blocks; Steel & cement sectors to
enhance, & to lessen @UPA2-created shocks.')

❖ ('2014-10-21 03:49:14',
The 'Ashwamedh-Yajna-Horse' ran Like #Tsunami of
#ModiWave, in 2 States: #MaharashtraElections &
#Hariyana- Sealed by @BJP4India their fates")

❖ ('2014-10-21 03:54:20',
@congressorg & @MNS were devasted; Even @
ShivSena was just Snubbed, checked and gated; @
Narendramodi_PM had called @MNS "Naturally
Corrupt."')

❖ ('2014-10-21 04:04:07',
@PawarSpeaks & @ajitpawarpawar Report Through
eloquent @prafullapatel1, @MNS's 'Unconditional
Support' To BJP, lest they should be in Jail!.")

❖ ('2014-10-21 04:16:00',
What a height of opportunism @sharadpawar57
scales-up, purely under fear! "Pawar is where Power is"-
-this aphorism Is patently present here?')

❖ ('2014-10-21 04:19:56',
#Haryana is aptly the land Where the GR8 @
Mahabharat War Was fought some 5000 years ago, and
This New Kurukshetra is once again on the radar')

❖ ('2014-10-21 04:26:15',
History is made, repeatedly, On the Earth, with each
passing day And moment; and surely & ironically,
Once again,"@satyamevjayate!," we say.')

❖ ('2014-10-21 04:31:53',
@Narendramodi_PM is the Grand Sire, Like Satyavrati
Bheeshma, and also Karma-Yogi Arjun's aglow fire He
carries in his bosom--very much so!")

❖ ('2014-10-21 04:40:48',
Thus @Bheeshma and @Arjun @Narendramodi_PM is
--a Two-in-One! This Modern @Mahabharat opportune
He will surely for @BJP4India have well-won!')

❖ ('2014-10-21 04:49:13',
Next R the battles 4 @Bihar_BJP & @TourismJK--
Jammu&Kashmir, And @UP, with Big Drama 4 all 2
C; And 2 spread the hue of the #Saffron Color!')

❖ ('2014-10-21 04:55:55',
In the meantime the GR8 Campaign for @Swachh_
Bharat_ Abhiyan is on! @Narendramodi_PM surely has
in store Many a GR8 Magical Dream well-sown!')

❖ ('2014-10-22 00:21:54',
RT @HPStorage: Add highly available shared storage
to virtualized #Intel servers. Get your free 1TB of HP
#storage to get going. https://t\u2026')

❖ ('2014-10-22 00:23:12',
RT @Swamy39: Black money names will embarrass
Congress, says Arun Jaitley : India, News - India Today
http://t.co/8MyBmuQAhT via @IndiaToday')

❖ ('2014-10-22 00:32:12',
@Swamy39 @IndiaToday @Narendramodi_PM Ji,
#blackmoney is a Black Spot in #India's #economy And
bringing it back to our country Is necessary")

❖ ('2014-10-22 00:53:18',
@Narendramodi_PM @arunjaitley @Swamy39 @
IndiaToday,"ONLY MODI, OR NO @BJP4India," @
babaramdev4 roared & a genuine Support Grew 4
His Idea')

❖ ('2014-10-22 01:06:08',
@Swamy39 @IndiaToday, our @VisVp Or @arunjaitley'd
not keep their Word 2 keep @SoniaGandhiG Or @
congressorg unembarrassed--THAT'd B ABSURD!")

❖ ('2014-10-22 01:14:24',
@Swamy39 @IndiaToday, #blackmoney MUST Come
Back thru @PMOIndia's toil; @Ganga-PUTRA @
narendramodi is JUST! &His GR8 RESOLVE NO-1
can foil.")

❖ ('2014-10-22 01:26:26',
@Swamy39, @congressorg deserves 2 B EMBRRSSD 4
All the Black Deeds they did. If #blackmoney tops the
list,it serves Them Well-No PruoVidQuid')

❖ ('2014-10-22 01:31:35',
@Swamy39 @IndiaToday @Narendramodi_PM Ji, The
Whole Country Is All Ears 2 Get the some News That
#blackmoney is Coming Back, & it 2 Welcome!')

❖ ('2014-10-22 01:40:59',
Now a bit of News on the Front Of our Modern
Mahabharat, to which These Tweets (Even if they Don't
Qualify) submit tributes...poor or rich!")

❖ ('2014-10-22 01:48:07',
Mention must B made of the snap That stung @
BJP4India & @ShivSena unexpectedly: 25-year-old
alliance grew a gap Which broke the taut medley.')

❖ ('2014-10-22 02:02:23',
@ShivSena's @meeuddhavThackeray And @
AmitShahOffice of @BJP4India Couldn't agree on the
array Of Seats to B shared, & they parted their way.")

❖ ('2014-10-22 02:07:57',
@BJP4India won the Assembly Election magnificently
& #Maharashtra had #MahaDilemma: To form the
Govt -- to take, or not to take, #ShivSena')

❖ ('2014-10-22 02:14:34',
In #haryanaelections, the @BJP4India Won & got
majority votes, And there, no Hudda or Chautala- But a
non-Jatt CM is the new CM, one notes.')

❖ ('2014-10-23 16:57:08',
@APSMeetings I'd like to submit a paper for the March 2015 APS Meeting. I'm submitting an Abstract.and also applying 4 a Travel Grant. Thanx")

❖ ('2014-10-27 02:37:35',
New CM of Haryana, Manohar Khattar @bjpmlal'll win our hearts If Justice gets those who made the State a Banana Republic by criminal con-art")

❖ ('2014-10-27 02:46:01',
Horror stories R abuzz In media that the son-in-law of @SoniaGandhiG did merge The law in dust by huge illegal land-deals, dirtying his paw.')

❖ ('2014-10-27 02:57:47',
Ex-CM @Hudda Transferred the honest @IAS-Officer About 50 times--Poor Ashok Khemka-- He dared question this @congressorg's reign of terror.")

❖ ('2014-10-27 03:16:58',
@bjpmlal (Khattar), CM new Of #Haryana, promised that no-1 Who committed such a crime shall be Spared, be it @RobertVadra or @Hudda,on run.')

❖ ('2014-10-27 03:28:31',
Many things Happened for India for the very first time: @Narendramodi_PM played drum, as he brings To China new air ....this Minister Prime!')

❖ ('2014-10-27 03:35:50',
While all Indians in the whole world Celebrated Diwali @ home, our @Narendramodi_PM traveled To Siachin, India's North-Front at -49 Degree.")

❖ ('2014-10-27 03:42:39',
@Narendramodi_PM visited Bhutan Days after taking @PMOIndia, to show That the good old @Hindustan, Shall friendship 4 all neighbors bestow.')

❖ ('2014-10-27 03:50:50',
Drive 2 keep India clean- From allies 2 the heart of
the Capital-- That's @Narendramodi_PM's vow serene;
Cleanliness is a Revolution Total.")

❖ ('2014-10-27 17:42:14',
#BlackMoneyHolders Hold #BlackMoney tight, &
leaders of @congressorg & @BJP4India fight
Endlessly,accusing each Other beyond public's reach.")

❖ ('2014-10-27 17:47:57',
3 names have been revealed by @BJP4India's @
arunjaitley 3 small insignificant fries While, maybe, the
Big Fish could be netted if he tries.")

❖ ('2014-10-27 17:54:54',
Who R the Big Fish--asks The nation; R they putting on
masks Of Parties, or Power, or Donors, Redeemers? Are
there hidden Wheelers-Dealers?')

❖ ('2014-10-27 23:20:36',
@BJP4India made such hype, Says @ARNABGOSWAMI,
in Election-Campaign! Yet trepidation-type Step Holds
#BlackMoneyHolders' IDs,& 4 whose gain?")

❖ ('2014-10-27 23:28:55',
On #Jammu & #KashmirMillionMarch
#MillionMarchJoke @BBhuttoZardari's Show In
#London, there was a quick discharge of rotten eggs
& #tomatoe")

❖ ('2014-10-27 23:39:54',
#Plastics #bottles were hurled On @BBhuttoZardari;
it's a #MillionMarchJoke Of #Internationalization-bid in
the #World Thru #eggs & #Coke!")

❖ ('2014-10-27 23:53:32',
@ARNABGOSWAMI, U R doing A GR8 Service 2 #India
by cuing #TalkinCowboys like @Pirzada-type Baffons
& #RantOfTheDay #Entertainment at noons!')

❖ ('2014-10-28 00:03:53',
@Pakistan's @ZulfikaliBhutto's grandson, @
BBhuttoZardari #rants in hoarse-voice @Kashmir...in
home-spun Yarn, when @TourismJK is ri8 choice.")

❖ ('2014-10-28 00:51:04',
@ARNABGOSWAMl @HeadlinesToday, @
AMISHDEVGAN @bhupendrachaube, & Many
#mediawatch #hero4, KEEP UP THE GOOD WORK
& your Wonderful GR8 #TVShows')

❖ ('2014-10-28 01:06:54',
#India has emerged from Dark Age of @congressdotgov
& @SoniaGandhiG Dirty #paws by virtue of your
stark- @satyamevjayate-based Shows on TV')

❖ ('2014-10-28 01:14:28',
RT @Swamy39: I am sitting on the banks of Ganga
after yoga and mantra.I am in Rishikesh to address the
disciples of Swami Dayanada Sarasvat\u2026')

❖ ('2014-10-28 01:23:16',
@Babaramdev786 @Swamy39 #history Would
remember as new #yoga-Master & #Heroes Of the
2nd Indian #Independence & Glory-- This every1
Knows.')

❖ ('2014-10-28 01:28:11',
RT @timesofindia: BJP blames Nitish for Gandhi Maidan
serial blasts http://t.co/uvebpgSAT)

❖ ('2014-10-28 01:35:38',
How lure & mirage of Power Can make one fall is
illustrated By the Fall of @Nitish4Bihar A name soiled
in #patna #Bomb #Blast2014 ill-fated')

❖ ('2014-10-28 02:02:57',
RT @timesofindia: Eye test that predicts Alzheimer's
years before its symptoms appear http://t.co/
bMqeKTmCzn")

❖ ('2014-10-28 02:07:53',
@timesofindia Eye-test to reveal Potential #alzheimers
or @alzheimerssoc Should be publicized to deal With
this terrible affliction to man.')

❖ ('2014-10-28 02:08:58',
RT @Swamy39: UPA govt had given amnesty to about
100 black money illegal foreign bank account holders.
At least release that list')

❖ ('2014-10-28 02:14:39',
@Swamy39 The Politics of #BlackMoney Is GR8ly
damaging to country- 1 shows that making Billions in
Black And Donating 2 a #party'll Pay-back")

❖ ('2014-10-28 02:18:51',
RT @Narendramodi_PM: Dr Jitendra Singh Administers
Vigilance Awareness pledge in PMO http://t.co/
CSziqco2Ia via @narendramodi')

❖ ('2014-10-28 02:25:14',
@Narendramodi_PM @narendramodi May I humbly
Ask if @BarackObama did present A package of
books,in a GR8 hurry, To #WhiteHouse 4 U I'd sent?")

❖ ('2014-10-28 02:33:08',
@Narendramodi_PM @narendramodi Be it Your Love
Sportsmanship or Statesmanship, That U Congratulate
each Summit, O Captain of Nation's Ship!")

❖ ('2014-10-28 02:35:16',
RT @timesofindia: India should refrain from
complicating boundary issue: China http://t.co/
hhKm2PCCXo')

❖ ('2014-10-28 02:42:26',
@timesofindia &should #China feel free To
complicate #Border-Issues at will, Unopposed by
#Indian #democracy Or an #Indian #Military Drill?')

❖ ('2014-10-28 02:48:59',
@MazumderNirmal @timesofindia #China &
#Pakistan've grown Bold @ Free Aggression against
#India Because of @congressdotgov Complacency Old.")

❖ ('2014-10-28 02:56:14',
@Narendramodi_PM @Swamy39 @arunjaitley @
TIME @timesofindia @nytindia @timesnow @
ARNABGOSWAMl, 4 the medley Of Verse-Tweets, pls.
follow me.')

❖ ('2014-10-28 03:02:35',
A Book of @mysteryancient of 1000 Verse-Tweets
on #Indiansummer #Politics Will be Published by @
aksinh, and A Modern @Maha_bharat it depicts')

❖ ('2014-10-28 03:10:08',
I'm no Rishi-Kavi @Vedavyasa of @dwapara3rdyuga,
But I've passion for #history & Kavita, So I post
Verse-Tweets, I'm no Wordsworth or Keats")

❖ ('2014-10-28 03:17:11',
Yet I hope & wish To cast #EntertainmentPR
Humanistic trends and swish, To paint in #B&W
Pandora's Box ajar: Be it #politics Or #Economics.")

❖ ('2014-10-28 03:25:12',
The Nu generation of #Indians @adobeyv & voice
of #youthengage #YouthSpark Of the @jcyberworld
mighty May like this genre's contrast stark")

❖ ('2014-10-29 06:15:07',
VIDEO: \u0932\u0949\u0928\u094d\u091a\u093f\
u0902\u0917 \u0915\u0947 \u0938\u093e\u0925 \
u0939\u0940 \u0928\u093e\u0938\u093e \u0915\
u0947 \u0930\u0949\u0915\u0947\u091f \u092e\
u0947\u0902 \u0935\u093f\u0938\u094d\u092b\
u094b\u091f - International News - Samay Live http://t.
co/aoKUWSUQyR @aksinh @NarendraModi_PM @
NASA')

❖ ('2014-10-29 07:42:19',
@Sheeladixit1 has expressed anticipation &
Admiration for @Narendramodi_PM- What would B @
SoniaGandhiG' reaction? How'd she this deed deem?")

❖ ('2014-10-29 07:54:39',
On being asked abt @SoniaGandhiG & @
rahulgandhi2020 not talking much, @Sheeladixit1
said,"@indiragandhi84Ji & @RajivGandhi,too,were
as such"')

❖ ('2014-10-29 08:04:52',
"But Indira Gandhi & Rajiv Gandhi did work,"
Added @Sheeladixit1, wistfully. So, now,O Readers of
this perk, Draw your own conclusions duly.')

❖ ('2014-10-29 08:11:56',
Congrats 2 @Dev_Fadnavis, the youngest Mayor of
#Nagpur, on becoming the youngest CM of #Maharashtra,
the very best From #RSS & #BJP,4 test!')

❖ ('2014-10-29 08:23:34',
A boy, 6, to his mom went "I\'d go 2 school no more!"
Why? "Because its name is Indira Convent; And @
indiragandhi84 jailed my father before."')

❖ ('2014-10-29 08:29:03',
That boy, with a spark of righteous Rebellion is now
going 2 lead State of #Maharashtra valorous; Adding to
@Narendramodi_PM's grand creed.")

❖ ('2014-10-29 08:43:50',
#indiatoday, #Kashmir 2 #Kanyakumari Shall March;
@narendramodi PM & @AmitShahOffice leading
#BJP: A New Model #Development in #Democracy.')

❖ ('2014-10-29 08:54:49',
When @Narendramodi_PM & @Dev_Fadnavis Get
2gether 2 roar & move majestically, #Development
has but 2 follow its Planned course, No sully!')

❖ ('2014-10-29 09:06:45',
Let #BlackMoneyHolders Be fully punished 4 the
Country 2 see: B it Top Party-Leaders or top Business-
Earners, #BlackMoney buys No Immunity.')

❖ ('2014-10-29 09:11:49',
Some 800+ #BlackMoneyHolders In a country with so
much poverty- The #BlackMoney must go the folders Of
Treasury 2 help the poor &the needy.')

❖ ('2014-10-29 09:25:56',
Like Chanakya, @babaramdev4 resolved 2
campaign,& @narendramodi Like @Chandragupta
evolved 2 Bid Nandvansha good riddance,&set
#INDIA Free.')

❖ ('2014-10-29 09:34:36',
The promise made to @BabaRamdeo To bring
#BlackMoney Home Must be fulfilled; thanks to @
SCJudgments that gave Order 2 cut a delay-syndrome.')

❖ ('2014-11-02 18:00:08',
There R some acute questions Why W.Bengal CM,
Mamata Banerjee Any plan to curb the terrorism shuns:
How lure of power steals power to see !')

❖ ('2014-11-02 18:20:00',
There R many scandals 2 examine-- Sharda Funds
misuse, the Burdwan case-- Yet "Didi" is getting deeper
into the sin Of just saving her face.')

❖ ('2014-11-02 18:32:37',
Playing the lowly game of vote- Bank politics, siding
communal Muslims & Communists--a Sport of
holding CM's Fort, 2ward harm 2 Nation grim.")

❖ ('2014-11-02 18:39:35',
Then there is our good-old @Jai_AAP @AK49,
Busy churning out and playing with glee His
"#Shoot&Scoot" game fine To become the CM of
Delhi.')

❖ ('2014-11-02 18:44:56',
@akejriwal7 abandoned Delhi CM post In a hurry 2
fight @BJP @Narendramodi_PM, And having terribly
lost His luck, is now dealing cards again.')

❖ ('2014-11-02 18:59:14',
@Akejriwal has become a Big Joke; He thinks he can
fool All, All the Time. Sunk in the @RiverGanga, he plays
a stroke In @Yamuna flow Prime.')

❖ ('2014-11-02 19:11:24',
By blaming LG Jung,& @BJP4India 4 horse-trading
of @AAP MLAs, @ArvindKejriwal is like a "Triya-
Charittar" character who a fantasy chases.')

❖ ('2014-11-02 19:20:44',
No less strange is the character Bearing the name @
RobertVadra, @rahulgandhi2020's Brother- In-Law, a
Lord of @SoniaGandhiG's bygone era.")

❖ ('2014-11-02 19:31:28',
@RobertVadra had some shady land-deals in @
HaryanaPCC, sort of a loot, Where he made 600%
profit;yet feels He can gallop while on back-foot.')

❖ ('2014-11-02 19:38:44',
Being son-in-law of @SoniaGandhiG, His arrogance
knows no bounds. He mistreats a journalist with
impunity; With "R U Serious"-type Sounds.')

❖ ('2014-11-02 19:43:28',
#YesWeAreSerious" says Community Of journalists
across @India, With @ARNABGOSWAMl pronouncing
the Guilty Verdict for foolish @RobertVadra.')

❖ ('2014-11-02 19:52:08',
@congressorg's @DigvijaySingh__ @JhaSanjay @
renukachaudhar1 &all The sold-souls of @
SoniaGandhiG bring Words 2 save @RobertVadra from
Fall.")

❖ ('2014-11-02 20:01:39',
@JhaSanjay @renukachaudhar1 @digvijaysingh28
&Other Mindless slaves of @SoniaGandhiG Are
raving 2 save @rahulgandhi2020's In-Law-Brother.")

❖ ('2014-11-08 01:55:55',
So, now the controversial son-in-law Of @SoniaGandhiG,
@RobertVadra, Folded 4 fingers of Open Hand, we saw--
& still has on 2 his dirty paw.')

❖ ('2014-11-08 02:01:50',
What does the abrupt closing of yor 4 Companies mean,
Mr. @RobertVadra? That, with @congressorg's, 4 sure,
Gone, U lost voice of @SanjayJha?")

❖ ('2014-11-08 02:07:53',
The New Govt. should or shall not, Let U pack-up &
go nily-wily way. The Law of the Land must've U caught
Red-handed, and show U jail 1 day!")

❖ ('2014-11-08 02:12:13',
@Narendramodi_PM adopts #Jayapur As his village to
set on radar Of #development, a destination to tour 4
Indians & Foreigners, like a Star!')

❖ ('2014-11-08 02:17:09',
4 Village of #Jayapur, 4 sure, Achhe Din Aa Gaye Hain,
Hai Na? Let Writing of a New Parva (Chapter) Begin In
this Modern Little Mahabharata.')

❖ ('2014-11-08 02:27:12',
In hands O'@Narendramodi_PM India & #Jayapur
Village Would challenge--it may seem-- Each Other as to
who travels faster in the Digital Age")

❖ ('2014-11-08 02:32:32',
Queer Mr.@kejriwal_arvind Must be full of lot of
foul wind-- To use posters like @Narendramodi_PM,
Together with his own face as #Delhi CM.')

❖ ('2014-11-08 02:35:19',
Once again, this power-hungry little Fox is playing
games to fool Delhi-people, Who, sure enough to teach
him a lesson Not to so day-dream.')

❖ ('2014-11-08 02:45:32',
Like a pin-pricked big baloon, This Mr @AK49--@
ArvindKejriwal Should be flattened to 0 soon; &
take 'Sanyaas' from #politics & talking tall.")

❖ ('2014-11-08 05:33:56',
Today, @Narendramodi_PM performed Puja @ #Assi
Ghat of #Varanasi; And then, with a group of laborers
formed, He worked out a labor-odyssey.')

❖ ('2014-11-08 05:41:34',
Taking a \'Kodi\' in hands, he began Digging, as a part of
"Swachchh Bharat Abhiyaan (Clean India Campaign)" To
clean from that Ghat its Dirt.')

❖ ('2014-11-08 05:51:19',
A symbolic gesture it was, but not a show: Or Photo-Op,
as in #CheatingCleanIndia, Some had made a go In
#Delhi, primarily just 4 the media.')

❖ ('2014-11-08 05:57:03',
They\'d a laborer scatter dry leaves On road, &
then with a dozen "Leaders", brooms in hands, full
sleeves, Acted 2 sweep, publicity 2 gain.')

❖ ('2014-11-08 06:04:56',
#BJP #Delhi President Upadhyay was Architect of this
farcical drama. With such pretentious ways, how a good
cause Would he serve, Hii Rama?')

❖ ('2014-11-08 06:14:36',
It was such hard labor for @Narendramodi_PM on
the Ganga- Ghat that in 10 minutes his face bore
Perspiration aflow, like a true dirt-digger.')

❖ ('2014-11-08 06:20:58',
@Narendramodi_PM, in a short speech Nomed 9 people
2 continue the mission: @yadavakhilesh, UP-CM among
them, 2 beseech Help in work 2 B done')

❖ ('2014-11-08 06:29:17',
Comedian @rajusrivastav, Kricketer @ImRaina &
@muhammedkaif, and Singer @tiwarymanoj, Vice-
Chanceler Of Chitrakut were enlisted in the band.')

❖ ('2014-11-08 06:35:37',
Wiping drops of labor-borne water From his forehead
& his glowing face, @Narendramodi_PM then
made a stir To Mata Anandmayi's Hospital-place")

❖ ('2014-11-08 06:41:54',
Singer @Kailashkher, 1 of the nominees, Whose voice
is joy 2 hear in free flows, Said rightly, "When 1 sees @
Narendramodi_PM, one knows.')

❖ ('2014-11-08 06:50:28',
What a true leader means, who aids 2 revive the Nation,
2 do genuine service 2 others in true spirit, after
decades Of decay and duty amiss.')

❖ ('2014-11-08 06:57:52',
@Kailashkher'd now sing songs Of valor of rebuilding
this nation; Thinking he is lucky that he belongs To
State of U.P.,full of Inspiration.")

❖ ('2014-11-09 23:41:43',
@Narendramodi_PM's his 1st expansion O'Cabinet,
with 21 new young faces; @ramkripalsingh1 (@
laluprasadrjd's scion) Now in @BJP makes waves.")

❖ ('2014-11-09 23:54:10',
@manoharparrikar Minister O'Defense; @jayantsinha
in #finance; others include @sureshprabhu14, @
girirajsinghbjp,hence, A Nationalistic mood")

❖ ('2014-11-10 00:03:38',
"Those not in favor of @narendramodi," he\'d said,
"Should go to #Pakistan." @AMISHDEVGAN\'s
#BigStoryBigDebate Airing now @meemafzal Khan')

❖ ('2014-11-10 00:12:51',
"@girirajsinghbjp in @BJP cabinet," @MeemAfzalKhan
complains, "Is blackest spot for @narendramodi yet."
Why? He should suffer no such pains.')

❖ ('2014-11-10 00:34:47',
@meemafzal1 @Rashidalvi11 @DrAMSinghvi @
SanjayJha @renukachowdary9 @RitaBJoshi @
ManiShankarIyer should all take taxi Or train to
#Karachi.')

❖ ('2014-11-10 00:49:03',
Whatever one's Party- Politics or loyalty, If one plays
Dirty Game of @SoniaGandhiG's #PseudoSecularity, It's
Treason, W/o Reason We shun.")

❖ ('2014-11-10 00:54:48',
Enough of "Divide & Rule" Policy @
BritishMonarchy & @congressorg followed. Now
the time 4 #Development of country Is here with @
narendramodi')

❖ ('2014-11-10 01:03:46',
So, if you dislike @narendramodi, U dislike @
Development for our nation; Then U might well like
#Pakistan's chaos, stagnation, degradation.")

❖ ('2014-11-10 01:14:33',
So, @girirajsinghbjp said what he felt & said it
honestly. He might've with politics dealt Incorrectly;
but with patriotism, appropriately!!")

❖ ('2014-11-10 01:18:53',
Wisdom of @uddhavthackeray is open 2 question,
when he recognizes not That @Narendramodi_PM, time
&again, Is giving him considerate thought.')

❖ ('2014-11-10 01:25:16',
A man of his word, @narendramodi, 4 respect 2 @
uddhavthackeray's Late Father, is dealing fairly, though
he Must accept #ShivSena's new fate.")

❖ ('2014-11-10 01:29:12',
Not a towering leader, @uddhavthackeray, With much
lower electoral victory, Should heed to the call of the
day And walk by, yet behind @BJP.')

❖ ('2014-11-10 01:38:23',
But @meeuddhav, so full of ego, Wants @BJP4India to
walk behind, In @ShivSena's shadow-- Surely victorious
@VisVp'd it repugnant find.")

❖ ('2014-11-10 01:47:09',
@sureshprabhu14, jumping ship, Joined @BJP4India
in #NewModiCabinet; While @anitadesai, on a trip To
#Delhi, was recalled by @ShivSena GR8!.')

❖ ('2014-11-10 01:58:40',
Today, numbering many a 1000 People came out in
#delhi & #mumbai 2 take part In #RunForUnity,
and 4 Health,Warming themselves &many a heart')

❖ ('2014-11-13 20:41:16',
The Rolex Awards support inspiring individuals with
innovative projects that advance human knowledge or
well-being. http://t.co/YfsEouhehn')

❖ ('2014-11-14 09:13:43',
@Narendramodi_PM, in Maynmar for @ASEAN Conf,
calls that country 1ˢᵗ 4 INDIA 2 go 2 Eastern Shore Of
ASIA-attribute typical of Modi, only.')

❖ ('2014-11-14 09:24:36',
@Narendramodi_PM flies 2 #Brisbane In @Australia 4
partaking in #G20Summit. He is Special Guest 4 PM @
Abe of Japan, & also of PM,the Brit.')

❖ ('2014-11-14 09:43:05',
@USPresidents101 @BarackObama & Chinese
President 2gether commit 2 Lower CO2-emission--a
Drama Borne out of INDIA-like Forces, no Accident.')

❖ ('2014-11-14 09:47:22',
Indian community in #Sydney, @Australia Is GR8ly
Excited about visit By @Narendramodi_PM of INDIA;
No less than @madisongardenKY--so B it.')

❖ ('2014-11-14 09:54:26',
Collaboration btwn India & @Australia In many
fields,including #uranium-deal 4 #energy, a crucial
need of INDIA Wuld follow, of GR8 Appeal.')

❖ ('2014-11-14 09:59:37',
There comes an Indian student In #Brisbane, @
Australia, Running hard, Panting, Excited, Ardent 2 get
a glimpse of @Narendramodi_PM of India.')

❖ ('2014-11-14 10:06:33',
@Narendramodi_PM of INDIA, Is such a GR8 Wizard to
win every heart In India and of the the Diaspora, &
of Foreigners, as well--What an Art !')

❖ ('2014-11-14 10:12:40',
It is abundantly clear to the World- History: a GR8 GR8
World-Leader, Like a #diamond & an Emerald @
Narendramodi_PM is destined 2 B, 4 sure.')

❖ ('2014-11-14 10:26:46',
O New Captain of #Ship Of Nation of INDIA, @
Narendramodi_PM, Sail Well, with a fitting grip On the
Oars, Matters not Seas B in Pandemonium.')

❖ ('2014-11-14 16:31:59',
@HeadlinesToday @sardesairajdeep @rahulkanwal,
It's fool's paradise @SoniaGandhiG @rahulgandhi2020
Enjoy their cronies @JhaSanjay unwise.")

❖ ('2014-11-14 16:47:48',
Possessing tiny little brains full of ego, @congressorg's
people from @JhaSanjay To @ManiShankarIyer all go
To #bankruptcy, neigh & bray.")

❖ ('2014-11-14 17:04:46',
Silly poor little @rahulgandhi2020 Calls @
Narendramodi_PM a Tourist: He might benefit by taking
entry In KG or Asylum, his #Mom to assist.')

❖ ('2014-11-14 17:18:28',
B it @SoniaGandhiG or @rahulgandhi2020, her witless
son Or @JhaSanjay--@congressorg exists only for
Saving Family &Kursi, 4 no good reason.')

❖ ('2014-11-14 18:13:38',
Bankrupt of any good thought, @congressorg should
retire 4 good; No more #Corrupt rule in @Bharat!
Gandhi-Nehru family now B history should.')

❖ ('2014-11-14 18:19:47',
Poor @rahulgandhi2020 is Biggest Joke in Indian
history: Tied to #MoM's Pallu,this tian-tian-fiss Should
B ashamed 2 criticize @narendramodi")

❖ ('2014-11-17 05:29:15',
@Narendramodi_PM #ModiInAustralia #PMInOz 4
#Brisbane City Flooding the #Twitter Like Wizard of Oz
Chronicle @NaMo4PM's towering popularity.")

❖ ('2014-11-17 06:03:00',
$ @rahulgandhi2020,old kid O\'@congressorg,@VisVp
is "Tourist-PM" & sired @KhursidRahman @
congressorg\'s stupid Cronies see Cheerers as hired.')

❖ ('2014-11-17 06:10:54',
No wonder @SoniaGandhiG & her @congressorg
sank, a tattered ship: If so dumb be party's leaders, Why
shouldn't smart India crack the whip?")

❖ ('2014-11-17 09:07:56',
#SydneyStorm for #ModiInAustralia is a sight For
India & Whole @World To see! What Wonder and
Delight: A New Colorful Flag has been unfurled')

❖ ('2014-11-17 19:11:33',
"Modi...Modi.." Reverberations Through roof of
#AllphonesArena With 18000 Euphoric Indians In
#Sydney, like #NewYork\'s #Madison SQ.Garden!')

❖ ('2014-11-17 19:15:16',
Again, shower of Inspirational words That Modi alone
can make materialize! Again the #SwachhBharat is
heard As a challenge of national size!')

❖ ('2014-11-17 19:22:58',
Again a Reminder and Exhortation Of India being the
youngest country, With Way to take the @IndianNation
To Pinnacle--A Promise of History!')

❖ ('2014-11-17 19:31:56',
Again Refreshing, Awakening Dream 4 Diaspora 2 Lead
the world By Revolution by the Cream Of INDIA with
"BHARATA MATA KI JAYA" Mantra heard.')

❖ ('2014-11-20 03:49:12',
#AskDrH How about efforts to check denudation of the
Rain-Forest to help limit the Climate-Change effects
globally? http://t.co/Riv4XqTq3F')

❖ ('2014-11-20 03:54:15',
@WhiteHouse Why did it take so long for USA &
China to agree on reduced emission levels? Industrial
development without respect for nature')

❖ ('2014-11-20 03:57:00',
@WhiteHouse I wonder if the package of books I had
mailed for @Narendramodi_PM of India while he was
visiting @WhiteHouse was ever received')

❖ ('2014-11-20 03:57:00',
@WhiteHouse I wonder if the package of books I had
mailed for @Narendramodi_PM of India while he was
visiting @WhiteHouse was ever received')

❖ ('2014-11-20 04:01:18',
@WhiteHouse I would GR8ly appreciate any response/
feed-back concerning the gift-package of my books
mailed 2 @WhiteHouse 4 @Narendramodi_PM.')

❖ ('2014-11-22 00:36:58',
@narendramodi is not just Our PM, HE is King of
HEarts; Winning every HEart W/ Art Of Love, 2 redeem
W/ Sincerity & Finesse A Leader's Part")

❖ ('2014-11-22 00:46:22',
All the World's Leaders GR8 are His Cherished
Friends; from USA's @BarackObama 2 @Australia's @
TonyAbbottMHR Praise him in so many ways.")

❖ ('2014-11-22 00:52:14',
@BarackObama calls him #ManOfAction And yet @
congressorg's @SoniaGandhiG, still Calls him a Big
Talker, One Who can't his big dreams fulfill")

❖ ('2014-11-22 01:04:25',
Such petty views only reflect Small-heart, little-brain
& -mind @congressorg possesses, every subject Of
@SoniaGandhiG is spaghetti-spined.')

❖ ('2014-11-22 01:13:05',
@mulayamsingh Yadav & @yadavakhilesh--
Father&Son Duo celebrating Dad's B'Day!
#PartyLikeMulayam; & guess What they have 4
their Ride of Jay")

❖ ('2014-11-22 01:29:20',
#PartyLikeMulayam rides #VictoriaSecret Open buggy
drawn by two horses; A 75-foot Cake would set Party's
mood with alien political forces.")

❖ ('2014-11-22 01:37:46',
A word about #Haryana's #warzonehisar, Where an
Enemy Of State-- A Fraud-man wearing the garb Of A
#Godman -- murdered 6 human of late.")

❖ ('2014-11-22 01:45:53',
Now @News18Jharkhand And Jammu & @
KashmirWindow, Where, Back from @FIJIWater, at
hand Is now @Narendramodi_PM, 4 @BJP4India honor
2 bestow.')

❖ ('2014-11-22 01:55:28',
@AzamKhan82, the communal crony of @
mulayamsingh Yadav @AapGhumaKeLeyLo, Says @
TajMahal, the Top National Monument of India, Ab
Hamako De Do')

❖ ('2014-11-22 02:01:14',
He quips about the B'Day expenditure 4 @
MulayamSingh has been funded By @EyeOnTaliban
& @daudibrahim424-- Has by fluke upon truth he
landed?")

❖ ('2014-11-22 02:08:36',
@SaifOnline hearing you speak That there should B
Only ONE LEGAL CODE For the Whole Country, a Streak
Of Hope Shines-up: that THERE IS GOD!')

❖ ('2014-11-22 02:11:34',
Progressive thoughts like yours Can reform narrow
alleys of religion! For, yo d also said per-force: Why all
terrorists R only Muslim men?")

❖ ('2014-11-22 02:18:45',
Peaceful Muslims should raises voice 2 correct what's
wrong with Islam: Separate Laws,Sharia--such a choice
Isn't of interest 4 minds calm.")

❖ ('2014-11-22 02:21:33',
You @SaifOnline do not believe In conversion to Islam
in a mixed marriage: Young men like U have to give New
Direction to Islam in this age.')

❖ ('2014-11-22 02:27:42',
@SaifAlliKhan,We Congratulate you And @
KareenaOnline with all our heart: If only young Muslim
think & do What you think and do on your Part!')

❖ ('2014-11-22 02:35:42',
@SaifOnline, you also hold Quite Fair View of @
Narendramodi_PM, Not a Blind, Narrow, Biased, and Old
Untrue and Warped Image of Gujarat-CM.')

❖ ('2014-11-22 02:41:57',
For @Narendramodi_PM is a True Leader, living
4 India as a Whole, Without any communal view,
Differentiating Hindus & Muslims in his role.')

❖ ('2014-11-22 02:50:54',
B it @JammuKashmirNow or @News18Jharkhand, @
MahaBJP or @UPGovt or @BJP_Gujarat @Narendramodi_
PM Would Do Well, and Win for Justice & Truth!')

❖ ('2014-11-22 02:58:53',
Satya-Ahimsa-Prem--Mahatma Gandhi's Mantra,&
@swachhindia Campaign, @MakeinIndia, @
PMJanDhanYojana--All these Will Write @HISTORY
with Gain.")

❖ ('2014-11-22 03:09:51',
New History of INDIA in Kaliyug Shall be as engrossing
as Dwapar's Great Mahabharat epic--a book The World
will look @TripInATweet in Verse!")

❖ ('2014-11-22 03:18:49',
This modern @Mahabharata_ID Has @Bheeeshm and
@Arjun--Both in One: @Narendramodi_PM is That Man
Mighty Also @Bhagavad_Geeta's Lord Krishan.")

❖ ('2014-11-22 03:32:56',
@timesofindia @PIB_India @PTI_News @Timesnow @
IndiaToday @HeadlinesToday @india360_asia will all
choose Tributes 2 @Narendramodi_PM 2 pay.')

❖ ('2014-11-22 03:38:47',
The Modern Little Mahabharata-- not So much an Epic
but a Journal in Verse- @TripInATweet--should then
ought To catch people's eyes terse.")

❖ ('2014-11-22 03:44:44',
A simple citizen of the modern world, No Great Rishi
VedVyas I am! 2 tell the story somewhat curled I've
ventured here,of @Narendramodi_PM !")

❖ ('2014-12-08 01:25:02',
SBI - say no to the world's worst loan & save
the Great Barrier Reef @TheOfficialSBI https://t.co/
Jq1yaTtLF8 PM_NaMo,pls stop thisBlackBiz")

❖ ('2014-12-08 01:28:25',
Twitter Buttons https://t.co/ZgyQ1Szlp3 via @twitter
Ever heard of a modern epic in verse-tweets? Pls. follow
@aksinh 2 enjoy a modern epic')

❖ ('2014-12-11 01:25:37',
@sardesairajdeep @BDUTT @M_Lekhi @mjakbar I'd
B most GR8ful if U write a review of my book on India/
NaMo in the LINK: http://t.co/7qH5cToVaA")

❖ ('2014-12-11 01:30:55',
@ShashiTharoor @AnupamPkher @chetan_bhagat I'd
B most GR8ful if U write a review of my book on India/
NaMo in the LINK http://t.co/7qH5cToVaA")

❖ ('2014-12-11 01:34:54',
@FareedZakaria @AMISHDEVGAN @RealArnabHere I'd
B most GR8ful if U write a review of my book on India/
NaMo in the LINK http://t.co/7qH5cToVaA")

❖ ('2014-12-11 02:10:38',
@juniorbachchan @AishwaryaQuotes @aamir_khan @
PrakashJha I'd B GR8ful if U look at my book on India/
NaMo in the LINK: http://t.co/7qH5cToVaA")

❖ ('2014-12-31 07:27:06',
Pak wouldn't learn from Peshawar: 133 children lost
their lives. Cobras they hide in their drawer Would
surely bite them, like bees in hives")

❖ ('2014-12-31 07:41:28',
Pak is huge a terror factory, With rows of terrorists'
camps Along LOC, ISI training them in a hurry. They'd
catch fire, & burn Pak as Vamps")

❖ ('2014-12-31 08:00:31',
Need is ripe 4 United Nations To nip every terrorist's
root Urgently, as ISI, ISIS've made destinations World-
Citizens' Chests,as they shoot")

❖ ('2014-12-31 08:05:09',
For J&K, the only hope For attaining lost glory
and riches Is Development-centric scope With BJP in
Government, without political glitches.')

❖ ('2014-12-31 08:10:51',
@Narendramodi_PM in Japan, America, Australia,
Nepal, Bhutan... Is only a preview; & not an end--
"Picture Abhi Bahut Baaki Hai, My Friend!"')

❖ ('2014-12-31 08:18:58',
In Delhi, @AAPInNews, for sure; For, being in news is
their GR8est agenda-- Not to seek a lasting cure Of any
ills by AK49 and his frienda.')

❖ ('2014-12-31 08:22:44',
1 can confidently predict Delhi People Shall choose 2
have @BJP win big; They've seen @AAP's simple Plan of
quitting when things get thick.")

❖ ('2014-12-31 08:28:21',
@congressorg and whole group Of foolish MPs from
@Opposition combined Has no better wheels 2 grind
Than to try to get @BJP in hot silly soup')

❖ ('2014-12-31 08:34:33',
#ConversionRow Occupies the rows Of @congressorg
& @Opposition MPs While precious time in gutters
flows- Circus of clowns and animals jumpy.')

❖ ('2014-12-31 08:43:38',
@Narendramodi_PM has the right stance 4 Opposition
creating #ruckus In #parliaments--passing laws as
Ordinance! #ConversionRow is just fuss')

❖ ('2014-12-31 08:53:44',
Biased MPs making fuss Over De-Conversion as 'Ghar-
Wapasi' (Homecoming) said not a word when curse
O'Forced conversion fell on poor Hindus")

❖ ('2014-12-31 09:04:24',
For centuries, nay, over a millennium, Islamic sword
& tricky marriages, And evangelic missionaries,
like scum, Converted Hindus, for ages.')

❖ ('2014-12-31 09:08:16',
By 10s of millions, in their own country, Hindus were
forced or coerced to accept Islam or Christianity- Poor
Hindu men died and women wept.')

❖ ('2014-12-31 09:13:55',
Pages of History of India R soaked in blood of Hindus
who refused To adopt Islam; the idea Of respect 4 all
religions is never in Islam used')

❖ ('2014-12-31 09:21:23',
A valley in Himalayas Is called "Hindukush" because
The whole Valley was packed with unarmed Hindus
Who were massacred by Islamists en-mass.')

❖ ('2014-12-31 09:33:37',
@congressorg's & @SoniaGandhiG & &
the likes of @O'Brian, late Agents of #VoteBankPolitics
& of foreign-brand Argue against majority
mandate")

❖ ('2014-12-31 09:39:20',
My words and lines aren't Meant to create communal
tensions Or injustice or parochial front; But to promote
open, fair brotherly relations.")

❖ ('2014-12-31 09:44:41',
Recall Swami Vivekananda, His glowing words and
stance: No religion should indulge in false propaganda 2
propagate itself 4 world-dominance.')

❖ ('2014-12-31 09:48:30',
The Inclusive and Deep Secular Spirituality of Hinduism
(or Buddhism) Is open 4 all 2 examine, 2 usher An age of
peace, progress, optimism!')

❖ ('2014-12-31 09:53:13',
Out-of-Date, Unscientific, Terribly parochial, and
Dogmatic Religions' days are up; an open-minded
Seeker of Truth is Not by these blinded.")

❖ ('2014-12-31 10:03:53',
An era of fresh breeze is in For Knowledge, Progress,
and Univers- al Love on Earth: No vile scenes of sin-
Born or Hell for Non-believers.')

❖ ('2014-12-31 10:06:41',
The 21st Century is destined, they say, To ascend to a
new peak With Bharat leading the way On the path of
Scientific Spirituality we seek.')

❖ ('2015-01-03 08:38:23',
Pakistan believes there's no limit In aggression against
India, Nor in the depth of the pit Of lies, depravity,
shamelessness--its trivia.")

❖ ('2015-01-03 08:45:56',
A boat (from Karachi, Pak?) comes in sight Near India's
coast in Gujarat; It takes 2 a hasty flight Upon India
Coast-Guard's protocol tract.")

❖ ('2015-01-03 08:50:38',
Then, finding that it can't run Away from capture,
Pak's boat sets itself ablaze, to burn And, loaded with
explosive, explodes on the spur.")

❖ ('2015-01-03 08:54:34',
It's apparent that Pak sent its boat To India for a large
terrorist activity Like 26/11 of 2008 in Mumbai, with
remote Control from Karachi.")

❖ ('2015-01-03 09:06:25',
Now, Pak states with no shame That a boat just
happened 2 catch fire; & India was playing the
blame- Game --Will Pakistan itself ever mend?')

❖ ('2015-01-03 09:16:27',
On the J&K Line-Of-Control, Pak violates Ceasefire
daily, Firing on Indian BSF-posts & rural people;
While complaining about return-volley.')

❖ ('2015-01-03 09:28:57',
Pakistan: a terror-factory, failed nation, Known 2 all as
such, Is earning Despise and Isolation; Oblivious that it
can't fool others much.")

❖ ('2015-01-03 09:36:40',
I've 10 books published by Xlibris, 4 by others (in
English), and 6 in Hindi; 3 more to go (Xlibris). I'd make
a book of these verse-Tweets.")

❖ ('2015-01-10 19:04:26',
@BeboMalaysiaFC your name Isn\'t without the Title
"KHAN". Isn\'t it a shame! That\'s your contribution to
Raj Kapoor Khandan\'s Aan-Baan-Shaan?')

❖ ('2015-01-10 19:08:59',
@KareenaMania Is "Khan" Your new Avatar? Is this an
inducement by @SaifAli_Khan Or is it going to make you
a better Star?')

❖ ('2015-01-10 19:14:56',
@SaifAli_Khan U had declared That @kareena4u is
going 2 keep Her original name, & dared That
religious conversion in your lives won't creep.")

❖ ('2015-01-10 19:18:04',
@SaifAli_Khan, U seem 2 be a ray Of hope -- an
enlightened Muslim -- As you utter with dismay Why
only Muslim names show up in terrorism!')

❖ ('2015-01-10 19:20:13',
This question arise In every Muslim who stresses
Vehemently, with open mind and eyes, That Islam is a
religion of Peace!')

❖ ('2015-01-10 19:26:11',
Why, then, the biggest Begot of humanist Who massacre
innocent people as a test Of their being faithful
Islamist?')

❖ ('2015-01-10 19:31:59',
Do you see the connection Between your converting
in Hindustan Your Hindu wife into one @
kareena24514154 or @KareenaKapoorKhan?')

❖ ('2015-01-10 19:36:01',
There is an intimate connection, 4 sure Between
religious conversion under pressure & terrorist
activities violent That take lives innocent.')

❖ ('2015-01-10 19:39:01',
For 'religious conversion is Violence,' So said Mahatma
Gandhi, 'It kills the soul and cultural essence In a
person's life truly.'")

❖ ('2015-01-10 19:46:13',
Isn't the goal of a terrorist 2 terrorize mind and heart Of
Non-believers in Islam? The twist, @SaifAli_Khan, lies
only in murderer's art.")

❖ ('2015-01-10 19:51:53',
U say you believe in Love (as you ought) And 2 call your
marriage 'Love-Jihad' Is narrowness of thought. But @
SaifAli_Khan, it's mighty sad.")

❖ ('2015-01-10 19:59:42',
Your wife's face is half-covered Dark, in Burqa--a
Muslim woman veiled-- As #HimalayaDhwani magazine
pictured. @SaifAli_Khan, yo ve failed.")

❖ ('2015-01-10 20:03:35',
@SaifAli_Khan, U have failed In your promise, tacit or
explicit, That @KareenaK_FC'd be hailed As a Hindu
wife, & not her religion forfeit.")

❖ ('2015-01-10 20:11:09',
@SaifAli_Khan, Love-Jihad is meant 2 trick a Hindu
woman Into wedding, thereafter she is forcibly sent
Behind bars of Islam-become Musalman')

❖ ('2015-01-10 20:17:25',
Similarity between terrorist attacks & 'Love-
Jihad' is clear-- Both R meant 2 spread Islam's tracks,
Difference is only in the model of fear")

❖   ('2015-01-10 20:21:18',
You may say it's none Of anybody's business how you marry; But the sufferer - the Hindus--shun Conversion in any form or mode, I'm sorry!")

❖   ('2015-01-10 20:30:33',
Terrorists show intolerance To Democracy and Peaceful Coexistence; While Love-Jihadists, with elegance, Subvert Democracy by false pretense.')

❖   ('2015-01-10 20:38:27',
In essence both methods are foul; Both R Jihad--Islamic religion's spread & dominance; both kill--body and soul. @SaifAli_Khan, both invade")

❖   ('2015-01-10 20:40:50',
12 innocent men and women Were killed in Paris, France On January 7, 2015, By two Jihadist gunmen, for instance.')

❖   ('2015-01-10 20:42:43',
153 innocent men and women Were massacred on November 26, 2008, in Mumbai, India, when 8 Pakistanis opened the fire of terror.')

❖   ('2015-01-10 20:47:24',
3000 innocent men and women Died on 9th of November, 2001, as two highjacked planes Crashed into the Twin-Towers of the World Trade Center.')

❖   ('2015-01-10 20:51:57',
@SaifAli_Khan, numerous bombings in Spain, UK, India--killed 1000s of innocent people-- Recall you may & what's common in all these samples?")

❖   ('2015-01-10 20:55:08',
@SaifAli_Khan, all these heinous acts Of terror have been perpetrated By Muslims--and that's a fact! Non-Muslim terrorist you find not yet!")

❖ ('2015-01-10 20:57:24',
So, what's abhoringly wrong, My dear @SaifAli_Khan, Is that all these terrorists belong To Islam, who swear by Koran!")

❖ ('2015-01-10 21:00:51',
The book of religion in Islam-- This fact let's stress-- Unambiguously promises such terrorists the charm Of virgins lying on silken couches")

❖ ('2015-01-10 21:03:23',
Waiting 4 them by evergreen Gardens, by an ever-flowing stream Of cool waters, in Paradise, keen On pleasing them--like in a heavenly dream!')

❖ ('2015-01-10 21:05:53',
@SaifAli_Khan, not having much education, Devoid of knowledge Of human advances, for generations, The terrorists have these damsels in gaze!')

❖ ('2015-01-10 21:09:43',
@SaifAli_Khan, psychologically sick Preachings by blind Mullahs, Generates bands after bands of terrorists, Ready 2 undertake suicidal vows.')

❖ ('2015-01-10 21:15:23',
Terrorists R motivated 2 kill Innocent men, women & children In such a killing drill, To ensure his place in a couch in damsel-full heaven.')

❖ ('2015-01-10 21:18:23',
@SaifAli_Khan, sly politicians, to gain Extra power and territories, with such Terrorists, pursue the insane Conspiracy of dominating much.')

❖ ('2015-01-10 21:22:24',
In name of religion, such pursuits To build anew empires-- Like the Ottoman or Moghal empires, by brutes Who won the world, so 'inspired?'")

❖ ('2015-01-10 21:25:08',
By the Founder of Islam, In the 6th century. Now in the 21st century, without qualm, Terror outfits aspire a repeat of that ancient victory.')

❖ ('2015-01-10 21:29:24',
But Times have dramatically changed, My dear @ SaifAliKhan, Swift Arabian horse & estranged World there's no more...now Drones the sky span.")

❖ ('2015-01-10 21:32:26',
Telecommunications satellites Cover every inch Of the Globe...A piece of news takes strides Like lightning, going 2 every corner in a cinch.')

❖ ('2015-01-10 21:35:55',
Instantly, the world awakes To any such piece of news!... Swift electromagnetic waves is all it takes To inform all of it, in a short fuse.')

❖ ('2015-01-10 21:41:01',
So, @SaifAli_Khan, though piercing Arrows & powerful lances've Given way 2 serial bombs exploding, The warring Islamist is simply too naive.")

❖ ('2015-01-10 21:44:31',
Ill-intentioned schemes Of the Islamist to re-establish The Ottoman and Moghal empires will be illusory dreams 2 B buried, mere death-wish!')

❖ ('2015-01-11 07:38:19',
I am marching with Paris. Will you? #jesuischarlie #notafraid https://t.co/7b14ZvHb74 A War against Democracy is shear folly, a Death-Wish.')

❖ ('2015-01-11 07:46:03',
Twitter Buttons https://t.co/ZgyQ1Szlp3 via @twitter Stand and March With Paris, & wherever Terror tries 2 Parch Even One Freedom-Lover.')

❖ ('2015-01-12 20:19:08',
Be it Iran, be it ISI be it ISIS Or for Iraq or Syria, or any
region-- A war against Democracy Or Civilization just
can't win.")

❖ ('2015-01-12 20:21:39',
Times have changed--- It's been over 15 centuries; But
the Islamist mindset hangs In the hand of 6th century
victories.")

❖ ('2015-01-12 20:24:40',
Now Democracy shall rule Supreme, with science and
technology; And it's an utter fool Who still thinks like
religion-realm's Ponzi.")

❖ ('2015-01-12 20:28:07',
Scheming and dreaming to win The world with truck-
full Of explosives or AK47 --a tin-- Drum of Islam to
beat, attacking temples and schools.')

❖ ('2015-01-12 20:29:59',
Then, there are some Who foolishly think That by
playing the number-game, Democracy and demography
they would hoodwink.')

❖ ('2015-01-12 20:31:51',
One more thing, my dear @SaifAli_Khan A war against
Democracy is shear Folly, be it played in Europe or
Pakistan.')

❖ ('2015-01-12 20:33:37',
Some Muslim men, My dear @SaifAli_Khan, Marry
Hindu girls, and then By hook or crook, convert them
into Islam.')

❖ ('2015-01-12 20:36:59',
If the sword fails, then they create a facade Of marrying
out of love; But it's not love, but Love-Jihad-- Sword-
bearing hand wearing glove.")

❖ ('2015-01-12 20:40:58',
U think, my dear @SaifAli_Khan, That U R an
enlightened person, Asking your marriage-partner 2
change religion Is'nt part of yr wedding-plan")

❖ ('2015-01-12 20:46:16',
But, then. how @KareenaOnline Is led 2 change her
name Into @KareenaK_FC in time-- Whatever you call
it--the goal & net result is the same.')

❖ ('2015-01-12 20:50:25',
On this very earth, without Suicide-bombing in the
name of Islam, Getting a pretty Hindu girl, no doubt, To
convert cunningly-- Grand Slam!')

❖ ('2015-01-12 20:59:18',
& when 'Himalaya-Dhwani' Prints the cover-girl's
face Half with Hindu Suhagin's Sindoor (it's not funny)
1/2 covered in Burqa,U cry offense.")

❖ ('2015-01-12 21:07:06',
U say "It reflects narrow- Mindedness",But if U
were Truly fair, you\'d not show Your Hindu wife 2
masquerade 2 mosque 2 say Quranic prayer.')

❖ ('2015-01-12 21:11:43',
Or, yo d also heartily bow before (Without acting) the
Divine Image In a temple, keeping the door Of your
mind open, as when doing Namaz.")

❖ ('2015-01-12 21:13:41',
Now, such a calculation Of number-game conversion
Is equally devious -- to shun Non-Muslim population,
without a gun!')

❖ ('2015-01-12 21:15:14',
Slowly, a minority, you chance The numbers to drive
And turn Democracy's balance In your favor, upside-
down, and thrive.")

❖ ('2015-01-12 21:16:50',
You think no one suspects Any foul play -- and love
Governs your star, and spreads Good omens below and
above.')

❖ ('2015-01-12 21:19:46',
But such archaic shine Of the sword or echo of wedding
vows Would hold no longer, and yo ll find Yourself
marginalized because of such rows")

❖ ('2015-01-12 21:24:10',
So, my dear @SaifAli_Khan, If you\'re truly as
enlightened As U seem to claim, can You @KareenaK_FC
back home as Hindu ("Ghar-Wapasi") send?')

❖ ('2015-01-12 21:31:23',
If you read these lines, my dear @SaifAli_Khan, may I
request your, Ah! Reply (Should your soul hear) &
2 miss nothing, plse follow @aksinh')

❖ ('2015-01-15 11:30:25',
RT @NaMo4PM: Narendra Modi's Campaign
Supports Largest Mass Outreach in India's History
#AbkiBaarModiSarkaar http://t.co/81MYJIWCbg")

❖ ('2015-01-21 08:56:13',
@ArvindKejriwal says BJP 'parachuted' @thekiranbedi;
of course, He forgot--Bedi executed @dtptraffic as a
police-officer, & not by Airforce")

❖ ('2015-01-21 09:08:00',
Come Febr 7'15, @thekiranbedi will Catapult @
ArvindKejriwal to oblivion; & he'd murmur still:
His turn as @IAmAnAnarchist AK49 wasn't given.")

❖ ('2015-01-21 09:11:48',
Lure of chair so charms Poor little @ArvindKejriwal,
That, after putting his Gur s mission in harm's Way, he'd
@ his colleague's feet fall.")

❖ ('2015-02-01 08:13:54',
The 66th Republic Day Had a special Chief-Guest: @
BarrackObamaUS, @POTUS (President of USA) Invited
by @Narendramodi_PM on India's behest.")

❖ ('2015-02-01 08:21:10',
@BarrackObamaUS visit to India, January 25-27, 2015
Turned a New Page Of History--a friendly hug when @
VC25_AI touched down, for next 3 days')

❖ ('2015-02-01 08:25:39',
The friendship deep between @Narendramodi_PM
& @BarrackObamaUS was at par The spectacle
pristine For 3 full Day, caught fully in the radar.')

❖ ('2015-02-01 08:31:59',
Guard of Honor was presented To the @POTUS @
BarrackObamaUS (of America) By 150 men of 3
Services, led By a Lady-Officer Of India called Puja')

❖ ('2015-02-01 08:35:27',
Women's Battalions of Air-Force, Navy and Army were
part Of the Republic Day Parade, in course Of which
military might mingled with folk-art")

❖ ('2015-02-01 08:37:55',
In Delhi's Hyderabad House lawn The two world
leaders strolled And exchanged views; a new dawn Was
ushered in the politics of the world.")

❖ ('2015-02-01 08:45:10',
No abject cold formality, Or elements of political
protocol; But the joining of soul, heart & mentality
Of two Free Nations in a novel role.')

❖ ('2015-02-01 08:52:03',
China was visibly burned, Saying shamelessly they'd
side Pakistan:no principle or propriety they earned;
Just childish play of politics-ride")

❖ ('2015-02-01 09:00:07',
Pakistan was snubbed even before @BarrackObamaUS's
arrival in Delhi-- With U.S. warning to make sure That
no terror or mischief there be!")

❖ ('2015-02-01 09:04:10',
New significant Agreements were signed By India
& U.S. about Nuclear Deal, And greater cooperation
and trade Followed smoothly in its heal.')

❖ ('2015-02-01 09:08:27',
Delhi is now in the grips Of election-heat all over again--
With @thekiranbedi's name on everyone's lips, &
@ArvindKejriwal running in vain.")

❖ ('2015-02-01 09:13:28',
@thekiranbedi, the lady IPS Officer of Delhi some
time ago Would surely be the new CM, thus @
ArvindKejariwal will be out, twice in a row.')

❖ ('2015-02-01 09:20:16',
He had maneuvered to become The CM last time, but
only 49 days it took For him to run away, to run for PM
To grab the Kursi by hook or crook')

❖ ('2015-02-01 09:25:27',
This utter fool and opportunist Called @thekiranbedi
opportunist & himself a true leader--what a twist
Of logic, now Delhi'd show him a fist")

❖ ('2015-02-01 09:29:33',
The foolish chap thinks people Are fools & can be
fooled again & again--But "Janata" is not a fool. In
caricatures his story shall remain.')

❖ ('2015-02-01 09:34:39',
Another classic fool is our good Old @rahulgandhi2020,
showing Emblem of @congressorg, as if he could Many
Delhi voters in his favor swing.')

❖ ('2015-02-01 09:51:14',
@RahulGandi1\'s stupid words: "PM is playing
\'dholaki\' in Japan" Or "PM is busy in his personal PR";
absurd Remarks for advancing Hindustan.')

❖ ('2015-02-01 10:09:36',
A word for @SoniaGandhiG, too, Mother of
incompetency, avatar Of corruption, destroyer of India,
who Dares question @Narendramodi_PM's star.")

❖ ('2015-02-01 10:13:52',
How @SoniaGandhiG has a face To appear in public,
crowing For @congressorg and address A group of
people--her word she in vain is throwing.')

❖ ('2015-02-03 18:22:30',
Febr 2, 2015, a disclosure came to light: @
ibnlive etc.carried news That #AVAM disclosed a
#HawalaAtMidnight: By @AAP: MoneyLaundering
fuse.')

❖ ('2015-02-03 18:27:22',
At midnight, 4 donors Each give to @AAP 0.5 crore
rupees All at once, opening their purse Wide, while they
have no income nor any business.')

❖ ('2015-02-03 18:31:51',
AAP says: "We have Listed on our website every
donation." But @BJP4India argues: How does that save
AAP from this 2 crore fraud allegation?')

❖ ('2015-02-03 18:35:46',
If the source of election donations Itself is fake or AAP
has indulged In serious monetary manipulations That
Black Money into White fudged.')

❖ ('2015-02-03 18:40:26',
@AAP blaimed @BJP4India And @congressorg
corrupt, with unknown Donors; and now AAP, the self-
proclaimed messiah Itself 2 be a thief shown.')

❖ ('2015-02-03 18:44:33',
@arunjaitley, Finance Minister of @BJP4India said:
"AAP has been caught red-handed." Fake companies
have paid 2 crore Rupees @ night\'s dead.')

❖ ('2015-02-03 18:52:29',
@Narendramodi_PM, too, wondered How party like
AAP steeped in lies shall Serve #MissionDelhi.(Better 2
nip in the bud AAP & @ArvindKejriwa.)')

❖ ('2015-02-05 01:27:38',
@BJP4India should expose @kejriwal_arvind On illegal
donation And AAP's scams floating in the wind In
#DelhiFightClub, to fool the nation.")

❖ ('2015-02-05 01:32:38',
@ArvindKejriwal is a conman Hiding behind his
muffler--a scam Of a man--of far high order than One
can imagine, playing musical chair game.')

❖ ('2015-02-05 01:37:09',
If #DelhiFightClub people get to know The real @
ArvindKejriwal wrapped In muffler, they surely owe To
defeat him, have him simply scrapped.')

❖ ('2015-02-05 01:43:58',
In #DelhiFightClub everyone ought 2 know that @
ArvindKejriwal Gets foreign $ from Anti-India Groups
which've bought Him, 2 whom he's loyal.")

❖ ('2015-02-09 17:27:04',
@timesofindia My dear @Bristol- Church, You\'re afraid
Yoga is "too spiritual" 4 u, then who\'s stopping u 2 b
less spiritual, or not at all?')

❖ ('2015-02-09 17:34:45',
@timesofindia @Bristol-Church, How ridiculous &
incredible Could u go 2 oppose us-- re in a lurch That
Yoga'd attract your members sensible")

❖ ('2015-02-09 17:40:48',
@timesofindia Bristol church-goers, Here is open
invitation 4 U all-- Knock at Yoga's doors & see if yo
d rather B too spiritual, or fall?")

❖ ('2015-02-09 17:45:02',
@timesofindia @Bristol-Church is Mortally afraid of
Yoga's popularity, Just like fanatic Islamists, Who KNOW
YOGA CAN CURE their vulgarity.")

❖ ('2015-02-09 17:52:19',
@timesofindia @Bristol @BillGates is invited In
spreading YOGA, freely aid In the world, as U.N.said
June 21 as YOGA-DAY to be celebrated.')

❖ ('2015-02-09 18:35:05',
@timesofindia I take This opportunity 2 invite @
BillGates 2 help clean world's Waters & also make
Bigot people's minds clean: new Mandates.")

❖ ('2015-02-09 18:40:02',
@timesofindia May be I'd write 2 @BillGates for a grant
To explore how to get clean solar energy efficiently
& 2 clean river-waters upfront")

❖ ('2015-02-09 18:46:30',
@timesofindia @Bristol people need @yogrishiramdev
to demonstrate Just how spiritual Yoga-practice can
feed Humans with highest mental state')

❖ ('2015-02-09 18:54:31',
@timesofindia @nytimesworld Hear, Hear World! @
Bristol-Church Says 'Yoga is too spiritual;' O dear! Can 1
4 them anti-spiritual way search?")

❖ ('2015-02-10 07:51:43',
@ArvindKejriwal's massive victory in Delhi Is a historic
sign To learn from for Congress and BJP-- Arrogance
wins nothing but curse divine.")

❖ ('2015-02-10 07:56:56',
Now that public trust has blessed @ArvindKejriwal
& his @AAP, Let's hope that they'll do all they've
said They'd; & wash away their old Paap")

❖ ('2015-02-10 08:01:08',
As @annahazaresays, @ArvindKejriwal Must not repeat
his past Mistakes, and work with @Narendramodi_PM,
all the way, To make his days last.')

❖ ('2015-02-10 08:07:16',
Who'd've predicted such a sweeping Victory 4 @
ArvindKejriwal & his party? Never say 'never' in
politics, in keeping With lessons of history!")

❖ ('2015-02-10 08:16:16',
As long as Delhi is transformed Into a GR8world-class
city, Never tormented and stormed By corrupt @
congressorg--matters lile it loses BJP.')

❖ ('2015-02-10 08:29:12',
@Kejriwal4CM must remember: Power, water @ low-
cost Is GR8, but we've 2 clean Yamuna river; End crime,
corruption; regain Delhi's glory lost")

❖ ('2015-02-10 08:45:15',
Getting my website http://t.co/L7SwyN6Gg4
Redesigned, 2 b able 2 offer my books (e.g.,http://t.co/
JBwiNBwFkh) Online with ease, new looks.')

❖ ('2015-02-10 08:53:10',
A special addition 2 a list Of 21+ books published (or
close) Would b book of 1145+ verse-tweets-- A sweet
treat for readers hung on prose.')

❖ ('2015-02-10 09:17:45',
U mustn't lose heart, @BJP4India, @thekiranbedi!
All the world is a stage, & we play our part-- @
ArvindKejriwal's may b a comedy or tragedy.")

❖ ('2015-02-11 17:57:45',
@TimesNow #Feb10WithArnab & other Indian
news channels were abuzz With #AAPStorm &
#AAPSweep, & further Lines AAP' victory in Delhi
2 judge.")

❖ ('2015-02-11 18:05:47',
"BJP Caught Napping," said one; "AAP Romps Home,"
another. #AAPKiDilli had tsunami bigger than Modi-
Wave;&"Congress-Mukta Dilhi, O Brother!"')

❖ ('2015-02-21 18:53:36',
@SrBachchan All seems well On the socio-cultural
front, With @Narendramodi_PM hugging 2 spell @
AapGhumaKeLeyLo & @laluprasadrjd-no stunt.')

❖ ('2015-02-21 19:03:39',
Eating with the enemy at home & being friends
looks bizarre; But in the field, they carry syndrome Of
finishing one another, fighting a war')

❖ ('2015-02-21 19:09:12',
This"Dharma-Yuddha"is hardly New; Mahabharat war
was fought so, too! If you wished 2 glimpse the alley Of
Modern Little Mahabharat, pls do..')

❖ ('2015-02-21 19:15:34',
..Please do follow the collection Of @aksinh for verse-
tweets. Here significant information On "modern little
Mahabharat" offer one a treat.')

❖ ('2015-02-21 19:21:45',
@SrBachchan if you wished to read An engrossing
fiction to leisurely scan, I\'d cordially invite you &
lead To "Reincarnation of Iron-Man."')

❖ ('2015-02-21 19:25:54',
@SrBachchan Pls visit the Link: http://t.co/eu1JI9tYUb
Or the catalog of amazon.in Putting for author's name
'Kosha Ahnis' to get in store.")

❖ ('2015-02-21 19:28:43',
@SrBachchan 2 get in store A lot of interesting plots
with many Characters, including yours own in the core
Of the story, with skill uncanny')

❖ ('2015-02-21 19:35:15',
d C the characters Of @Narendramodi_PM & @
SoniaGandhiG, & @ArvindKejriwal and may be @
juniorbachchan that stirs Emotions as in a movie.")

❖ ('2015-02-21 19:40:50',
If yo d grace this novel With a few words of comments
heartfelt, I'd be most indebted, & tell Myself my
efforts were with greatness dealt.")

❖ ('2015-02-22 18:48:32',
Largest New Year's resolution of 2015 - follow 3
simple, powerful principles: http://t.co/giLNTLSYSc
->Wisdom, Kindness+Respect,& Gratitude.")

❖ ('2015-02-22 18:54:33',
Twitter Buttons https://t.co/ZgyQ1ShKgZ via @twitter
Modern Mahabharat of 2014+2015, with a collection of
1200 verse-tweets, follow @aksinh')

❖ ('2015-02-23 20:38:28',
#RSSQuestionsTeresa @ARNABGOSWAMl You get
entangled in wasteful \'Tu-Tu-Man-Man" Without
appreciating all sides of any Core issue oftentime.')

❖ ('2015-02-23 20:40:50',
No one questions the service aspect Of the Missionaries
here-- But their sole purpose is to convert By winning
through allurement, my dear!.')

❖ ('2015-02-23 20:45:01',
@ARNABGOSWAMl #RSSQuestionsTeresa For a reason:
Father Emmannuel, Is he a person from the heaven, or
West? No he is a converted Hindu.Well?')

❖ ('2015-02-23 20:48:58',
Bible asks Priests, Evangelists, Ministers to go
& spread Christianity in every land--I wish, @
ARNABGOSWAMI #RSSQuestionsTeresa, you read?')

❖ ('2015-02-23 21:48:04',
@ARNABGOSWAMI on #WhereIsRahulGandhi We must
recognize @SoniaGandhiG A Dozen Scams, a crushing
defeat, And a missing son-Fate's GR8 Treat!")

❖ ('2015-02-23 21:55:38',
#WhereIsRahul It's clear to us all That this man would
remain Mama's baby Forever, he isn't fit at all To be a
leader of our country.")

❖ ('2015-02-23 21:59:13',
Now just a oneliner on #WhereIsRahul: To Greece
& Italy via Bangkok? Couldn't find a direct flight--2
escape LandBill or any bill whatsoever")

❖ ('2015-02-23 22:43:14',
#WhereIsRahul @BrijeshKalappa yelling To tell @
ARNABGOSWAMI to stop Such inquiries--why is he not
telling Rahul's whereabouts, or just drop!")

❖ ('2015-02-23 22:48:17',
#WhereIsRahul O my God! What a great political fraud-
Bigger scam than #CoalGate & CWG, When'll @
congressorg quit such games @SoniaGandhiG?")

❖ ('2015-02-23 23:39:11',
@ManiShankarIyer @SalmanKhurshid_ @
AbhishekManu9 @ManishTiwari & all Company of
@congressorg should bid Going under, for it's bound 2
fall!")

❖ ('2015-02-23 23:49:50',
It was hard 2 resist rhyming @congressorg @
SalmanKhurshid_ With insulting adjective (e.g.,'Stupid')
Just as #WhereIsRahul's junket-timing.")

❖ ('2015-02-23 23:55:55',
All those who still lick @SoniaGandhiG's worn-out shoes
Or dream of @congressorg,s revival, are sick Of slavery
to white skin as their woos!")

❖ ('2015-03-02 07:07:34',
New Novel Presents Glimpses of Both Ancient
and Modern Day India http://t.co/8waN7nLE56
via @PRWeb @aksinh @TimesNow @ndtv @
NarendraModi_PM')

❖ ('2015-03-03 08:27:13',
Is @MuftiMohammadSaeed a snake Up in ur sleeves,
@Narendramodi_PM Ji? Is PDP to turn out to be fake,
Singing praise of #terrorism Pakistani?')

❖ ('2015-03-03 08:27:13',
Is @MuftiMohammadSaeed a snake Up in ur sleeves,
@Narendramodi_PM Ji? Is PDP to turn out to be fake,
Singing praise of #terrorism Pakistani?')

❖ ('2015-03-07 01:32:11',
@NarendraModi_PM for GangaClean-upProject -How to
Clean Up Our Water & Reduce Water Pollution
| NRDC from @NRDC: http://t.co/uXDHrY3DP4')

❖ ('2015-03-07 02:01:07',
RT @americanrivers: Is Your Favorite River
Endangered? Find out April 7! - Heron on the Haw River
| Haw River Assembly As 2015 continu... h\u2026')

❖ ('2015-03-07 02:07:56',
RT @americanrivers: Recreation business owners point
to why healthy river flows needed in #CoWaterPlan. @
MayaJRodriguez http://t.co/Nn7kjwX\u2026')

❖ ('2015-03-07 02:10:02',
RT @americanrivers: RT @wrirvin8 @GinaEPA says @
EPA will get #ProtectCleanWater rule done http://t.co/
XaW5w1JXRr http://t.co/nRZeW9thED')

❖ ('2015-03-07 02:39:41',
@NarendraModi_PM @aksinh Water resources
development of Himalayan Countries! http://t.co/
ApUd4lBuHA This article may be useful 4 Ganga work')

❖ ('2015-03-08 07:47:23',
@K_BoumaGregson I'm eager to learn abt technologies
to clean up polluted rivers. Please send any pertinent
material to kosha.ahnis@gmail.com")

❖ ('2015-03-08 08:09:01',
@NarendraModi_PM an example in River Cleanup and
Revitalizing Local Communities through Recreation a...:
http://t.co/G4kpLrA8FG via @YouTube')

❖ ('2015-03-08 08:21:25',
@NarendraModi_PM A Socio-Political Novel about India
http://t.co/2Sr7PbKY5I #Reincarnation via @aksinh @
amazon.com and other book websites')

❖ ('2015-03-08 08:26:09',
A Socio-Political Novel about India #Reincarnation via
@aksinh')

❖ ('2015-03-08 08:28:04',
Blue Trails Webinar: Revitalizing Local Communities
through Recreation a...: http://t.co/G4kpLrA8FG via @
YouTube @PMO @IndianExpress 4Ganga')

❖ ('2015-03-09 19:02:47',
@MufteeSaeed becomes a CM after Alliance &
turns @MasaratAlamBhatt loose-- Is Saeed a CM in full
defiance Acting just as a Pakistani Stooge?')

❖ ('2015-03-09 19:12:47',
Did @BJP4India goof in allying With PDP &
choosing a #ProPakCM, Giving Pak ammunition f4 lying
& 2 disrupt Peace-Plan of @Narendramodi_PM?')

❖ ('2015-03-09 19:24:34',
The unity and sovereignty can't be Compromised in @
Kashmi or elsewhere-- @Narendramodi_PM holds this
as does BJP; Yet Pak stops not 2 dare.")

❖ ('2015-03-09 19:32:32',
Kashmir remains bone of contention Between India
& Pak since 1947-- The final dissolution of tension
Is to charge Pak with a reverse 26/11.')

❖ ('2015-03-15 07:21:58',
@Narendramodi_PM returns Home after three-nations
tour-- Only a leader like him earns Great ties with all
neighbors, for sure!')

❖ ('2015-03-15 07:28:22',
For 20-30 years, it didn't occur 2 any Ex-Indian Premier
2 visit These countries in our very neighbor- Hood, or
they viewed them as unfit?")

❖ ('2015-03-15 07:37:19',
Leaders not large-hearted at all, Nor farsighted like @
Narendramodi_PM May be thought of them as small
Countries, not worthy of their time')

❖ ('2015-03-15 07:50:43',
True Friendship with China,Japan, Nepal,Sri-
Lanka,Bhutan,Pakistan-- All is @Narendramodi_PM's
mission That, for all, should bear fruit soon!")

❖ ('2015-03-15 08:01:10',
@rahulgandhi2020, @SoniaGandhiG Of @congressorg,
or @ArvindKejriwal Of AAP--little minds--do not C How
GR8 @Narendramodi_PM is, above all.')

❖ ('2015-03-15 08:08:22',
@rahulgandhi2020 goes away, hiding For lone musing
what to do next; And @ArvindKejariwaI is riding On
public sympathy for his cough, vexed!')

❖ ('2015-03-15 08:14:22',
Frail hearts & small minds-- It's pity some people
think of them As leaders; their labor only grinds Vote-
bank politics, a national shame!")

❖ ('2015-03-15 08:29:31',
@rahulgandhi2020 & @ArvindKejrlwal R
escapists, unable to govern; Dynastic call or fooling all,
Or horse-trading 2 win is their net concern')

❖ ('2015-03-15 08:34:53',
@congressorg only knows how to Hamper and block
progress and scam. Recent internal quibbles, break-ups
do Leave AAP to be totally damned.')

❖ ('2015-03-19 00:19:13',
ElectronMicroscopyIsBeautiful Book- utm_
source=Physics+Today&utm_
medium=email&utm_campaign=5444306_
Physics+Today+The+week+in+Physics')

❖ ('2015-03-19 00:20:57',
RT @asana: Say goodbye to email, calendars, notepads,
status updates, and sticky notes. And say hello to Asana.
https://t.co/8EGvm2XZ1t')

❖ ('2015-03-26 10:56:06',
@MSDmahi: a #cricket-wizard in #AUS-tralia--
Undoubtedly #JeetegaBhaiJeetega #JeetegaIndia!')

❖ ('2015-03-26 10:59:00',
You wish @rahulgandhi2020 was on hand To cheer
#TeamIndia, & not bury his face in sand!')

❖ ('2015-03-26 11:07:10',
Poor @rahulgandhi2020 has simply vanished from the
scene; @SoniaGandhiG, your pushing him into politics is
absolutely obscene.')

❖ ('2015-03-26 11:10:12',
@Narendramodi_PM's plan and vision for the country
For Development is kept hostage by @SoniaGandhiG!")

❖ ('2015-03-26 11:14:17',
@SoniaGandhiG, for putting position first, Is selfishly
hurting India's vital need & thirst!")

❖ ('2015-03-26 11:25:37',
In their long rule over India 4 many a decade, @
SoniaGandhiG had little concern 4 farmers' aid. &
suddenly now She's championing the show !")

❖ ('2015-03-26 11:33:06',
@BJP4India's #LandAcquisitionBill Is being resisted
with all might & will By @SoniaGandhiG, the GR8
loser keen, Becoming beggar from queen.")

❖ ('2015-03-26 11:38:49',
@SoniaGandhiG,not being able 2 control even her own
son, Wants to turn the table By protesting against @
Narendramodi_PM's Development vision")

❖ ('2015-03-26 11:45:29',
In the illusive hope of coming 2 power again by hook
or crook, @SoniaGandhiG is becoming The biggest
obstacle to #Development, a pure joke!')

❖ ('2015-03-26 11:51:54',
The short-sighted and selfish bunch Of @cpimspeak
& @SamajwadiSocial today Are shouting, throwing
punch In vain in @Narendramodi_PM's way.")

❖ ('2015-03-26 11:56:36',
How can anyone foolishly say That @Narendramodi_
PM'll hurt or ignore Farmers' interest,and sway The day
only the rich to unfairly favor for")

❖ ('2015-03-26 12:05:46',
If, instead of '@WeAreOpposition' slogan, Just for
political gain, Others cooperated with @BJP4India, a ton
Of goodwill they'd gain again.")

❖ ('2015-03-26 12:10:28',
Parties that lost the 2014 election R bent upon
becoming hurdles 2 @BJP4India & @
Narendramodi_PM Merely for dirty politics in their
skulls.')

❖ ('2015-03-26 12:16:14',
In the long run,or even in the short one, @
WeAreOpposition'd lose even more As @Narendramodi_
PM gets undone Their anti-national stand & core")

❖ ('2015-03-26 12:21:00',
Now, today, @annahazaresays he wants Open debate
with @Narendramodi_PM, This surely warrants
Excellent outcome for everyone's satisfaction")

❖ ('2015-03-26 12:30:54',
Coming back 2 #IndvsAus cricket match, I hear India
lost by a small margin- Well, @msdhoni must dispatch
No gloom, as some U lose, some win!')

❖ ('2015-03-27 23:07:17',
@ArvindKejriwal's lesson to his gang Backfired
in #AAPKaSting With @AapYogendra & @
PrashantBhusha5, O Dang- Attacking in #WarInAAP the
king.")

❖ ('2015-03-27 23:13:29',
#AAP, the party preaching clean Politics &
transparency & all that Is wrapped in ugly
discipline #AAPBreakUp & #WarInAAP like a rat
vs. cat.')

❖ ('2015-04-08 05:13:20',
@rahulgandhi2020--a figure in cartoon! Missing in
action in his fight with @BJP4India. @SoniaGandhiG
says, "he\'ll come soon" (via Alitalia?)')

❖ ('2015-04-08 05:20:09',
@SoniaGandhiG these days Is pretending to champion
the cause Of farmers & trying to oppose &
chase The Land Bill on streets & in the House')

❖ ('2015-04-08 05:25:55',
During her regime 4 a decade, She & her family
had no care or concern But for Robert Vadra-led Drive
to amass their own family-wealth & urn.')

❖ ('2015-04-08 05:32:41',
How desperate & depressed and Bankrupt of
ideology of a true Opposition is @congressorg's stand!
They oppose for opposing with not a clue.")

❖ ('2015-04-12 19:30:17',
India-vs-Pakistan seems to remain A burning topic for
@TimesNow anchored by @3DArnab, trying, time and
again, To reflect on misdeeds of ISI')

❖ ('2015-04-12 19:38:31',
The 26/11, Pak's terrorist attack On Mumbai, killing
156 innocent men And women, and Pak's total lack Of
sensibility; denial, now and then.")

❖ ('2015-04-12 19:49:26',
Now #PakFreesLakhvi, the terrible Mastermind of that
attack & much more; India trying hard to mend the
little Minds of Pak Reps' views gore.")

❖ ('2015-04-12 19:52:42',
#Kashmir is uppermost in Pak's mind; And all the
terror plots and killing They think naught about--a kind
Of proxy war, with border-firing.")

❖ ('2015-04-12 19:56:51',
Friendship with India isn't at all Their goal, but
capturing territory; As if they wish 2 re-install The
Moghal empire in India's periphery.")

❖ ('2015-04-12 20:03:34',
They miss no occasion to reiterate, (As @P_Musharraf
did himself) that Pak is a nuclear-capable state-- A bad
boy bullying in idle chit-chat')

❖ ('2015-04-12 20:11:32',
Once an irate Indian Rep, in a previous @TimesNow
discussion or debate Pronounced: If Pak even dreams 2
attack India, they'd blow their fate")

❖ ('2015-04-12 20:18:30',
No sooner Pak'd start an N-war With India, Pak'd be
wiped out From the map of the world, by far! Yet the
Pak blockheads continued to shout.")

❖ ('2015-04-12 20:26:08',
India has to simply understand That Pak is never going
to digest Friendship--4 they dream of a grand Victory
over India by terrorist mindset')

❖ ('2015-04-12 20:38:25',
In this, not only the terrorist troupes And ISI are
partners active; But also the civil government &
groups Of bureaucratic system furtive.')

❖ ('2015-04-12 20:44:23',
India keeps hoping & trying, That Pak PM (a
Musharraf or a Nawaz Sharif) Would cooperate in
drawing A line and picture of peace & friendship')

❖ ('2015-04-12 20:47:50',
Lessons of history R forgotten Again & again under
such hope; Yet it dawns not that this'll happen NOT, and
one must reckon the end of rope.")

- ❖ ('2015-04-14 06:32:44',
Today @ibnlive's @sardesairajdeep was unjust 2 @
BJP4India, abt @ShivSena State- -Ment that Muslim
#vote-bank trend must Go, calling it Hate!")

- ❖ ('2015-04-14 06:42:30',
@sardesairajdeep didn't call Kashmiri Separatists'
demo against settling #KashmiriPandits in their own
city; For better security&surrounding")

- ❖ ('2015-04-14 06:47:16',
@sardesairajdeep didn't find such Hateful act of the
Separatists A statement of Hate--how much Injustice
the Muslims do: isn't in his lists")

- ❖ ('2015-04-14 06:51:47',
Such blatant & barbaric act Some Muslim groups
dish-out (Like throwing K-Pandits out of Kashmir, in
fact) & @ZoomIndianMedia aren't fraught.")

- ❖ ('2015-04-14 06:55:17',
If the media kept even eye on both Hindu and Muslim
excesses,impartially, Only then they have a right 2 take
oath 4 protecting the minority')

- ❖ ('2015-04-14 07:00:24',
But media generally, indeed, Takes fancy in shouting a
GR8 deal In favor of minority, & rarely heed 2 how
marginalized of the majority feel')

- ❖ ('2015-04-14 07:04:11',
Ya, India is a secular country, 4 sure; And there should B
no partiality By religion or caste-galore-- But majority
is snubbed--what a pity!')

- ❖ ('2015-04-14 07:12:23',
Muslims have #Hajj subsidy, special laws (Like many
wives--multiplying to gain In population) wouldn't this
cause Democracy to go in vain?")

❖ ('2015-04-14 07:15:36',
So, if far-sighted Hindu leaders & MLAs Voice
concern (in whatever words), U in the media promptly
raise Din and bustle, like foolish nerds.')

❖ ('2015-04-14 07:24:37',
Please pay a little attention To India's history: the
subjugation By the Mughals & the British has done
To our great people & to our nation!")

❖ ('2015-04-14 07:32:47',
They looted this land 2 render India a poor country.
They've converted Hindus; remember Today's Muslims
& Christians R mostly Hindu progeny.")

❖ ('2015-04-14 07:38:05',
These converts become zealots Of Islam &
Christianity in the name Of equal rights; they've bought
The media & Congress-leaders with no shame")

❖ ('2015-04-14 07:42:08',
Jaychands & Mir Kasim sold the country In total
blind-selfishness; & disunity has caused slavery Of
all of us, 4 centuries, we must confess!')

❖ ('2015-04-14 07:45:28',
The trend continues, with a new twist: Now the media,
western education And slave-mentality, happily exist 2
continue Hindu-bashing, no pun!')

❖ ('2015-04-14 07:53:52',
Hindus R naturally a Secular lot, Respecting all
religions: Even those who wronged us & fought To
kill us--Non-violence against their guns.')

❖ ('2015-04-14 07:58:19',
Yet the media finds it easy To show disdain against the
Hindus: It is the fashion, and they act silly And yet they
feel proud of their woos.')

❖ ('2015-04-14 08:04:51',
If @sardesairajdeep #CNNIBNNews & @
IndiaToday's @rahulkanwal & @TimesNow
@3DArnab, with their oblique views, Decided to save
Justice--Wow!")

❖ ('2015-04-22 08:59:37',
@rahulgandhi2020, Hello! Hello!! Long Time, No C,my
dear fellow! After a Leave of Absence of 59 days, Lo And
behold, @congressorg is mellow.')

❖ ('2015-04-22 09:09:58',
@SoniaGandhiG hid the fact That @rahulgandhi2020
isN'T up 2 the act Of acting as @congressorg's VP- He
Prefers Thai-party 2 @Congres-Party.")

❖ ('2015-04-22 09:15:07',
Poor chap had 2 B back 2 his mother's bidding of
wearing the crown: So, helplessly he gropes 4 a track;
Yet succeeding in acting as a clown")

❖ ('2015-04-22 09:19:19',
@congressorg party-members R So thrilled--here
comes their star! And, aided by Khadge & Scindhia,
@rahulgandhi2020 seeks his place in India.')

❖ ('2015-04-22 09:21:50',
He managed to somehow repeat The line his mother, @
SoniaGandhiG towed That @Narendramodi_PM's treat-
Ment of Farmers is hitting a sour node")

❖ ('2015-04-22 09:28:47',
@SoniaGandhiG blazed the trail, -B it a drama or put-up
job poor- That @BJP4India is going to fail Poor farmers
& serve only the rich's door")

❖ ('2015-04-22 09:31:12',
So the faithful son, in turn, Reiterated the same line
dutifully; And the mother-&-son tried to earn
Farmers' favor in next election coolly.")

❖ ('2015-04-22 09:37:17',
In Parliament, the absentee son, In a tongue he'd lost 4
so many years, Repeated the good old slogan, Claiming
2 have seen farmers in tears")

❖ ('2015-04-22 09:47:22',
The next day, in his new sulky & ill-fitting,
unnatural avatar silly, He raised question-rather bulky
For his stature-of net-neutrality.')

❖ ('2015-04-22 09:51:15',
With Scindia by side, coaching @rahulgandhi2020 with
curt whispers, @congressorg VP proceeded,touching
On his mother's reference,on twitter.")

❖ ('2015-04-22 09:54:57',
And Facebook & Internet--the net: Saying @
Narendramodi_PM--much Praised by @P0TUS,
Amreeka's President, Wants to give it to the rich as
such")

❖ ('2015-04-22 09:59:13',
@rahulgandhi2020z, @intanetz Is automatically open 2
all without Restriction, how can U say it's easy 2 gift it
to only a Group with clout?")

❖ ('2015-04-22 10:05:24',
& if it's a matter of allotting Its spectrum 2 only
the chosen-- Then the 2G scam and its plotting Took
place under @SoniaGandhiG's regime")

❖ ('2015-04-22 10:10:40',
@rsprasad of @BJP4India replied You well: may B U
seek publicity & Scindia eggs U on, & U tried--
But Parliamentary affairs allude U--pity!')

❖ ('2015-04-22 10:14:41',
Outside, talking to the media, U put on a brave face,
making claims That U won the battle--but phobia Of @
Narendramodi_PM on yr face remains')

❖ ('2015-04-22 10:22:17',
How can #development with infrastructure B executed
expeditiously, say, If 1 of those whose land turns a
super- Hurdle for a super-highway?')

❖ ('2015-04-22 10:36:10',
This simple facet seems 2 B beyond Those who oppose
the clause Of Government's right to respond Using the
land 4 the project with no pause.")

❖ ('2015-04-22 10:40:25',
@SoniaGandhiG & @rahulgandhi2020, Your
political maneuvering of @Narendramodi_PM Shalln't
work-there're plenty Of other issues 4 your game.")

❖ ('2015-04-22 14:41:16',
Then, there is this party called @AAP Which, acting
like the village @KHAAP Has turned out four of its GR8
Members out to an uncertain fate.')

❖ ('2015-04-22 14:46:40',
@AapYogendra @PrashantBhusha5 of AAP Have been
turned out of the #Jhadu-Chhap Party, of which @
ArvindKejriwal Is the Hitler-type All-in-All')

❖ ('2015-04-22 14:49:51',
@ArvindKejriwal, in his majestic Sweater &
Muffler & coughing throat, Was holding a meeting,
a patent trick To get some media and a few vote')

❖ ('2015-04-22 14:54:28',
At New Delhi's Jantar-Mantar, @ArvindKejriwal was
giving A majestic lecture or address, to stir The public
against #LandBill, like a sting.")

❖ ('2015-04-22 15:01:33',
#LandBill is bad for farmers; they're So dependent for
their Life and all- Land is his Life; his Ghar-bar His all-
-so said @ArvindKejriwal!")

❖ ('2015-04-22 15:05:17',
And, then a poor farmer, desperate, passed right in
front of his eyes; & he climbed over the tree next 2
him, as if to execute an exercise.')

❖ ('2015-04-22 15:09:18',
And the poor farmer, right in front Of @ArvindKejriwal,
proceeded To hang himself -- it was no stunt! Yet our
GR8 leader of AAP not heeded.')

❖ ('2015-04-22 15:15:09',
Our GR8 @ArvindKejriwal, unmoved Continued his
address without a pause! He did call a cop &
proved That he carried a concern for his cause !')

❖ ('2015-04-22 15:20:33',
So, the poor farmer whose cause @ArvindKejriwal was
busy bringing 2 light, in his very sight, 2 rouse The
public, hung himself, like a sting')

❖ ('2015-04-22 15:26:13',
So the poor farmer, hanging From a branch of the very
next tree-- & @ArvindKejriwal said he'd bring
Freedom 2 all, as the farmer gets free")

❖ ('2015-04-22 15:36:19',
The hanging farmer in presence, & in plain view
of AAP audience, Becomes free from woes about crops
& land, as Arvind talks & watch the cops')

❖ ('2015-04-22 15:52:44',
@ArvindKejriwal, busy in a harangue, Was defended by
@ashutosh83B of AAP: "Next time if a man tries 2 hang
Himself, CM would surely adapt')

❖ ('2015-04-22 15:56:59',
Says @ashutosh83B, Ex-media chap, Who\'s now a
top AAP-man, "The CM of Delhi, the leader of AAP,
Himself\'d climb the tree & go 2 its branch..')

❖ ('2015-04-22 16:01:29',
"& the CM of Delhi himself would Rescue a man intent on committing Suicide for want of land and food," Said @ashutosh83B, openly grinning.')

❖ ('2015-04-22 16:08:52',
@ArvindKejriwal is a majestic fool, All now know that! But this man- @Ashutosh-did he ever go 2 school Of journalism? Is he human?or Insane?')

❖ ('2015-04-22 16:13:36',
All this tragedy & political Drama has been played on stage-- Shakespeare would have no lull, But a bumper crop of words in this Modern Age!')

❖ ('2015-04-27 07:37:02',
@googlecloud I\'m interested in your offer:"Build ..Google-Get $300 in credit..60-day free trial." Pls send me details: kosha.ahnis@gmail.com')

❖ ('2015-04-27 07:52:32',
@narendramodi doubtlessly Media Like @TimesNow @HeadlinesToday & more Have heroically stood 4 India, Projecting well from Everest to Shore.')

❖ ('2015-04-27 08:00:36',
@narendramodi We in India or Overseas R so Jubilant & Proud 2 have You As Captain of our Ship, to Ease India's Journey thru Storms & Cruise.")

❖ ('2015-04-27 08:28:16',
@narendramodi Our sisters & brothers All over World, & now in #Nepal, Thank God that after years Of avalanches, we've a Navigator GR8,Tall!")

❖ ('2015-04-27 08:50:06',
@ndtv @TimesNow @HeadlinesToday @DalaiLama, Saddened by @NepalEarthquake, We rather wish @ UN4FreeTibet-Nama Made China wake-up and shake.')

❖ ('2015-04-27 08:58:29',
@SanjayAzadSln @msisodia @kumarvishwas1 @
Aashutosh_LKO- Yo re a shame 2 @AAP & to @
India Murdering an innocent farmer for your dirty
show!")

❖ ('2015-04-27 09:13:09',
@ArvindKejriwal, posing as a GR8 #AAPatWork folks'
leader Is just a fox with power-lust: #AAPRallyMurderer
at #aapkisanrally @jantarmantar.")

❖ ('2015-04-27 09:22:47',
What 2 say about @rahulgandhi2020, a naive late-
bloomer teenage- Rebel, totally without A feel for fitting
politics, now afoot a pilgrimage!')

❖ ('2015-04-27 09:27:56',
Is it desperation 2 draw Attention of Hindu voters that
@rahulgandhi2020 Travels to Kedarnath, or awe Of
deity that @SoniaGandhiG has seen?')

❖ ('2015-04-27 09:37:59',
Now, is it threat to @BJP4India that in Opposition Of
#landacquisitionbill 4 the sake Of farmers, or simply to
stun @SoniaGandhiG,or a fake?')

❖ ('2015-04-27 09:45:13',
Whatever the reason, @rahulgandhi2020 Plans 2 travel
thru India, on foot! 4 taking landscape & the scene;
Or @SoniaGandhiG'll beget a loot!")

❖ ('2015-05-01 07:17:41',
@GoogleForEdu Interested in signing up; Pls sign me!
For learning by all means is my cup of tea.!')

❖ ('2015-05-01 07:28:17',
@GoogleForEdu Have you heard Of Verse-Tweets?Pls
follow me @ @aksinh, 4 poetry in tweets: No absurd
Talk, but A Modern Little Mahabharat!')

❖ ('2015-05-01 07:34:34',
A very grave crime AAP's committed : They killed @
gajendr1 by hanging Him from the nearest tree, and
called it A Farmer's suicide, laughing.")

❖ ('2015-05-01 07:43:04',
@ArvindKejriwal: it is laughable That AAP is blamed
4 it. A phantom prisoner of politics, able 2 commit
gruesome murder, 4 society is unfit!')

❖ ('2015-05-01 07:48:42',
AAP top leadership involved In this heinous crime of
murder Should be hanged, if the mystery is solved 2
show if guilty of it is any member.')

❖ ('2015-05-01 07:51:44',
At least a life-imprisonment Should be the sentence, if
the suicide- Note is found 2 B fake document! &
AAP should be thrown by the wayside.')

❖ ('2015-05-01 08:00:22',
@ndtv Now @babaramdev4 is accused Of selling
a #RamdevMalePill: To defame him, dimwit @
kctyagimprs used Such a silly issue, out of ill-will!')

❖ ('2015-05-01 08:13:06',
With no real issues, Yogis like @babaramdev4 & @
Narendramodi R maligned by @kctyagimprs's & @
rahulgandhi2020's, Thru false fear in country.")

❖ ('2015-05-01 08:20:28',
@timesofindia #CNNIBNNew @ndtv @kctyagimprs\'s
accusation nilly-willy Of @babaramdev4 is as silly As @
rahulgandhi2020\'s "Save Kisan" rally!')

❖ ('2015-05-01 08:29:40',
@rahulgandhi2020's is an evil If not stupid plot
of toppling @BJP4India By raising hell about
#LandAcquisitionBill, Like vote-bank by Sonia")

❖ ('2015-05-01 08:36:09',
People of India R far more smarter Than the likes of @
rahulgandhi2020 & @kctyagimprs--these silly
characters R rejected by people a-plenty.')

❖ ('2015-05-01 23:27:49',
@penguinpress @FrankWilczek @DeepakChopra It is
praiseworthy On part of a physicist to take A view of
Art, Literature, Culture and beauty')

❖ ('2015-05-01 23:32:32',
@FrankWilczek @DeepakChopra @penguinpress
Indeed more of Math,Chemistry&Physics Should
come to rescue from duress Analysis of Consciousness')

❖ ('2015-05-01 23:40:42',
@penguinpress @FrankWilczek @DeepakChopra When
a Physics Nobel Laureate and a Social Leader and the
media Close together--that is a fix GR8.')

❖ ('2015-05-01 23:44:22',
@penguinpress @FrankWilczek @DeepakChopra,
may I beg 2 state, I 4 one Would be gratified to elk A
membership in such an august commission!')

❖ ('2015-05-01 23:59:03',
@penguinpress @FrankWilczek @DeepakChopra,
Having written books in Literature, Physics, Religion,
etc. I'd B grateful to get critiques your!")

❖ ('2015-05-02 00:04:15',
@penguinpress @FrankWilczek @DeepakChopra, if you
kindly consent, I'd B delighted to stake My reputation
& have 2 you a few samples sent.")

❖ ('2015-05-02 00:12:54',
@3DArnab 1 notices in @TimesNow A GR8 % of time
you\'ve yr guns Blaring "Just a minute" or so While
2-3-4 of the debaters shout all at once')

❖ ('2015-05-02 00:18:56',
@3DArnab @TimesNow It wouldn't be a crime To
make a rule that only one Debater speaks at one time,
Allowing equitable time for all, in turn.")

❖ ('2015-05-02 00:23:00',
@3DArnab @TimesNow U seem Heavily bearing upon
all participants So yo ve your own views 2 redeem,
Refuting a debater's points significant.")

❖ ('2015-05-02 00:33:42',
Take, e.g., @babaramdev4 Whose #PutraJeevakBeej
was in splash By @kctyagimprs, just 2 score A non-
issue, as an Ayurvedic name was in clash.')

❖ ('2015-05-02 00:37:43',
@3DArnab @TimesNow, should we Now think that you
R a herder Or owner ("Swami") of cow ("GO")? You see,
Your name is just a traditional word.')

❖ ('2015-05-02 00:46:48',
People who try 2 prove that U, "Goswami", R "Owner
of Cow" R @ fault for having the view That your
traditional name is misleading @timesNow')

❖ ('2015-05-02 00:50:40',
@3DArnab @HeadlinesToday @ibnlive @
sardesairajdeep & the bunch Seem stubbornly
anti-Hindu, 2 say The least, the majority always in a
crunch')

❖ ('2015-05-02 00:55:11',
Secularity is fine, no one Opposes equal rights of all
citizens. But minority-appeasing, and 2 shun Genuine
Hindu rights is art of your pens')

❖ ('2015-05-02 01:00:32',
This is a natural result of your fancy With Convent-
Education & distorted View of Secular Democracy,
Where ridiculing Majority is exhorted.')

❖ ('2015-05-02 01:06:41',
To look down upon your heritage & Fine Age-
old Culture and Tradition, In Macaulley-type foreign
bondage, U churn wheel in ape-like fashion.')

❖ ('2015-05-02 01:19:06',
@3DArnab did you ever hold Your pen upright 2 write
the fate Of millions of Hindus converted by old Tactics:
terror, pressure & deceit GR8?')

❖ ('2015-05-02 01:32:31',
But a small case of "Ghar-Wapsi" Makes endless
headlines for Your camera--@3DArnab @TimesNow, see
How twisted,unfair stories U\'ve in store?')

❖ ('2015-05-02 01:41:58',
Take @Iam_rahulgandhi\'s lame Words like "Suited-
Booted" Sarkar, @3DArnab this parliamentary shame,
This hapless chap is reincarnated a star!')

❖ ('2015-05-02 01:47:13',
Don't U C shallow and fake Form of @SoniaGandhiG's
son, with No brains of his own, conniving 2 take The
center-stage because of your wreath.")

❖ ('2015-05-02 01:55:15',
@rahulgandhi2020 innocently asks: "Kya Kisan \'Make
in India\' Nahin Karta?" @3DArnab, ignorant silly fellow
basks In media\'s attention, O Ya!')

❖ ('2015-05-02 01:58:51',
@rahulgandhi2020 doesn't understand Difference
between Agriculture & Industry in national life,
and Shouldn't he be painted as a caricature?")

❖ ('2015-05-02 02:03:08',
@rahulgandhi2020 makes jibes like: @Narendramodi_
PM is on India's tour 4 few days--does this strike As a
foolish remark on PM, India's hero?")

❖ ('2015-05-02 02:09:57',
Sheltered upbringing, dynastic Ambition, crushing
defeat at poll Have turned @rahulgandhi2020 a plastic
Batman, & @SoniaGandhiG an acid-doll')

❖ ('2015-05-02 02:22:34',
It's by great fortune That @narendramodi &
@BJP4India won! Otherwise @congressorg @
SoniaGandhiG scam-ridden Would've for India hell
earned!!")

❖ ('2015-05-04 22:22:19',
Bartolomeo Cristofori\u2019s 360ᵗʰ Birthday
#GoogleDoodle https://t.co/nE91jqjv28 @aksinh')

❖ ('2015-05-05 01:16:06',
Getting up to speed in molecular biology
?utm_source=Physics+Today&utm_
medium=email&utm_campaign=5636391_
Physics+Today..27+April GR8')

❖ ('2015-05-08 16:57:10',
Gr8 film about relationship betwn a father & son,
how #CORiver & #GrandCanyon was the thread to
reconnect them http://t.co/zrBKDsPCwJ')

❖ ('2015-05-10 08:57:41',
@OfficeOfRG VicePresident Of @congressorg, U &
your mom @SoniaGandhiG've looted India, 2 Gr8
extent; Unashamedly, U fi8 4 a lost kingdom!")

❖ ('2015-05-10 09:02:18',
Timid Rahul Baba, @OfficeOfRG, You go vacationing 2
Thailand, & now R posting hurdles horribly; After
burying for decades your head in sand.')

❖ ('2015-05-10 09:10:18',
@OfficeOfRG, have U read The Mouse That Roared-if
not, U should. Flexing your weak muscles, instead Of
helping in nation-building; NO GOOD!')

❖ ('2015-05-10 09:14:07',
Suddenly, appearing as if a new Avatar after
disappearance for 2 months from Parliament's pew, @
OfficeOfRG should read these Tweets 4 sure.")

❖ ('2015-05-10 09:25:04',
@OficeOfRG, in anticipation Of being @congressorg
President, U act as a joke 2 Nation, Hindering @
Narendramodi_PM's Development-Plans Decent")

❖ ('2015-05-10 09:32:03',
Since when @SoniaGandhiG Has cared about land-
reform or Farmers' lot? Getting an address @
OfficeOfRG, Hardly makes RVadra or U worth a dot.")

❖ ('2015-05-10 09:37:38',
@OfficeOfRG, may be,if U work Sincerely 4 the country
without Petty lil politics--from which U should shirk-- U
might gain a bit of clout.')

❖ ('2015-05-10 09:41:50',
@OfficeOfRG, getting a twitter-address Is a good start;
now U should proceed 2 acquire some experience 2
ward-off your immature word & deed')

❖ ('2015-05-10 09:51:50',
Here is a small advice @aksinh (follow me): I\'m writing
"Modern Little Mahabharat," with verse- Tweets on
Indian Politics, a new epic, anew!')

❖ ('2015-05-10 09:56:07',
It's up to you @OfficeOfRG, my dear! Whether you wish
to appear In it as a villainous character Or as a good
fella--a hero of toil shear!")

❖ ('2015-05-10 10:08:48',
Quit yr policy of protesting 4 the sake of fishy
protesting, @OfficeOfRG; @timesofindia is watching U;
get out O'@SoniaGandhiG's sick wing!")

❖ ('2015-05-10 10:14:37',
Be not under the illusion that @Congressorg'd gain
more seats; U might even lose 44, fat Chance--unless
you heed to these @aksinh tweets.")

❖ ('2015-05-10 10:24:51',
@congressorg @SoniaGandhiG @OfficeOfRG, To
know @Narendramodi_PM & how he\'s serving
the country, Read Novel "REINCARNATION OF THE
IRON-MAN'")

❖ ('2015-05-11 09:00:28',
.@SUBWAY Eat fresh, live green? Show us by phasing
out antibiotic-raised meat. Lives are at stake! This
applies to steak. Vegetarianism wins')

❖ ('2015-05-11 09:05:40',
Twitter Buttons https://t.co/ZgyQ1ShKgZ via @twitter
see My "MODERN LITTLE MAHABHARA",a Collection of
1300 verse-tweets on Indian Politics')

❖ ('2015-05-11 09:12:03',
Twitter Buttons https://t.co/ZgyQ1ShKgZ via @twitter
See "MODERN LITTLE MAHABHARA":My collection of
1300+Verse-Tweets on Indian Politics!')

❖ ('2015-05-11 09:16:31',
Twitter Buttons https://t.co/ZgyQ1ShKgZ via @twitter
There was THE MAHABHARAT by Rishi VEDVYAS. Now
"Modern Little Mahabhara" on Twitter 4)

❖ ('2015-05-11 10:54:01',
https://t.co/R5dqOUCQV1 Please sign this petition
on http://t.co/Cz6n3we0ul for 1.25 Billions of people
coexisting peacefully in the world.')

❖ ('2015-05-11 11:53:19',
@JagranNews Hamlogon ko Hindi ko UNO ke 'official
languages' me shamil karane ke liye prayas karate
rahna chahiye. https://t.co/8R6y7xgjNd")

❖ ('2015-05-11 12:01:39',
@tavleen_singh I\'d like to contact you for help in my
literary endeavor for readership of Indian Diaspora; e.g.,
"REINCARNATION OF IRON_MAN"')

❖ ('2015-05-11 12:07:23',
@Narendramodi_PM I was so happy about your
interview with Hindi @JagranNews ; My novel
"REINCARNATION OF THE IRON-MAN" may be of
interest.')

❖ ('2015-05-16 02:33:51',
Drilling in the Arctic? #ShellNo! Join the call to Seattle's
Mayor & RT: https://t.co/sgHr1egLNY for climatic
health of the world.")

❖ ('2015-05-18 06:02:32',
Facebook has a right to save its Face; and possibly to get
an uplift for it. https://t.co/kEXJ8uiOvb')

❖ ('2015-05-18 06:15:54',
1 couldn't have said it better. Let all remember oft:
#developmentinpractice of mindset, Sir, Must b hard,
not soft. https://t.co/sYrXxZVUqB")

❖ ('2015-05-18 06:33:29',
@BJP4India has right 2 teach @OfficeOfRG a lesson
or 2 If he taunts #MakeInIndia,#ModiInChina 2 reach
#Amethi-Farmers or FoodCourt an issue.')

❖ ('2015-05-18 07:00:56',
@ArvindKejriwal should face FIR 4 murdering a farmer
4 #AAP-ralley, Instead, Facing-off Delhi-Governor, Now
wants 2 meet Prez, shamelessly!')

❖ ('2015-05-18 07:07:45',
Computers can rule the world If only given a chance;
Only ? is: Would that herald New nuances 2 decline or
advance! https://t.co/2VAAF8C0mJ')

❖ ('2015-05-18 07:17:29',
@TheEconomist More spirituality Is needed, not more
corrupt religiosity; "Religion" differs from spirituality--
This many don\'t know:a pity!')

❖ ('2015-05-18 07:26:50',
@kuffodog @TheEconomist To know Divinity, yo ve to
look within Yourself, not 2 Supercomputers! O God, Your
Cloud now hides Dharma vs.sin!!")

❖ ('2015-05-18 07:40:48',
@TheEconomist Man's highest Innovation is God; His
image Is Man's Spirit or Dharma, yet the Quest 4 Him
the Church limits-a pitiful mirage!")

❖ ('2015-05-18 07:58:30',
@TheEconomist %age of Religiosity Or #Innovation
hardly measures Man's own Spirit:The Entity Is True
Spirituality, one's Innermost Treasure!")

❖ ('2015-05-18 08:06:04',
@OfficeOfRG,even now,thinks That @congressorg can
win By fooling Indian Voters, & by winks- Knowing
not that they're far far wiser than him!")

❖ ('2015-05-18 08:14:28',
More satellite capacity is the inherent trend, &
legacy of @INTELSAT. Every #Region will bask in it
sooner or later. https://t.co/v4WgkUQYni')

❖ ('2015-05-18 08:29:20',
All over world--from East 2 West, @narendramodi's
& India's image is having a feast; Poor @
congressorg @OfficeOfRG C only his suit's brand!")

❖ ('2015-05-18 08:47:18',
@congressorg @SoniaGandhiG shall Lose even
seats they now have, For India watches their fall--
#CongressMuktBharat shall rise, word my save!')

❖ ('2015-05-18 09:01:04',
@OfficeOfRG asks,"Don\'t Farmers \'@MakeInIndia?\'
The poor chap knows not The difference between
#agriculture & @elearnindustry, lamp &
diya')

❖ ('2015-05-18 09:08:49',
Immature @OfficeOfRG thinks just By using pompous
name, public Will become impressed enough to vote 4
@congressorg, playing a monkey-trick')

❖ ('2015-05-28 04:10:29',
I've 2 get my book & Papers giving simple model
of Higgs boson(s) reviewed by a few open-minded
physicists in CERN. https://t.co/mvARiwz0BJ")

❖ ('2015-05-28 04:12:08',
The Shear Beauty of It! https://t.co/Ti5hZ3EjAP')

❖ ('2015-05-28 04:12:08',
The Shear Beauty of It! https://t.co/Ti5hZ3EjAP')

❖ ('2015-05-28 04:15:29',
This (Graphene) is the miracle of the Six-sided close-
pack figure in two-dimensional (Plane) spatial
configuration. https://t.co/Z8riGw6mYZ')

❖ ('2015-05-28 04:20:02',
Can 1 imagine the miracle of six-dimensional space-
time (6-D ST) close-pack structures? "New Dim..." by
Ashok Sinha. https://t.co/Z8riGw6mYZ')

❖ ('2015-05-28 04:26:47',
#Modi365 is a Crest; #aap100 is a down the alley!
@Narendramodi_PM's journey is world's best; @
congressorg's 10 years, a depression-valley!")

❖ ('2015-05-28 04:37:17',
Eating @ Farmer's hut Is @OfficOfRG's GR8 glory!
Farmers' GR8-Days is #Modi365-Dream; but A Farmer's
hanging, @ArvindKejriwal's story gory!!")

❖ ('2015-05-28 04:42:55',
So many Domestic and Foreign-Policy GR8
Achievements #Modi365 mark; Yet myopic @
OfficeOfRG see Nothing but the rings around their eyes
dark.')

❖ ('2015-05-28 04:50:35',
@congressorg kept INDIA in dark ages, No vision,
no growth, only scams! Even @Plaid_Singh, now in
#scamnesia phase, G2, Coal-Gate, CWGames!')

❖ ('2015-05-28 04:58:51',
Height O'honesty 4 @Plaid_Singh Is:his family didn't
partake the loot! Landslides & Hurricanes in the
wind, Yet Chief's proud he'd no boots.")

❖ ('2015-05-28 05:03:26',
All those who looted or caused Or Oversaw the Loot
& Downhill Slide of the Nation's Fate, and used
Amnesty of Power must now Pay the Bill.")

❖ ('2015-05-28 05:11:31',
History'd judge those who ushered & fostered
poverty thru MANREGA & the like Harshly, for
they brutally crushed Poor people's lot & psyche.")

❖ ('2015-05-28 05:19:51',
If top @congressorg's leaders R tried & proven
guilty & jailed, That'd bring Justice to feeders Of
the country whom they so utterly failed !")

❖ ('2015-05-28 05:34:42',
@SrBachchan @juniorbachchan 2 add another
GR8 feather In yr rich caps, pl.play \'AMIT\' &
\'MANOJ\' in fiction: "The NEXT LIFE (2nd Ed.)", Sir!')

❖ ('2015-05-28 05:41:24',
Re-tweeting a boring tweet Does little justice 2
yr strife! 2 paint with blood & sweat, Pick up
Novel"The NEXT LIFE" https://t.co/ckM8Hv5qMM')

❖ ('2015-05-28 05:52:20',
@BachchanWorld @SrBachchan, my Humble Challenge
to your genius: Playing "Amit"(under @SubhashGhai1?),
Of "The Next Life,"U\'d B immortal thus')

❖ ('2015-05-28 06:00:02',
@BachchanWorld @SrBachchan, if U Play "The Next
Life\'s" "Amit Kumar", I can guarantee India\'d erect a
statue Of yours in Image of Pole-Star!')

❖ ('2015-05-28 06:05:17',
"The Next Life,"also titled "REINCARNATION OF THE
IRON-MAN," is the Tale Of Millennia, and today\'s nation
Of India,too,never ever 2 go stale')

❖ ('2015-05-28 06:13:55',
@BachchanWorld @SrBachchan,monument 2
history & Society of past & present &
Future o'India Is presented to an extent As never b4,
effulgent.")

❖ ('2015-05-28 06:17:58',
@BachchanWorld @SrBachchan U R presented
herewith Verse-Tweets Of "Modern Little Mahabharat"
2 Celebrate New Era and happenings bittersweet.')

❖ ('2015-05-28 06:22:28',
A Book of 1400 Tweets in Verse Is soon 2 appear-the
very first Creation of this kind, in terse Reason &
Rhyme, depicting events best & worst')

❖ ('2015-05-28 06:31:21',
@narendramodi,What a GR8 Fortune & 'Sumati'
Bharat had 2 Elect a Leader 2 Usher so soon 'Achche
Din,' ending an era so horrible, bad & sad!")

❖ ('2015-05-28 06:35:43',
@Gahmar3 @narendramodi If I say That our new
PM shall excel Even Lincoln in many a way, That'd B
Exaggeration Not, Let the world see & tell.")

❖ ('2015-06-01 06:35:37',
I signed the McGraw Hill "DOCUSIGN" for using 10 Fig
from Lee\'s book and 1 Fig from . Richharia\'s, charges
($550) to be paid by Nov 15, 2015')

❖ ('2015-06-01 06:38:43',
McGraw Hill Edu\'s Ms Ebony Lane is contact point for
granting permission to use 11 Figs in my book "THEORY
OF SATCOM" published by XLIBRIS..')

❖ ('2015-06-01 06:42:51',
I think there should be easier and less costly rules
& regulations for academic exchanges. I'd not
charge a cent for using part of my books.")

❖ ('2015-06-05 09:14:33',
@POTUS Universe is a curious place Smiling @ Man's
finds and quests- Here a dense crowd O'stars in case;
There, oceans O'galaxies in chests!")

❖ ('2015-06-05 09:22:31',
@POTUS @NASA surely deserves Our standing ovations
& admiration, 4 Sending up the Hubble 2 God's
turfs, Matching Man's Zeal for Exploration.")

❖ ('2015-06-05 09:33:39',
@POTUS 100s of Billions of Galaxies, Each with 100s
O'Billions of stars, 4 100s O'millions of years, cease Not
to coexist--say man's radars.")

❖ ('2015-06-05 09:47:15',
@POTUS If only man learned 2 coexist
Peacefully,lovingly,with neighbors: That'd B Existence's
true gist-- Heaven--descend 2 Earth & immerse!")

❖ ('2015-06-05 09:56:52',
Today I sent a few lines To @POTUS on @NASA's @
Hubble's GR8 Achievements in Space that shine Through
stars and galaxies strewn like pebbles.")

❖ ('2015-06-05 10:10:34',
@Narendramodi_PM How India is jubilant &
Proud 2 have U as our GR8 leader-- After 10 years of
disastrous winter, pleasant Spring is in air!')

❖ ('2015-06-05 10:19:14',
Your planting a tree is so symbolic, @NarendramodiJi,
not just for environment, But also to sow New Hope, to
pick New speed for Development.')

❖ ('2015-06-05 10:26:13',
New speed 4 Development is Indeed the Ace of Spade to
play Your hand, & dig deep @narendramodiJi, To
unearth diamonds in the country's clay!")

❖ ('2015-06-26 10:24:32',
@SrBachchan Yet you hibernate, Sir, on my request 2
read,"REINCARNATION OF THE IRON-MAN;" @ any rate
Consider your role in it of no concern.')

❖ ('2015-06-26 10:40:31',
@INTELSAT might consider starting with the South
Pacific Island countries, where INTELSAT's VISTA
service was launched, 31 years or so ago.")

❖ ('2015-06-26 10:48:04',
@Swamy39 Rahul & Sonia are the Rahoo &
Ketu of the Asur-Group, who have stolen half-a-gulp of
Gandhi-Amrut - all the rest are mere mortals.')

❖ ('2015-06-26 11:04:11',
@narendramodi Suggestion: these should be called
"ATNA" (ATal-NArendra) cities, like Pataliputra
(PATNA), glorious Capital of Maurya Empire.')

❖ ('2015-06-26 11:10:09',
@narendramodi Under your great leadership, India will
surely regain not only friendship but also leadership of
the world, we hope and pray!!')

❖ ('2015-06-26 11:16:51',
@narendramodi Congress: first it was Monopoly, then
Emergency, then Bhrastachar--Sonia embodying all
these traits.Congress-MuktaBharat! NOW!')

❖ ('2015-06-26 11:19:13',
@maneeshfilmdir @narendramodi Here is an humble
suggestion:Make a film on the novel "REINCARNATION
OF THE IRON-MAN" written by Ahnis Kosha.')

❖ ('2015-06-26 11:29:20',
@INTELSAT So INNOVATION=Square-Root
(GEOxLEO)=Sq.Rt(LEO)xSq.Rt(GEO)=? Is the answer
MEO?Does this optimize the number of orbited
satellites?')

❖ ('2015-06-26 11:33:23',
@INTELSAT One question: If the Igloo is turned upside
down, would it work as an efficient earth station
antenna at sub-zero temperatures?')

❖ ('2015-07-02 03:42:15',
@POTUS What assistance incl. insurance is available for
an Alzheimer's patient (my wife--63 years-old,who lost
her job due to dementia)?")

❖ ('2015-07-02 03:47:59',
@POTUS CONGRATULATIONS for success in your
endeavor to make healthcare available and accessible to
all at lower cost --a GR8 service to USA.')

❖ ('2015-07-04 02:21:35',
@NASA @Space_Station Can U send data transmission
details(Data-Rate,Xmit & Recv.Antenna
Sizes,Range,Eb/No,etc.)for #SpaceToGround to @aksinh')

❖ ('2015-07-04 02:23:35',
@NASA @Space_Station I'm interested in getting info
about Xmission Parameters, if public, as part of my
study of space-telecommunications.")

❖ ('2015-07-04 02:28:49',
@SrBachchan Thodi baat zindagi ki ho jai, Yam ke
badale (pl. see yourself in "REINCARNATION OF THE
IRON-MAN" by Ahnis Kosha(aka Ashok Sinha)')

❖ ('2015-07-04 02:34:00',
@SrBachchan I\'ve tweeted 2 U b4 abt my GR8 Filmable
novel "REINCARNATION OF THE IRON-MAN" featuring
real events and characters, like U & PM.')

❖ ('2015-07-04 02:39:58',
Just curious-tweeted to NASA for info on Xmission
paramtrs on Pluto flyby; so I could view data quality.
Should perhaps contact NASA Moffet.')

❖ ('2015-07-04 02:42:52',
Tweeted to @SrBachchan inviting him 2 look into my
Novel "REINCARNATION OF THE IRON-MAN", to see
himself and others (@Narendramodi_PM) in it')

❖ ('2015-07-04 02:49:56',
@BillGates @TheEconomist Need better seeds,
fertilizer (Organic), technology, edu. Only if countries
produced more corn, rather be war-torn.')

❖ ('2015-07-04 02:53:47',
Intensive research 4 a new Green Revolution was never
more critical. Generous and judicious research grants
would surely help beyond measure')

❖ ('2015-07-04 02:56:30',
Also tweeted to @BillGates concerning stagnant wheat-
production data during (2005-2015); and critical need 4
research 4 New Green Relolution')

❖ ('2015-07-04 03:02:02',
Now back 2 Modern Little Mahabharat War; I've yet to
contribute many lines. History is written every hour; Be
it @OfficeofRG or #coal-mines.")

❖ ('2015-07-04 03:05:41',
Poor @OfficeOfRG, with a small Level of Intelligence,
Still moving desperately on the beck and call Of @
SoniaGandhiG, with very little sense')

❖ ('2015-07-04 03:08:54',
Of politics & good conduct, @OfficeOfRG knows
very little indeed. He may adopt trash-can-like abrupt
Action, like vanishing with high speed!')

❖ ('2015-07-04 03:12:53',
To try to counter @narendramodi, The PM, for him is
like a sweeper Of @Plaid_Singh's 'Raddi'- -Basket, acting
as @congressorg house-keeper.")

❖ ('2015-07-04 03:17:41',
@rahulgandhi2020 is like a mouse, That roared seeing
typhoon In the tea-cup, pretending as if the House Is
his, talking like a buffoon.')

❖ ('2015-07-04 03:22:55',
Nothing better @OfficeOfRG could Come up with than
"Suit-boot ki Sarkar." A Shame of House, he should
Retire than engage in a Twitter-War !')

❖ ('2015-07-04 03:26:23',
Trying 2 catch up to somehow find A place in
#DigitalIndiaWeek super-plan, He is like a kid hiding
behind A smoke-screen all his life-span!')

❖ ('2015-07-04 03:31:41',
Now, what 2 say of #DigitalIndiaWeek, & "MAKE
IN INDIA" campaign-- @Narendramodi_PM is here to
seek An India that can B a Super-Power again.')

❖ ('2015-07-04 03:36:22',
1 truly wishes and prays That @Narendramodi_PM
succeeds In all his endeavors, so new brilliant rays Of
Hope & Success become India's Creeds.")

❖ ('2015-07-04 10:26:14',
@BJP4India What a glorious picture! And source of
inspiration-- Reminds us of the celebration we treasure
Of Swami Ji's 1893 participation.")

❖ ('2015-07-04 10:31:26',
@BJP4India Swami Vivekananda's oratory In 1893
in the World Parliament of Religions-- We celebrated
Centenary in 1993 In USA, in Washington!")

❖ ('2015-07-04 10:39:08',
@BJP4India I'd the assignment Of Editing &
Publishing the Book 2 mark the superb occasion, that
went Pretty well, many months though it took")

❖ ('2015-07-04 10:47:01',
@BJP4India Every word that Swami Vivekananda
uttered in Chicago then (In 1893) is still true, as @
Narendramodi Ji Has wonderfully penned.')

❖ ('2015-07-04 10:52:33',
Specially, Swami Ji's admonition That no religion should
predominate Over others in the World, in the Nation:
And terrorism's doomed is fate")

❖ ('2015-07-04 10:58:06',
This Age has so much to give: @Narendramodi_PM's
Initiative Of #DigitalDialogue we'd share & live;
His #DigitalDreams would so much achieve")

❖ ('2015-08-11 16:35:12',
Congress killed itself (Harakiri) and now it is digging
a grave to bury itself. Good riddance! https://t.co/
ftxb7xGuSA')

❖ ('2015-08-11 16:41:29',
@Swamy39 If good and sensible Muslims recall that
their ancestors were most likely Hindus converted to
Islam by force, they'd worship Ram.")

❖ ('2015-08-11 16:43:47',
@BJP4India This'd hopefully teach a lesson to Congress, too, to wake up and stop negative politics if they want to remain relevant at all.")

❖ ('2015-08-11 16:48:35',
@ISS_Research @NASA Let's move on from Lettuce and thinks of lots of harvest, so the inflation and food-shortage on earth could be remedied.")

❖ ('2015-08-11 16:50:42',
@narendramodi @poonam_mahajan Lots of people are complaining why the present PM, known for his transparency and straight talks, balks now.')

❖ ('2015-08-11 16:53:35',
@narendramodi @poonam_mahajan Looking forward to your Independence Day speech to reply to Congress and others to give them all a good "Maat"')

❖ ('2015-08-11 17:07:25',
@NASA How about an International contest with big Prizes for the Smallest-Sat Design and Lowest-Cost Launch to promote Small-Sat program.')

❖ ('2015-08-11 17:11:53',
@Ahmd_AbdAllah_ @NASA Collapse of Theory of Evolution? From what Age do you come from, man, Stone-Age? Take 1000 Questions (instead of 20).')

❖ ('2015-08-11 17:16:03',
@narendramodi If the youth of today become "Fighters-for-Development" of the country, the dreams of the Freedom-Fighters would be realized.')

❖ ('2015-08-11 17:19:08',
@narendramodi Hasn't @rahulgandhi2020 claimed in the Parliament yet that he was one of the great freedom-fighters under the leadership of S.")

❖ ('2015-08-11 17:24:02',
@narendramodi @NitishKumar blundered by leaving
BJP, otherwise he might have some good to his name.
Now he should go the way @SoniaGandhiG.')

❖ ('2015-08-11 17:25:29',
@BJP4India @narendramodi @narendramodi @
AmitShahOffice @SushilModi @RajivPratapRudy @
ShahnawazBJP @irvpaswan @nkishoreyadav @
byadavbjp GREAT')

❖ ('2015-08-11 17:31:14',
@vhsindia @Swamy39 @AseerAchary @
ARangarajan1972 @KiranKS Not enough to mention the
amount, the culprits MUST be brought behind bars, soon.')

❖ ('2015-08-11 17:36:20',
@AmitShahOffice @BJP4India A more apt slogan would
be more direct: "@NitishKumar @laluprasadrjd Baahar
Jaao; Bihar me Bahaar Laao."')

❖ ('2015-08-11 17:43:55',
@Balsanskarsewa @Swamy39 @HMOIndia \'Rapist\'
may be a foreign word here--use "Balaatkari Jo
Chamatkari Banaa ghoom raha tha; Jhoom raha tha."')

❖ ('2015-08-11 17:51:16',
@Balsanskarsewa @Swamy39 @HMOIndia Paid by
foreign elements, part of media may turn "Balaatkari" 2
public and Truth, & must pay 4 it dearly.')

❖ ('2015-08-11 17:55:39',
@BillGates You & your Foundation R doing such
wonderful good 2 the world of good cause, 1 wishes all
who have means followed your footsteps.')

❖ ('2015-08-11 18:01:14',
@Dilir123 @narendramodi Independence by
negotiations? Have you been sleeping all these years,
Robinson Cruso? Peace by negotiations: maybe!')

❖ ('2015-08-11 18:06:21',
@Swamy39 @narendramodi Poor @rahulgandhi2020
dreaming of 2020. He's going 2 disappear 1 of these
days (south of Thailand, 2 the South Pole)."')

❖ ('2015-08-11 18:12:17',
@BJP4India @narendramodi "Parivartan lakar hi
rahega Bihar : Bhajapa Sarkar hai samay ki pukar!')

❖ ('2015-08-11 18:18:33',
@ganesh_thore @Swamy39 @AShetty84 Hindu Unity
ka abhav hi Bharat ki durdasha ka mukhya karan hai.
Sabhi Hindu ek ho jayen, to Bharat Mahaan!')

❖ ('2015-08-11 18:23:13',
@SrBachchan No, I think this "Beta-Beti ka phark"
reflects tradition of male-dominance in our society, that
should be abolished in this age.')

❖ ('2015-08-11 18:27:31',
@SrBachchan Is that why the sons demand Ten Lakhs
as dowry 4 marrying a single daughter, Sir? Why cover
the harsh reality with sweet words?')

❖ ('2015-08-11 18:30:34',
@SrBachchan Dressed like a professional mountaineer,
you look great, Amitabh Ji (I'm same age as you, so I can
address you so (by your name)")

❖ ('2015-08-11 18:32:55',
@SrBachchan This is because when alive, everyone is
somebody, but dead, he or she is nobody! He ceases to
exist, only his or her body exists')

❖ ('2015-08-11 18:37:48',
@BillGates This nearly linear relationship (Power
consumption Vs.GDP) simply asserts that the more you
consume, the more you produce.')

❖ ('2015-08-11 18:40:35',
@BillGates A more innovative and efficient system would permit a high level of production even with lower level of consumption, I think.')

❖ ('2015-08-11 18:46:00',
@BillGates Actually producing more food in the right manner should have a great impact on the environment --it would lead to a better world.')

❖ ('2015-08-18 07:31:14',
Subscribe to Positive News From India - The Better India http://t.co/XkNXjUJHpu via @thebetterindia My Discovery of 'The Better India': GR8.")

❖ ('2015-08-26 17:27:35',
Why Do Dementia Patients Wander? http://t.co/X0JDE46vsZ')

❖ ('2015-09-15 08:04:28',
HILLARY FOR AMERICA "DEBATE CONTEST\u201d SEPTEMBER OFFICIAL RULES http://t.co/cuBvF1StFI (Any role 4 Hillary in my "Modern Little Mahabharat"?).')

❖ ('2015-09-16 04:22:16',
Apple patent adds magnetic drive actuation to UK-style folding pin USB adapter http://t.co/tRQIQX5bq9 via @AppleInsider CONGRATS 2 VIKAS---D')

❖ ('2015-09-24 17:11:52',
#PMModiInCA: What a wonderful Joy for the #SiliconValley Indians 2 play a Great Part in the Home-Rule In @makeinindia with @Narendramodi_PM')

❖ ('2015-09-24 17:22:57',
@PMOIndia @narendramodi It's Time Pak and Bangladesh, In their own interest, Chime The Bells of Peace and Friendship with India and Cherish!")

❖ ('2015-09-24 19:17:59',
When India & USA become True Friends in UNO, in Business and Diplomacy, in ending Poverty, too, Then Peace'll stand. https://t.co/gyLBkrbRK0")

❖ ('2015-09-24 19:27:34',
CEOs of Apple,Google,Facebook,GE, & Other Giants of Industry meet With @Narendramodi_PM, and Destiny Of a new world-order shall have a treat')

❖ ('2015-09-24 19:33:31',
Now the \'Modern Little Mahabharat\' Is not just limited to the shores Of India, but would freely "Chat" With Sky\'s Clouds, and Oceans\' floors')

❖ ('2015-09-24 19:40:08',
"DIGITAL INDIA" will surely Connect With @ DigitalGlobe, to "@MakeInIndia" A Reality circumspect; And a Revolution will take place in India')

❖ ('2015-09-24 19:44:10',
@narendramodi @PMOIndia Your Vision and Energy we felicitate With folded hands; it's sure That India's Wisdom shall save the world's fate.")

❖ ('2015-09-24 19:56:50',
@narendramodi @PMOIndia! Sail on O Captain of the State, to Seek Victory -- Be it America's Deep Silicon Valley or India's Himalayan Peak")

❖ ('2015-09-26 22:21:14',
@Narendramodi_PM,#DigitalIndia- Incarnate, is visiting Indian Diaspora in San Jose, California, The Silicon Valley's very Fountain-Spring!")

❖ ('2015-09-26 22:32:40',
Tomorrow the whole world will see The Cream of India melt and clap, Felicitate the hero, @narendramodi, In the City's Center called the @SAP")

❖ ('2015-09-26 22:50:29',
In New York, @Narendramodi_PM Hosted 4G Nations,
@UNSC to reform! With @Brazil, @GermanyUN, &
@japan, Taking bull by horn, world by storm!')

❖ ('2015-09-26 22:56:53',
@Narendramodi_PM performs miracle After miracle,
blowing the trumpet Of victory, smashing every
obstacle, Spreading for Future, red carpet!')

❖ ('2015-09-26 23:15:25',
Pakistan, just spreads lies ("India is building a wall
along the LOC"), As if world has no eyes; & @
NawazSharif\'s no face 2 C @narendramodi')

❖ ('2015-09-26 23:30:01',
Sail on, O Captain of State! @Narendramodi_PM...O
NaMo...NAMO, From Pole to Pole, thy call'll reverberate,
To obliterate Poverty's sly flow")

❖ ('2015-09-26 23:36:24',
@narendramodi's Clarion Call To build a Future for
today's world And for future generations, all in all, With
Care for the Nature unfurled.")

❖ ('2015-09-26 23:51:08',
We need to understand and tame The Climate to protect
the vital Interests of the Farmer; the blame-game Must
end among nations of the world!')

❖ ('2015-09-26 23:57:37',
Indeed, 'Vasudhaiva Kutumbkam' (The Whole World is
a Family)-- So pronounced @Narendramodi_PM-- And
that we're but Mother Earth's progeny!")

❖ ('2015-09-27 00:02:32',
Dealing with ease with Top Leaders of the world,
touching their souls, @narendramodi excelled in the
pin-drop Silence, as in digital tumults')

❖ ('2015-09-27 00:18:59',
At home, in the media, the rag-tag Army of the
Opposition raises @rahulgandhi2020's tattered flag
('Suit-Boot Ki Sarkar') & in such ways.")

❖ ('2015-09-27 00:22:04',
Poor @rahulgandhi2020...packing up His own suitcase
he disappeared again. Politics is not his cup Of Tea, but
for @SoniaGandhiG's foul reign")

❖ ('2015-09-27 00:28:08',
Now, Election is due in the State Of Bihar; and @
Narendramodi_PM'd Campaign for @Bihar_BJP, the fate
Of Bihar, however, everyone does elude.")

❖ ('2015-09-27 00:37:42',
On the one hand, the Mahagathbandhan Of @
lalooyadav, @NitishKumar, and @congressorg, like
Duryodhan Challenge @biharbjp in a jungle-brand.')

❖ ('2015-09-27 00:48:22',
In the State of Delhi, on the other hand, @
ArvindKejriwal, the old fox, Blames @PMOIndia, and
The Governor, while Dengu plays in the stocks.')

❖ ('2015-09-28 14:50:36',
New Online Exploring Tools Bring NASA's Journey to
Mars to New Generation http://t.co/JtGZvVbUB2 Today,
to Mars; Tomorrow, to Stars! No Bars")

❖ ('2015-09-28 15:00:36',
Send Your Name to Mars on NASA's Next Red Planet
Mission http://t.co/ZouVrBNF54 What's in a Name? Or
Fame? Child's game! Focus on the Aim!!")

❖ ('2015-09-28 15:19:39',
I plan to send to Gov. Brown (and others) some systems
concept on how to easily PREVENT AND CONTROL
Forest Fires!!! https://t.co/aA4bicGVtp')

❖ ('2015-09-28 15:25:49',
@narendramodi YOUR SPEECH IN SILICON VALLEY,
CAlifornia on Sept. 27 was superb, as all your speeches
always are, anywhere on this planet !!')

❖ ('2015-09-28 15:33:49',
@narendramodi Your words are electric--they charge
and energize the Youth of the country (and also give
shocks to convulsing Congress Party)')

❖ ('2015-09-28 15:41:36',
ISRO and NASA should act as partners in space, and
play 'Jugalbandi' in curbing global terrorism and Global
Warming https://t.co/aNMoxHP3Cy")

❖ ('2015-09-28 15:48:29',
A small contribution in the GR8 \'YAJNA\' of DIGITAL
INDIA:my Book "THEORY OF SATELLITE AND MOBILE
TELECOMMUNICATIONS" https://t.co/Yk8G94JQx)

❖ ('2015-09-28 15:53:01',
@Narendramodi_PM @narendramodi @isro INVITE
YOUR ATTENTION AND COMMENTS ON THE NEWLY
PUBLISHED BOOK:"THEORY OF SATELLITE AND
MOBILE TELECOM"')

❖ ('2015-09-28 15:58:28',
@Mdshamim786Mm Apane muhalle ko sudharane ke
liye aapane abtak kya kiya hai? Ya sarkar ke bharose hi
baithe rahenge, Garibi mitane ke liye?')

❖ ('2015-09-28 16:03:36',
NAMO-NAMO reverberates in the West, & East,
& North, & South--- WHO IS THE WORLD
LEADER BEST? "@Narendramodi_PM" roared every
tongue & mouth')

❖ ('2015-09-28 16:19:57',
#ModiInSiliconValley, #ModiInUSA, or @Narendramodi_
PM in Bharat or overseas #MakeInIndia, from shore to
shore-- Is in the making, in breeze')

❖ ('2015-09-28 16:28:53',
"JAM" 4 @Narendramodi_PM eloquent: "J for JanDhan,
A for Aadhar, M for Mobile", Central for the New
Government! For @congressorg, it\'s JAMai')

❖ ('2015-09-29 22:15:52',
I just supported What's Satellite Done for You? on @
ThunderclapIt // @sspi http://t.co/TFicdaQaBZ IT WAS
GREAT TO HAVE BEEN A PART OF IT ALL")

❖ ('2015-09-29 22:29:14',
@AVPbroadcast There exists a simple solution to make
satellite systems for broadcast, mobile, & other
applications more efficient !! @aksinh')

❖ ('2015-09-30 00:54:59',
@AVPbroadcast Pls. send catalog and info about
program details on satellite broadcast and multimedia
services ASAP to: kosha.ahnis@gmail.com')

❖ ('2015-09-30 01:11:34',
@AndOneTech @sspi Silicon Valley event at @sslmda
facility. Please send info and details ASAP for attending
to kosha.ahnis@gmail.com Thanks.')

❖ ('2015-09-30 01:52:46',
@sspi I enjoyed my membership in the Washington DC-
based SSPI organiz--must become a member again, and
campaign for making it International.')

❖ ('2015-09-30 01:57:04',
@sspi Why NASA does not mentioned that the person
making this GR8 discovery is a young man of Indian
origin (born in USA) working in Nepal??')

❖ ('2015-09-30 02:14:39',
@talkee_NASA THE DISCOVERY OF MARS HAVING
WATER was made by LOJENDRA OJHA, a 25 years
young man of INDIAN ORIGIN, IN NEPAL, reports
CNN-IBN')

❖ ('2015-09-30 02:18:48',
@satellitenetw Immense possibilities exist for
enhancing satellite network capacity yet to be
exploited. Many avenues come to mind. EXPLORE.')

❖ ('2015-09-30 02:29:52',
@xlibrispub @XlibrisUK U Published 1 dozen of my
books, advertized by all book-websites for new &
old copies; but I never hear from U, Why??')

❖ ('2015-09-30 02:41:28',
@Narendramodi_PM pronounced in #SiliconValley, US:
"No Good Terrorist (ONLY BAD)" Where\'ll @defencepk
@USAID_Pakistan @ISI @TheGoodISIS go?')

❖ ('2015-09-30 02:45:41',
@Narendramodi_PM called for global collaboration
(USA, UK, France,…) to rid the world of terrorism. @
UNO must act. Get India in @UNSC ASAP')

❖ ('2015-09-30 02:49:20',
@nepalitimes Is it true that the news from @NASA that
#MarsWater is a discovery made by Lojendra Ojha, 25,
of Indian origin, now in @NEPAL?')

❖ ('2015-09-30 03:00:13',
Back to my Modern Little Mahabharat! @
rahulgandhi2020 is absconding; no doubt He's a @
congressorg brat - As @mjakbar rightly pointed out.")

❖ ('2015-09-30 03:12:34',
A part-time politician @rahulgandhi2020, As @
BJP4India called that Dimwit,arguing against @
narendramodi, Then running away like a little rat')

❖ ('2015-09-30 03:23:11',
@rahulgandhi2020 called the Nation- Al BJP-Govt
"SUIT-BOOT KI SARKAR" As he packed his suitcase 4
vacation In USA (or @azzurri) in hotel5**')

❖ ('2015-09-30 03:31:41',
Then there is @ArvindKejriwal advising @
Narendramodi_PM that he should First "Make India"
before calling For #MakeInINDIA-foolish @AAP dude')

❖ ('2015-09-30 03:44:02',
Small-minds like @rahulgandhi2020 & @
arwindkejrriwal criticize @Narendramodi_PM--it's is
like silly Stupid (b)rat & sly fox vs a lion-size")

❖ ('2015-09-30 03:55:28',
@googlecloud Your promise is GR8! Endow
my nonprofit "General Education, Economics,
& Technology Associates," a Global Network
Organization')

❖ ('2015-09-30 16:00:22',
Satellites run the world - Book Just published:"THEORY
OF SATELLITE AND MOBILE TELECOMMUNICATIONS"
by Ashok Sinha http://t.co/8m7dTs3jd)

❖ ('2015-10-15 04:03:05',
@rameshnswamy @Swamy39 @vbsingh60 @swamilion
@jgopikrishnan70 @rvaidya2000 @SoniaGandhiJi and
@rahulgandhi2020, must pay for their crimes.')

❖ ('2015-10-15 04:09:16',
@Swamy39 bring @SoniaGandhiG and @
rahulgandhi2020 to the judiciary. This wud be a GR8
service to the nation--they must pay for their crimes.')

❖ ('2015-10-15 04:21:57',
Art 370 is a notorious page created by Nehru (his
motive is suspect). It must go as a new history is being
written. https://t.co/2i4eme0btt')

❖ ('2015-10-15 04:24:58',
All the pseudo-secularists and pseudo-nationalists
writers should form a Trade-Union; they are not worth
their salt https://t.co/ChnFUXbw0C')

❖ ('2015-10-15 04:30:22',
Preservation of Rama-Setu is most important,
because,being underground, it is pristine, untouched by
invaders' hands https://t.co/YLO7I805c1")

❖ ('2015-10-15 04:34:45',
Calling a Dakini 'Chachi' is giving respect to a person
who has harmed India more than anyone else in recent
history https://t.co/XH8gj1JVU0")

❖ ('2015-10-15 04:39:55',
I, for one, wish Congress should merge with dust in
shame for all their unjust and anti-national, selfish
activities https://t.co/qJAttZ9Fl0')

❖ ('2015-10-15 04:44:53',
This'd set history right and show how self-centered
Congress has been over years. Congress-Mukta Bharat
is called 4. https://t.co/eE3nNCTGo4")

❖ ('2015-10-15 04:48:47',
Ye buddhu (or inake Samadhi) are too dense to realize
they are wrong. Ghar-Wapasi? Vote-Bank is all they
think about https://t.co/LcK3MaQNP9')

❖ ('2015-10-15 04:54:23',
Back to My Modern Little Mahabharat! Many incidents
happen daily in a large Country like India, but some are
such that A writer must charge')

❖ ('2015-10-15 05:00:01',
A tragic event happened in Dadri, UP, and the
Opposition and the Media toiled hard to make it like
Babari Masjid, cursing PM & @BJP4India.')

❖ ('2015-10-15 05:08:08',
A UP incident (Dadri) is a Law-&-Order Problem
--the State machinery Is responsible for it, but they
managed to stir & make it all too muddy')

❖ ('2015-10-15 05:13:51',
Then there was a huge hue and cry: Why is @
Narendramodi_PM silent About it, why he doesn't decry
The culprits and any statement pertinent?")

❖ ('2015-10-15 05:24:20',
Lo & behold, today when @Narendramodi_PM his
sadness aired, The Opposition & Media yet remain
Indignant: Why he spoke so late if he cared !')

❖ ('2015-10-15 05:26:56',
So the Opposition and the Media just Want some excuse
to criticize @Narendramodi_PM --they'd adjust Their
barometer for all seasons & eyes")

❖ ('2015-10-15 05:32:30',
Media people have a serious Responsibility of
preserving the sanity & sanctity of the nation;
nervous- Ness shouldn't make'em run in frenzy")

❖ ('2015-10-15 05:44:03',
A general observation About media: By and large,
anything That puts Hindus in good light stuns Them;
and Hinduism's ills they endlessly sing")

❖ ('2015-10-15 05:49:41',
Why is this so: only they can tell! May be, as they're
mostly educated In Missionary schools and dwell Much
on painting Hinduism discredited")

❖ ('2015-10-15 05:59:54',
British colonialism is still with their Soul & pen--
they compete With 1-another, being unfair To the faith
of the Rishis--journalistic feat!')

❖ ('2015-10-15 06:05:29',
The more harsh a journalist is To a genuine Hindu
cause, the more Professional he or she is, and his Or her
credentials enrich his/her store')

❖ ('2015-10-15 06:11:16',
It's a well-accepted trait Or fashion for journalists
to show Disdain toward Hinduism; the fate Of the
overwhelming majority suffers,though.")

❖ ('2015-10-15 06:16:44',
They're mostly ignorant of the majesty And universal
benevolence of the spirit Of Hinduism, nor do they have
decency Of learning ABC of it.")

❖ ('2015-10-15 06:23:43',
It's a trend that motivates'em; Ill-mouthing Hinduism,
being unfairly Biased to the minority satiates'em. They
r like foreign agents unruly.")

❖ ('2015-10-15 06:28:11',
It must b stated that not every single Journalist is in the
above category. There are some who deserve to mingle
With highest honor & glory.')

❖ ('2015-10-15 06:38:53',
But a half-baked journalist Unabashedly exhibits unfair
bias Against Hinduism and Hindus, blatantly to twist
Reports & shows verging on lies')

❖ ('2015-10-15 06:47:00',
Now a pragmatic suggestion to all Journalist:
@3DArnab @anjanaomkashyap @sardesairajdeep @
rahulkanwal Yo ve to time speakers & ration-up.")

❖ ('2015-10-15 06:54:50',
For the benefit of TV viewers, truly It's waste of time
when more than 1 Person speak simultaneously; Just
permit equal time 2 them, 1-by-1")

❖ ('2015-10-15 06:58:51',
Use of simple electronic time-keeper Could be used to
tally each the time Spent talking by each speaker To end
chaos without reason or rhyme')

❖ ('2015-10-15 07:08:37',
Today, Netaji Subhas Chandra Bose's Family met @
Narendramodi_PM And he announced that the forces
Keeping history hostage won't win the game")

❖ ('2015-10-15 07:12:19',
File kept secret as classified Would be disclosed and the
world Would know what @congressorg tried to hide;
Let Nehru in his grave be curled')

❖ ('2015-10-15 07:17:30',
Truth has a way to be vindicated, No matter how much
they (The ill-doers) try to cover it, their ill-fated Game
ends, and 'SATYAMEV-JAYATE.'")

❖ ('2015-10-30 07:21:25',
Came across websites with info/pictures of famous
people in any field, and @BrainyQuote -It's like
discovering diamond mines in my backyard.")

❖ ('2015-10-31 16:56:20',
People-2-People Positive interaction in #India &
#Pakistan can foil venomous designs by @ISI &
#ISIS 2 unify 4 ever. https://t.co/XVmBnSj8SM')

❖ ('2015-10-31 17:01:28',
If CRT, TDK, Buddhu were spelled out, the transparency
of your Tweet would b enhanced, unless the lid is OK for
now. https://t.co/nfZnwRIJf0')

❖ ('2015-10-31 17:10:28',
The whole Indian Diaspora is watching #BiharElections,
hoping that #BJP4Bihar wins to bring #AcheDin (really)
there. https://t.co/S6V1wSMWta')

❖ ('2015-10-31 17:16:24',
SHOULD'NT @NASA refrain from sectarian references
to eerily creep into scientific revelations and
interpretations?.? https://t.co/55gxidhuMW")

❖ ('2015-10-31 17:20:56',
Tribute to Saradar Patel as GR8est Unifier of Bharat
after Chanakya is so true. Enemies of the nation: @
SoniaGandhiG https://t.co/DO4GyFHzAL')

❖ ('2015-10-31 17:28:44',
Blind @congressorg leaders(?) & media-Reps (@
ManiShankarIyer, @JhaSanjay, @manishtiwaridp, etc)
should pack-up & GO. https://t.co/DO4GyFHzAL')

❖ ('2015-10-31 17:32:13',
Indian masses should be made more aware of life
& gifts of Pt.DeenDayal Upadhyay--let's celebrate
his B'Day big way. https://t.co/YKOGNOEuq)

❖ ('2015-10-31 17:35:40',
What we really need is a 'Run 4 Unity' 2 get a 'Swachha
Bharat' (physically, socially, politically) every single day
https://t.co/pB88FY2w1t")

❖ ('2015-10-31 17:39:03',
To make the GR8 DREAM of "Ek-Bharat" and "Shrestha
Bharat" a Reality.....we need to take the dream 2 every
Indian.. https://t.co/pB88FY2w1t')

❖ ('2015-10-31 17:42:14',
Just as Gandhiji took Dream of Independence 2 every
Indian...But this time the task is harder as the enemy is
within https://t.co/pB88FY2w1t')

❖ ('2015-10-31 17:53:01',
Nehr s GR8 mistake-#Kashmir; @RajivGandhi's
big mistake-@SoniaGandhiG; hers--getting @
rahulgandhi2020 in politics.. https://t.co/
Ltsn5MMNkN")

❖ ('2015-10-31 18:00:19',
For dynastic rule, @laluprasadrjd and many others trying, @congressorg is mainly guilty; & @ SoniaGandhiG must pay.. https://t.co/Ltsn5MMNkN')

❖ ('2015-10-31 18:03:33',
Your idea of tallest statue of Sardar Patel is wonderful; let it not b dissolves or diluted by @congressorg's noise. https://t.co/Bw6v60cnds")

❖ ('2015-10-31 18:10:20',
In India, meaning of 'secular' is distorted 2 suit @ congressorg's vote-bank politics; truly Secular must B redefined https://t.co/bGl5smKRjB")

❖ ('2015-10-31 18:18:09',
Pl.visit https://t.co/YVYIR6iSpT, use prom-code 12400000025411 for Free Download of "REINCARNATION OF THE IRON-MAN". https://t.co/ Y5extjhlok')

❖ ('2015-10-31 18:18:09',
Pl.visit https://t.co/YVYIR6iSpT, use prom-code 12400000025411 for Free Download of "REINCARNATION OF THE IRON-MAN". https://t.co/ Y5extjhlok')

❖ ('2015-10-31 18:35:25',
Pl. see https://t.co/pUMNXvxBRb (ASHOK SINHA) or https://t.co/YVYIR6iSpT, promo-code 12400000025411 for free dwnload https://t.co/UoxYBkoRu3')

❖ ('2015-10-31 18:39:54',
Please recall most successful and economic "MARS ORBITAL MISSION (MOM)" by ISRO (INDIAN SPACE RESEARCH ORGANIZATION) https://t.co/NqArla4XCq')

❖ ('2015-10-31 18:44:00',
I think you canceled a big step toward Bikaneris to become aware of national issues of GR8 interest and importance. https://t.co/yV3lPFVsN)

❖ ('2015-10-31 18:49:30',
Book ("THEORY OF SATELLITE AND MOBILE (CELLULAR) TELECOMMUNICATIONS") by Ashok Sinha is now available; Pl.pass it on https://t.co/FYg67z14ys')

❖ ('2015-10-31 18:52:14',
Picture used here is fantastic. I\'ve used a similar picture in my book ("REINCARNATION OF THE IRON-MAN", Ahnis Kosha https://t.co/Y5extjhlok')

❖ ('2015-10-31 18:56:43',
@Via_Satellite @northropgrumman @AstroAerospace I believe there exists a method to further optimize any and all antennas(in satellite, E/St)')

❖ ('2015-10-31 19:01:08',
You neglected to mention where (Space/Earth segment) this observation has been made, or if the energy could be used. https://t.co/uqtFGvNao6')

❖ ('2015-10-31 19:05:07',
This looks like a new dawn in the space (and in related research programs); such explorations would turn a new leaf. https://t.co/1myiQztozI')

❖ ('2015-10-31 19:11:51',
Indian cinema is reaching a new zenith in terms of use of technology in sets & scenes. Stage-deco is fantastic, too. https://t.co/TzMOc2wJU0')

❖ ('2015-10-31 19:15:00',
Once again, Please see https://t.co/pUMNXvxBRb (ASHOK SINHA),or https://t.co/YVYIR6iSpT, promo-code 12400000025411 https://t.co/53QhRjB9gY')

❖ ('2015-10-31 19:18:28',
He Bhagwan, kya Neeteesh Kumar itana gir chuke hain,
"Kursi" ke liye? Agar yah bat sach hai to Janata ko bhi
batayen https://t.co/Iq5m7kSKjz')

❖ ('2015-10-31 19:22:14',
4 obvious reasons: They have more trust in India than
in China or USA, I think. Nurturing of this relation'd be
GR8. https://t.co/YQ52FVTtlR")

❖ ('2015-10-31 19:33:23',
Resuming the Modern Little Mahabharat, Two events
deserve mention here: #AwardWapsi and #BiharBattle
with the rat Of #CastePolitics, O Dear!')

❖ ('2015-10-31 19:41:12',
Atha #AwardWapsi Katha: A large Number of Writers,
Film-Makers, & Historians happened to barge Into
collective shows, becoming Protesters.')

❖ ('2015-10-31 19:45:48',
These artists-- of Word, Camera, & Reviewers of
the passing events Of import for the Nation, sounded
the band Of dissent against @NaMo4PM.')

❖ ('2015-10-31 19:51:09',
The protest was 4 growing Intolerance Induced by @
Narendramodi_PM, they said, Citing #Dadrilynching as
an instance! Were they true or paid ?')

❖ ('2015-10-31 19:55:59',
They might be paid stooges In the sense that they
mostly belonged To Left-wing thoughts, and the pages
Or films or @HISTORY probably ranged-')

❖ ('2015-10-31 20:05:18',
They delved into bias for communism; (They painted
glory of Red Revolution)! Of history they made mockery,
and of Hinduism! Using pen as gun')

❖ ('2015-10-31 20:09:30',
Gun that taunted or transgressed Truth and better
judgment for the good Of the country and the country;
stressed The masses as masters rude.')

❖ ('2015-10-31 20:13:36',
Lo and Behold! These dissenting And protesting
celebrities in letters, And art of film-making, and
writing @HISTORY hid behind them fetters.')

❖ ('2015-10-31 20:21:14',
Indeed, they were mostly tied To favoritism by @
congressorg, and they Were against @SupportNamo,
and tried Hard to defeat Modi B4,too,anyway')

❖ ('2015-10-31 20:24:57',
Who knows? Maybe these dissenters Of #AwardWapsi
\'Returning" their honor Were stooges of @congressorg,
beggars Or recipients of unfair honor')

❖ ('2015-10-31 20:28:56',
@arunjaitley, Finance Minister Under @Narendramodi_
PM, rightly Said, "The dissent might be Manufacture-
-Ed," fanned by @congressorg, U see!')

❖ ('2015-10-31 20:34:04',
Now, a word about #BiharBattle, Where #CastePolitics
is at peak! All selection of leaders is settled By what
caste 1 belongs 2, so to speak!')

❖ ('2015-10-31 20:37:24',
The present leadership in Bihar Wrecked the system of
administration; And corruption is rampant-- a Star Of
the past history of the Nation!')

❖ ('2015-10-31 20:41:52',
Bihar, during the Gupta Empire Was a center of
learning:Nalanda University was world-famous, now a
satire Of the old glory, its revival, Ha!')

❖ ('2015-10-31 20:48:53',
@laluprasadrjd took the State Of Bihar Backward
during his years of regime ! @NitishKumar, present
Chief Minister's fate Hangs rather grim")

❖ ('2015-10-31 20:53:05',
@NitishKumar earned a reputation Of bringing some @
GdnDevelopment But his alliance with @laluprasadrjd'll
shun People's favor for him 100%")

❖ ('2015-10-31 20:57:09',
The #MahaGathBandhan Or "Grand Allianc" of
@laluprasadrjd With @NitishKumar & @
congressorg is fun To talk about, paving the way for @
BJP !')

❖ ('2015-11-04 10:21:01',
To neutralize a poisonous seed Is essential before it Has
a chance 2 germinate and feed Spiders a cobweb to knit.
https://t.co/Faspi3CsVn')

❖ ('2015-11-04 10:30:36',
Only if BIHARIS appreciated This + acronym, there is no
doubt NDA there will win By a landslide, Throwing (-)
out https://t.co/puvi2KcTBK')

❖ ('2015-11-04 10:37:14',
Are Bhai, @congressorg ke liye Ab kya bacha hai; falatu
Obstructionism, Protest ke siwa, Aur karana main-
main-tu-tu! https://t.co/SpErpUtyx8')

❖ ('2015-11-04 10:45:58',
The Immortal,Luminous spirit Of Jnanyodha,
Karmayodha & Sthitprajna shall B lit In every true
Indian Soul's Prajna! https://t.co/THPp85F4Ge")

❖ ('2015-11-04 10:53:00',
4 1 so blessed as U With riches boundless &
humane Heart, nothing is loftier than to Give, on earth
paradise 2 gain! https://t.co/xdRP1nczia')

❖ ('2015-11-04 11:34:16',
#AwardWapsi is no good; #GharWapsi is far far better,
Since, someone stray should Return home; but an
awardee has no business causing fetter')

❖ ('2015-11-04 11:39:05',
This #ToleranceTussle Is unparalleled boring hussle!
#IntoleranceWar is stupid struggle Created by @
congressorg, with much din and bustle?!')

❖ ('2015-11-04 11:43:11',
Lo and Behold! @SoniaGandhiG Is on march to @
RashtrapatiBhvn Since she feels @BJP4India is her
enemy, While @Pranavmukharjee is her FM man')

❖ ('2015-11-04 11:47:37',
March! March Left-Right! @SoniaGandhiG May you
suffer the Heat of June And the Icelandic cold, you see,
Your legacy is India's bad fortune!")

❖ ('2015-11-04 11:59:12',
@rahulgandhi2020 Marches with his Mom, @
SoniaGandhiG with men Of @congressorg in file; the
show-biz Of politics floats a cracked egg (w/ hen')

❖ ('2015-11-04 12:02:52',
What's this 2020 in the twitter- Address of @
rahulgandhi2020? May be he, asking for a baby-sitter,
Hopes he'll be grown by the year 2020 !")

❖ ('2015-11-04 12:07:39',
Chorus goes on in the camp Of #AwardWapsi & @
congressorg: "Why doesn\'t the @Narendramodi_PM
Speak up!" If he does, he\'ll show\'em to morgue!')

❖ ('2015-11-04 12:15:31',
@congressorg March led by @SoniaGandhiG hits the
Press, Where @rahulgandhi2020 speaks, shy But
prompted by her, verbatim, so eager 2 impress')

❖ ('2015-11-07 05:50:02',
This is not just the Golden Day But also start of a
Golden Era When again world\'ll say "India is \'SONE KI
CHIRIYA!" https://t.co/opqhpItiJS')

❖ ('2015-11-07 06:00:01',
Thanks a Million to @Narendramodi_PM Leading
the country to excel In every front & realm; @
congressorg!Behave,Well. https://t.co/7AjSmBelK4')

❖ ('2015-11-07 06:13:42',
Thanks to our Heroes:@AnupamPkher, @
imbhandarkar, @ashokpundit, and Silent Majority, who
prefer To #MarchForIndia, Assert #IndiaIsTolerant!')

❖ ('2015-11-07 06:17:50',
March to India's @RashtrapatiBhvn By @SoniaGandhiG
@rahulgandhi2020 And 'Chamachas' in desperation
Was a Comical and Pathetic commentary.")

❖ ('2015-11-07 06:29:41',
@congressorg's terrible account Of treacherous &
traitor-like Acts in Parliament & Outside, amount
To terrorism, @HISTORY's foulest strike.")

❖ ('2015-11-07 06:46:37',
The Nation shall not forgive @congressorg & @
rahulgandhi2020 For trying to derail @BJP4India thru
negative Words in Parliament, aplenty.')

❖ ('2015-11-07 06:54:34',
The #LandAcquisitionBill and #GST Suffered blockage
in the UpperHouse, Hampering progress of the country,
@congressorg biting like a mouse!')

❖ ('2015-11-07 07:00:59',
May God give a bit of commonsense To @SoniaGandhiG
& her clan, So they think of the country, and hence
Stand not in way of progressive plan!')

❖ ('2015-11-07 07:28:02',
#ToleranceTussle & similar instances Are
contrived issues, just to defame @Narendramodi_PM,
for circumstances For which he shares no blame!!')

❖ ('2015-11-07 07:53:06',
Law and Order mechanism Of a State happens to
miserably fail, And @congressorg, calls it a schism,
Ranting '#Intolerance',

unity to derail")

❖ ('2015-11-07 08:03:34',
The Campaign of Discord & Hate By @
SoniaGandhiG against @Narendramodi_PM Is
slanderous; It'd drive her fate & of @congressorg
further down!")

❖ ('2015-11-07 15:24:26',
#Nov8WithArnab era of Caste-based Politics may not
be over; yet The era of #development is a fast-paced
Dawn among the young of Bihar State')

❖ ('2015-11-07 20:47:34',
@SoniaGandhiG lecturing #BJP Govt as "Intolerant"!
Lo And Behold!Shame to @Congressorg party! Sau-sau
choohe khakar billaiya chali Hazz ko!')

❖ ('2015-11-07 20:52:40',
@abdullah_omar of #Kashnir Tweeting Against @
Narendramodi_PM's visit To the State--or is he eating
His heart out, or having desperation-fit!")

❖ ('2015-11-07 21:07:04',
@SaeedMufti, #Kashmir-CM has a change Of heart
when he shows accord With #BJP and @Narendramodi_
PM, Praising his vision, forgetting discord')

❖ ('2015-11-07 21:15:35',
In TV Program "#UparWala- Dekh Raha Hai", a gala,
Religious leaders\' assembly, the Ala- Imam quiets
warring Hindu Gurus, praising Alla-Tala')

❖ ('2015-11-08 17:34:32',
Vedic Framework and Modern Science https://t.co/
OANzojUeJS Article by Rajiv Malhotra. Articles on
SUPER/CONSCIOUSNESS to follow (Archive)')

❖ ('2015-11-08 17:45:24',
High gain+NO (low) off-axis radiation also possible; to
revive my Patent Application for Forest Fire Control
(FFiCS) https://t.co/S9V6ngFefq')

❖ ('2015-11-08 17:50:21',
Science in India- Brief account in Appendix of
my book "NEW DIMENSIONS IN ELEMENTARY
PARTICLE PHYSICS AND COSMOLOGY" https://t.co/
EixAUMDGwv')

❖ ('2015-11-08 17:53:47',
In ancient Indian scriptures, "Other Worlds (\'Lokas\')
Described--Could be other celestial bodies (Planets,
galaxies) https://t.co/Rp6lfSIOB2')

❖ ('2015-11-08 17:57:11',
There should be more vocal expressions by the Silent
Majority on such problems/events (#ReawrdWapsi
#TolerantTussle) https://t.co/tg9aJPT5S8')

❖ ('2015-11-08 18:01:00',
Active Interest on part of the World's Richest Man
for solving global problems is venerable and highly
praiseworthy! https://t.co/3MYnIZweGg")

❖ ('2015-11-08 18:11:44',
2day a surprised Indian Nation Saw with awe @
BJP4India in #Bihar Election Lose-Is it manifestation Of
Caste-Politics or Falling of a Star?')

❖ ('2015-11-08 18:22:12',
Now @NitishKumar is once again CM by this
#BiharVerdict. Let's Hope Development'll remain Alive
as envisioned by @narendramodi,without rift.")

❖ ('2015-11-08 18:27:38',
For @BJP4India, it is a moment For GR8 introspection:
Why This awful defeat of Central Government In spite
of @Narendramodi_PM utmost try!')

❖ ('2015-11-08 20:50:04',
BUFFER Acct to archive Articles (e.g., Rajiv Malhotra\'s
"Vedic Knowledge and Modern Science") + Articles on
BRAIN, SUPER/CONSCIOUSNESS, etc.')

❖ ('2015-11-09 06:42:38',
@3DArnab I repeat a page from my "MODERN LITTLE
MAHABHARAT" (1600+ Verse-Tweets) Kindly TRY To
control every Debate So 1 can hear each guy.')

❖ ('2015-11-09 07:01:36',
@AnupamPkher @aksinh SAARANSH was GR8,
Inspiring. Please also read 1500+ Verse-Tweets
(MODERN LITTLE MAHABHARAT) On Indian political
creed!')

❖ ('2015-11-09 07:09:42',
@AnupamPkher Could you scan "REINCARNATION OF
THE IRON-MAN" A modern novel, to make a FILM, if you
can, It\'d be a true tribute to HINDUSTAN.')

❖ ('2015-11-09 07:21:34',
@AnupamPkher Tributes 2 You 4 strengthening @
Narendramodi_PM's Hands, 4 U & he march 2
Revive India of our dreams, Foiling adverse schemes")

❖ ('2015-11-09 07:31:43',
@AnupamPkher I\'d be all THANKS If U scan BOOK
(Novel) "REINCARNATION OF IRON-MAN" 4 a MOVIE
on the Plot it does dwell On--It\'d sell well.')

❖ ('2015-11-09 07:42:36',
@NarendraModiruv @AnupamPkher I repeat a line
of "MODERN MAHABHARAT" A Verse-Tweet Book on
Twitter : SAIL ON, O CAPTAIN OF SHIP OF STATE!')

❖ ('2015-11-09 07:47:02',
@NarendraModiruv @AnupamPkher Perhaps AAP
would make a better Opposition Than vicious MAHA-
GATHBANDHAN, Though both suffer with holes &
gaps')

❖ ('2015-11-09 08:06:35',
@hasnjun @AnupamPkher Money 4 March? Hasan, This
is NOT funny; Your mind is truly filled With dirt, 2 B
cleaned (4"Swachh Bharat" drilled)?')

❖ ('2015-11-09 08:17:43',
@naishadhvyas @AnupamPkher @narendramodi_in
Fascist is @rahulgandhi2020 actually (And his mom,
coming from Italy, The Land of true Fascism)')

❖ ('2015-11-09 08:28:42',
@3DArnab In your DEBATE, No 1 can get a word, at any
rate, When 2-3-4 people shout 2gether; U must facilitate
so they communicate Better!!!')

❖ ('2015-11-09 08:44:32',
@3DArnab This I must state: Journalistic Excellence has
saved Fate Of India, and 2 Anchors like You The country
owes much--that's very true")

❖ ('2015-11-17 17:05:45',
@ByAzamkhan @ManiShankarIyer and All those who
justify #ParisAttacks #terrorism should b fed desert-
sand And drowned in the oceans in sacks')

❖ ('2015-11-17 17:11:27',
#Terrorism is the biggest threat 2 humanity: new
Jihad and crusades; In 21st Century one expects GR8
Advances, not innocents' bloody trades")

❖ ('2015-11-17 17:16:54',
In States #Bihar, #UP, regional parties Via to block
@Narendramodi_PM; In Center, @Opposition @
SoniaGandhiG & @rahulgandhi2020 do the same')

❖ ('2015-11-17 17:23:09',
Such Opposition-agenda to derail @Narendramodi_PM,
to cause just Destructive -ve moves are bound to fail,
For People in #development trust.')

❖ ('2015-11-17 17:28:19',
@SatyamevJayates & true endeavors Toward
#development Shall Win; Opposition might gain some
odd favors; But eventually it would be done In.')

❖ ('2015-11-17 17:35:19',
@viren56002 @Swamy39 @WithCongress 4 @
rahulgandhi2020 ANYTHING is possible; He is British
& Indian & Italian at once; Thanks 2 Nehru
uncle.')

❖ ('2015-11-17 17:41:02',
@Swamy39 @WithCongress Nehru-Gandhi name
carries a miracle By which 1000 clerical errors about
address, Name and nationality he can tackle.')

❖ ('2015-11-17 17:49:25',
@DavidBCohen1 @Swamy39 Good to know That finally
the Brits are realizing The injustice & cultural
blow They heaped on India, that now sting.')

❖ ('2015-11-17 18:00:40',
@DavidBCohen1 @Swamy39 @GREATBritain must
now rectify The \'Clerical Error\'(Ha!Ha!)is to Fine
& make @rahulgandhi2020 say :"India, Goodbye."')

❖ ('2015-11-17 18:07:13',
@aaptardno421 @DavidBCohen1 @Swamy39 A
Second Freedom Revolution Must include throwing
@rahulgandhi2020, (son And mother) OUT OF
HINDUSTAN!')

❖ ('2015-11-17 18:16:45',
@Narendramodi_PM @BJP4India @M_Lekhi shouldn't
there be a Law That anyone Deliberately standing in
way Of #development shall b put 2 thaw")

❖ ('2015-11-20 17:15:22',
#BiharElections done & set is the stage For
return of @laluprasadrjd's Black Page: Worse yet than
#JungleRaj Is, Lo & behold:#LaluBetaRaj.")

❖ ('2015-11-20 17:23:59',
First it was RabadiDevi, the wife Of @laluprasadrjd,
into whose hand Helm of Rule over life Of #Bihar fell
and now it's #LaluBetaRaj-Brand.")

❖ ('2015-11-20 17:35:18',
#dynasty-rule like the moghal Emperors and old-style:
king's throne 2 b occupied by king's son--and all Good
people left cold: under a drone")

❖ ('2015-11-24 15:17:54',
@aamir_khan made a statement That his wife said, may
be they Should leave India as their descendents Might
face intolerance, as some say!!')

❖ ('2015-11-24 15:22:49',
Where's this #IntoleranceIndia slew Is originating?
Who is really behind It all? All seems well but for a few
Prominent persons words unkind")

❖ ('2015-11-24 15:31:03',
#DemocracyNow isn't harmed by A few ill-motivated,
@congressorg-cell Inspired, persons' biased outcry. @
Narendramodi_PM has done quite well")

❖ ('2015-11-24 15:36:15',
The country's economic base Is sounder and upward-mobile. The prestige of #India has had a raise! @congressorg is hindring in its own style")

❖ ('2015-11-24 15:50:46',
@AMISHDEVGAN's #BigStoriesBigDebate Had big discussion: How @aamir_khan's #IncredibleIndia suddenly became #Intolerant? @congressorg's Hand?")

❖ ('2015-11-24 15:57:31',
In Hindu-majority Indian nation, Top 3 #Bollywood Stars're all Muslims: @aamir_khan, @iamsrk, @BeingSalmanKhan; Yet some cite #Intolerance!")

❖ ('2015-11-24 16:05:52',
Many a careless, callous word By a few shan't shape the country This #IntoleranceDebate is absurd @congressorg lost, @BJP4India has victory.")

❖ ('2015-11-24 16:11:21',
It's apparent that #IntoleranceRising- Argument has been engineered by @SoniaGandhiG; defeated in the Poll-Ring @congressorg's making a try!")

❖ ('2015-11-24 16:23:47',
Poor @rahulgandhi2020, being A good son, is trying hard, too! But beyond "Suit-boot" slogan & acting Like a parrot, what else can he do?')

❖ ('2015-11-24 16:32:29',
@yosoyelara @sspi I take satisfaction In having made small contribution: Being a part of this revolution, And with book on SATELLITE TELECOM')

❖ ('2015-11-24 16:39:48',
GR8 having been part Of @INTELSAT, always with a look Of grandeur, with Science & Art Of SATCOM (Also see my book)! https://t.co/ihMBJEvt9h')

❖ ('2015-11-24 16:47:59',
In Self-publicity, just a bit, I'm here being led: But this
is called 4, as the digit Is not by itself transmitted
https://t.co/ihMBJEvt9h")

❖ ('2015-11-26 18:58:34',
Nov 26, 2015 is our #ConstitutionDay! @
BJPRajnathSingh but had to say That #Secular is a
misused--Nay, The Most Misused word in India today')

❖ ('2015-11-26 19:18:07',
#IntolerantSonia blamed #BJP for violating
#secularism--this from @congressorg Prez who to
Imam claimed That '#Secular' votes b 1 as a norm")

❖ ('2015-11-26 19:23:40',
The concept of separation of State & Church
(Faith)--the original intent Vanishing from the
#SecularDebate-- She now preaching to #BJP Govt!')

❖ ('2015-11-26 19:31:21',
In @congressorg's wicked mind, #secularism in India
means Treating Hindu majority most unkind- Ly,
appeasing Muslim minority and Christians!")

❖ ('2015-11-26 19:37:54',
Flagrant violation of #secularity, Purely for Vote-bank
politics, And British-type divide-and-rule policy, Played
havoc on Hindus & Sikhs.')

❖ ('2015-11-26 19:50:28',
Kashmiri Pandits in millions're made Refugees, exiled
from their home; And 1000s of Sikhs're dead In Delhi,
victims of @congressorg pogrom!")

❖ ('2015-11-26 20:00:03',
Atrocious, Usurpers @the_hindu devotees' gifts to their
temples, #hazzies & #conversions supporters--
Now explain #secularism's principles!")

❖ ('2015-11-26 20:11:42',
@NASA We surely can live In peace in the #ISS, but unfortunately Down on ground, r bent upon reprieve 4 #ISIS, taking world 4 a ride lately')

❖ ('2015-11-26 20:30:08',
A Tweet on @ManishankarAiyer in Modern Little Mahabharat (by @aksinh) Just to remind him of the sin Of calling @NaMo "Chaiwala," offering-')

❖ ('2015-11-26 20:35:47',
To open tea-stall, when NaMo started Campaigning for @BJP--how shamelessly Intolerant was that, O Congress-stalwart? U Apologize 2 country')

❖ ('2015-11-26 20:42:21',
Was NaMo outcast 2 u just because He came from humble background socially, Yet rose to be PM, free from jaws Of Intolerance, ManyAiyer JI?')

❖ ('2015-11-26 20:46:53',
Writing in verse-tweets, Instead of Sanskrit Shlokas as Rishi-Samrat Vedvyas did, I've such treats Chronicled in Modern Little Mahabharat.")

❖ ('2015-11-26 20:57:07',
It'd b good 2've comments on 1800 Tweet-verses: Go 2 https://t.co/nISy3IK4Tu; follow the song by @aksinh, 2 view story of new BHARATVARSH's")

❖ ('2015-11-26 20:59:46',
In world of social media, In MODERN DIGITAL INDIA, These verse-tweets'll remain immortal For all posterity--from Janpath to every Tea-stall!")

❖ ('2015-11-29 08:48:19',
@narendramodi @COP21 It's most crucial That Developed countries dare And comply in moral & legal Terms their responsibility, in fair share.")

❖ ('2015-11-29 08:51:45',
@narendramodi @COP21 to say That higher levels of
industry require Greater environmental pollution is no
way 2 prove their greatness, Sire!')

❖ ('2015-11-29 08:57:54',
@narendramodi Ji, I think The example of @Noorjehaan
in Your Today's #MannKiBaat should link Even in
highest world-forum like @COP21,& akin.")

❖ ('2015-11-29 09:18:05',
@narendramodi @COP21 #ParisAttacks: History's
black-spots, cracks, Dark as #carbon global foot-print-
#SIIS's Finger-print, blood-red tint!")

❖ ('2015-11-29 09:25:51',
@BJP4India @arunjaitley Who could Forget Jaychand,
Mir Kasim, inviting Invaders and Colonizers? Indians
should Learn History's lessons grim")

❖ ('2015-11-29 09:31:36',
@BJP4India @Narendramodi_PM @arunjaitley
Ji, undoubtedly somewhat Manufactured &
engineered seem All the fuss & talks on
#IntoleranceDebate')

❖ ('2015-11-29 09:43:54',
@NARENDRAMODlPM Your #MannKiBaat And
#Parliament-speeches, & 'Chai-par Charcha'
(Statesman-like top-level tea-chat) Make us proud,
inspire")

❖ ('2015-11-29 09:55:13',
@StationCDRKelly @NASA @Space_Station U C Earth's
silver-lining (austere Diamond-ring at total eclipse of
sun) But a diamond not-for-ever!")

❖ ('2015-11-29 10:06:17',
@Swamy39 That's leela o'Lalu! Past all the name-calling
(likely rightly), People R curious if still there's aalu In
samosa, outing nightly")

❖ ('2015-11-29 21:28:18',
@thebetterindia @Narendramodi_PM, I\'m yr fan!
My small Shradhanjali 2 thy theme sweet: Book
"REINCARNATION OF THE IRON-MAN" & my 2000
Tweets')

❖ ('2015-11-29 21:34:34',
@thebetterindia Keep up the GR8 work! INDIA needs
your GR8 campaign. @Narendramodi_PM is godsend-a
Perk To the Nation standing much to gain!')

❖ ('2015-11-29 21:39:06',
@thebetterindia I seek yr valued assistance To
publicize kosha.ahnis@gmail and @aksinh 2 reach out
to the public, be it India or France! Ya!')

❖ ('2015-11-29 21:48:55',
@thebetterindia I ask yr favor:if U can, Review Novel by
Ahnis Kosha, "REINCARNATION OF IRON-MAN," +1800
Verse-Tweets(Little MAHABHARATA!)')

❖ ('2015-11-30 06:00:24',
@the_hindu Let me propose That I'd love to regularly
write a column In your great newspaper, if you chose
Me 2 do so, b it on top or bottom!")

❖ ('2015-11-30 06:07:11',
@the_hindu I love writing (22 books Published, more
on the way.) On poetry, fiction, plays, religion...,it looks I
could serve well the day!')

❖ ('2015-11-30 06:29:42',
@ManiShankarIyer My dear Sir, yo d b Unhappy as long
as u live For saying & doing what u should Not
have, in India or Pak, in yr reprieve!")

❖ ('2015-11-30 06:35:54',
@BeingSalmanKhan U R indeed The spirit of India
-SwachhBharat, in Body and Soul-Be it Holi or Eid,
Projecting yr best in Veer & Bajarangi!!')

❖ ('2015-11-30 06:44:25',
@ManiShankarIyer So you have fallen So low as
to be stupid mud-slinging On a national hero, @
Narendramodi_PM, For his historic accomplishing')

❖ ('2015-11-30 06:49:48',
@ManiShankarIyer, shame on you! U call yourself a @
congressorg leader? Unable to b of any value, You should
"Doob Maro Pani Me Chullu Bhar"!')

❖ ('2015-11-30 07:13:48',
@Swamy39 Buddh ll remain A Buddhu, no matter what!
He is truly a wayward adventurer insane, Citizen of UK
or India--he's not worth his salt")

❖ ('2015-12-08 16:25:52',
A new chapter has opened up for @congressorg, when
@Swamy39 Filed a legal case in the Patiyala Court
Questioning @SoniaGandhiG & her son!')

❖ ('2015-12-08 16:37:14',
@indiragandhi84's Bahu(daughter-in-law) @
SoniaGandhiG, Sonia's son @rahulgandhi2020,
& her son-in-law Acting funny!! https://t.co/
Wz98YHXGd0")

❖ ('2015-12-08 18:20:14',
@SrBachchan Sir, you of course R not 'wrond'--but U
may be wrong If yo re saying 'Chup' and 'khamosh' To
people in support of @congressorg")

❖ ('2015-12-08 18:27:43',
@hebabachchan @SrBachchan Now Who's @
hebabachchan? Whose Hugs and kisses does he miss?
How Is all this related to your, picture & your pose?")

❖ ('2015-12-08 18:34:51',
One'd preliminarily think That we should keep Space
Free of mundane business, with no link With earthen
marketplace! https://t.co/NpEM1N4tfo")

❖ ('2015-12-08 18:41:44',
@NadkarAmit @SrBachchan 8th of Jan --that's a special
day for me, Sir! So let me join others, as your fan, And
wish you all the best 4 Wazir")

❖ ('2015-12-08 18:50:27',
@bigb21bigbshiv @SrBachchan @SONIYALUVSU
@guestlist_in @ShailendraS7 @HARDWELL @
MagicBusIndia--All of U 4 adding 2 tweet-count, R GR8
help')

❖ ('2015-12-08 18:55:28',
@AMITADAHEUR2 @SrBachchan I'd suggest 2 keep
something 4 yourself, too! It's not unwise to freely
invest All you have, but tell me: Who R U?")

❖ ('2015-12-08 19:00:38',
@hebabachchan @SrBachchan Let me Again join
the fan-club, Sir, & wish you a life full of happy
Moments and memories, each second a new spur!')

❖ ('2015-12-08 19:14:26',
@CokyCrazyByAB @SrBachchan This Picture must be
from a film in which U played a double role, unless U
always keep an extra face 2 bewitch!!')

❖ ('2015-12-08 19:23:50',
@Bharatiyata @Swamy39 If Chanakya Didn't happen,
we wouldn't have Had the Golden era of the 'Maurya-
Samrajya', getting rid of Nanda knave!")

❖ ('2015-12-08 19:32:11',
#NationalHerald is 'bought' by The duo
(Mother&Son--Maa-Beta) & a lot of Gol-Maal
they try, And when caught, they cry: Political Vendetta!!")

❖ ('2015-12-08 19:38:14',
So now #GandhisInDock deep As #HeraldHauntsCong
badly, But instead of saying "sorry", they keep
Disrupting Democratic Process Parliamentary')

❖ ('2015-12-08 19:44:18',
@SoniaGandhiG & @rahulgandhi2020, It seems U
think U are above the law-- U commit a criminal 420,
Then hold country's progress hostage, Wah!")

❖ ('2015-12-08 19:50:39',
The country is watching U both, @SoniaGandhiG &
@rahulgandhi2020, Yo d not be forgiven of wrath Of the
people, U R no good 4 this country!!")

❖ ('2015-12-08 19:56:47',
But before U are banished 4 good, O sly Mama &
your Buddhu Lalla, U 2 have to pay 4 betrayal, you
should Do time for #NationalHerald-Halla!!')

❖ ('2015-12-08 20:03:40',
A Daughter of Fascism is come To India on a marriage-
plank (No palanquin, no surprise!) but have U no
shame, @rahulgandhi2020, a think-tank?')

❖ ('2015-12-08 20:08:42',
@rahulgandhi2020 U claim 2 be An intellectual, a GR8
champion of Farmers' interest and @SoniaGandhiG
Simply used you 2 be the Queen, Scoff!")

❖ ('2015-12-08 20:12:01',
This revelation and litigation Is just A beginning, now
@Swamy39 Should expose you so yo re punished
Properly for all your heinous crime!")

❖ ('2015-12-08 20:20:01',
@rahulgandhi2020 we had some Hope that being a
young man, Yo d be idealistic and become Good citizen,
not a part of @youngindia24-scam!!!")

❖ ('2015-12-08 20:28:53',
Nehru-Gandhi dynasty must feel Ashamed of your black deeds! Drunk Of power & impunity, now you must kneel B4 the law, forgetting your rank!')

❖ ('2015-12-08 20:41:23',
@congressorg spokespersons: @JhaSanjay @ ManiShankarIyer @GauravGogoiAsm @ GhulamNabiAzad @anandsharmamp--R guns Of empty words, useless arms!')

❖ ('2015-12-08 20:49:03',
@congressorg spokespersons, king\'s "Chamachas" (of Nehru-Gandhi dynasty) Speak like firing, w/o listening 2 others, autocratic, sad irony!')

❖ ('2015-12-10 09:09:51',
#SalmanVerdict is out, acquitting The Man of Action, Bajarangi-Bhaijan. Congratulations to the "Veer", the King- Actor, @BeingSalmanKhan!')

❖ ('2015-12-10 09:34:00',
@StationCDRKelly @NASA @Space_Station Glory & Halleluiya!(wrong spelling?) Let there be joyous celebration Of Spirit of Man! A Star-Thing!')

❖ ('2015-12-10 09:42:22',
@Swamy39 That's exactly right! Buddhu with foreign DNA Is a curse--trying 2 turn the plight Of National politics sour! He's no good 4 India!")

❖ ('2015-12-10 09:49:02',
@Swamy39 The country is indebted to you 4 helping 2 weed out roots Of dynastic rule by corrupt, much-ado-For-nothing guys! 2 them, 3 Hoots!')

❖ ('2015-12-10 09:52:04',
@narendramodi Your book Will surely be a distinguished Mile- Stone for Present and Future, to look Into a genuine leader's legacy and style")

❖ ('2015-12-10 10:00:40',
@narendramodi Ji, Our Beloved PM! It's a gift 2 Nation
& world! Your book reflects Grand Neeyat, Niyam
And Neeti for Reform-Progress-Herald!")

❖ ('2015-12-10 10:11:48',
@narendramodi @fhollande @UN Soon @BarackObama
& every world-leader The whole world, Mr @
Bankimoon1 Too, would admire U, 2 read U, be eager!')

❖ ('2015-12-10 10:17:13',
It\'s a time for merriment and joy For all the fans of @
BeingSalmanKhan, #SalmanWalksfree! The "Bad Boy Of
#Bollywood, our #Bajrangi-Bhaijan!')

❖ ('2015-12-10 10:23:22',
Stalling #Parliament by Maa-Beta Of @congressorg;
with #ParliamentRuckus, Calling it #PoliticalVendetta,
When their crime stares'em in face!")

❖ ('2015-12-10 10:44:12',
@congressorg's become a scum Of #politics--Mama
& Buddhu Abusing all: @BJP4India, #mediafreedom,
#Judiciary, #Parliament..@Swamy39 must sue!")

❖ ('2015-12-10 10:50:02',
@SoniaGandhiG & @rahulgandhi2020 Have NO-
Right 2 hamper Progress Of @India, #development of
Country By Stalling #Parliament, Aye #Congress!')

❖ ('2015-12-10 10:54:25',
Future generations of #Indians, U C, Shall curse
@SoniaGandhiG & Son For subverting @
openDemocracy; The Maa-Beta must be punished,
shunned!')

❖ ('2015-12-12 20:06:00',
@Swamy39 Congrats on your victory In cases for
national interest! Your fight against highest territory Of
corruption'll stand time's test!")

❖ ('2015-12-12 20:16:40',
@narendramodi @RashtrapatiBhvn, 4 sure, @
PranabMukharjee, Like Aacharya Dron Of Mahabharat,
was on wrong side b4, as @congressorg's scion.")

❖ ('2015-12-12 20:24:03',
@narendramodi @RashtrapatiBhvn Now @
PranabMukharjee, like Vidur, Spins wisdom in words,
showing how A seasoned Head should shine as
Kohinoor')

❖ ('2015-12-12 20:37:02',
@BeingSalmanKhan @narendramodi Both of you, on
the world's stage, Continue 2 enact supremely, boldly,
Turning every day in2 a golden page!")

❖ ('2015-12-12 20:45:47',
@BJP4India O what a scene it was-- @AbeShinzo &
PM @narendramodi, Amid resonant mantras 4 the
cause Of worshiping @RiverGanga in #Varanasi!')

❖ ('2015-12-12 20:55:57',
@BJP4India @narendramodi @PMOIndia @AbeShinzo!
It was a festival, a feast For the eyes: reaffirming idea:
The Sun also rises--in the East!')

❖ ('2015-12-12 21:01:43',
@NASA @Space_Station Be it For rejuvenation or
celebration Of Christmas--Earth remains our home, fit
For travelers in space of every nation!')

❖ ('2015-12-12 21:07:51',
Now, coming back to the Modern Little Mahabharat, @
rahulgandhi2020 on face Said @PMOIndia did turn The
@JudicialWatch on #NationalHeraldCase')

❖ ('2015-12-12 21:15:27',
After much bad press & public Opinion cursing @
rahulgandhi2020, He took about-turn, sick With a wish
for a showdown with PM @Narendramodi!')

❖ ('2015-12-12 21:24:30',
@rahulgandhi2020, claiming that @Narendramodi_PM
left suit-boot Because of his comments, is a fat Chance,
like my Tweets rescuing his loot!')

❖ ('2015-12-12 21:28:37',
Turning around, taking a U- Turn, @rahulgandhi2020
announces calm- Ly: #NationalHeraldCase has nothing
2 do With stalling #parliamentlogjam')

❖ ('2015-12-12 21:35:18',
@rahulgandhi2020\'s stunts Are based on belief that
Janata Is foolish enough to take his rants 4 granted, so
he cried "Political Vendetta!"')

❖ ('2015-12-12 21:39:52',
After arguments by @arunjaitley That he must fight his
case In Court, now @rahulgandhi2020 Gets the logic,
and winds up his blind race!')

❖ ('2015-12-12 21:47:21',
@rahulgandhi2020, no doubt, is Pushed by his mother,
Maharani, @SoniaGandhiG, who thinks his Only destiny
is with 10-Janapath, her Rajdhani!')

❖ ('2015-12-12 21:58:02',
#ReformsRoadblocks by Maa-Beta #parliamentlogjam,
national wastage In #Summer & #Winter, by
dimwit Neta Of @congressorg evokes public rage!')

❖ ('2015-12-12 22:02:02',
@congressorg'd b lucky 2 get Single seat in the next
election In view of their rampant and net Irresponsible
conduct damaging the nation!")

❖ ('2015-12-12 22:06:59',
A self-proclaimed champion Of Farmers' & the
poor's cause, @rahulgandhi2020, acting as a buffoon,
Stands to make @congressorg totally lose!")

❖ ('2015-12-12 22:22:15',
@congressorg'll regret Its #parliamentlogjam, its
stupid mistake! Now digressing from Modern Little
Mahabharat A peak outside let's take!")

❖ ('2015-12-12 22:31:30',
It's time 2 view & rejoice Abt #ClimateForChange
Summit in #Paris2015, Where India's @Narendramodi_
PM's voice Rings on #COP21DoOrDie theme!")

❖ ('2015-12-12 22:44:11',
@PrakashJavdekar, India's Minister Of #environnement,
painted the doom Lurking if the threat, the sinister
Outcome, if ignored, shall loom!")

❖ ('2015-12-12 22:48:45',
The developed, rich nations Must do more 2 abate the
disaster-- For they cause more Carbon-emission, Said @
PrakashJavdekar, with many others')

❖ ('2015-12-12 22:57:08',
#India & #China, developing countries Have taken
GR8er share of burden; And it's turn of #USA and
#Europeennes Their take on it to sharpen!")

❖ ('2015-12-12 23:07:11',
#India's Capital, #Delhi, Is suffocating With pollution,
smog choking all; #LetDelhiBreathe, people r saying,
& @ArvindKejriwal made a call")

❖ ('2015-12-12 23:13:07',
An #OddEvenFormula is 2 b applied 4 cars in #Delhi--
success Of this #OddEvenPolicy is dubious, all sighed,
Hope this doesn't create a mess!")

❖ ('2015-12-12 23:17:40',
On #Pakistan-policy, @BJP4India, Under @
Narendramodi_PM assumes A breakthrough, many
in the media And #Government say, with talks to
resume!')

❖ ('2015-12-12 23:17:40',
On #Pakistan-policy, @BJP4India, Under @ Narendramodi_PM assumes A breakthrough, many in the media And #Government say, with talks to resume!')

❖ ('2015-12-12 23:21:09',
In general #Pakistan is hardly ever 2 b trusted, they violate the ceasefire Without any rhyme or reason, never being a trustworthy neighbor.')

❖ ('2015-12-12 23:25:54',
@Narendramodi_PM had a close Chat with #NawazSharif, Prime Minister of #Pakistan; & he chose To send @ SushmaSwaraj for some reason and rhyme')

❖ ('2015-12-12 23:36:32',
@Sanjay_singh76 @Swamy39 My dear Sir, Do you also believe in such an offense For other faiths,too? Such a rule will stir A world of violence')

❖ ('2015-12-15 00:50:46',
@NASA @theAGU An epitome of Man's Quest for Knowledge & Spirit For Exploration of all that Space Pans! Your Contributions live in every bit.")

❖ ('2015-12-15 00:59:48',
@Swamy39 @ucanews @news_va_en Should Note in no uncertain terms: Their encroachment upon the Indian Soil--Dalits--no God's favor will earn.")

❖ ('2015-12-15 01:10:45',
Now it's #NationalHerald,now Assam's Temple,now #Kerala CM,now...Er.. Now #PunjabAgainstBadals--it seems @rahulgandhi2020 is a manufacturer!")

❖ ('2015-12-15 01:14:38',
@arunjaitley said it well-- it's a cry- Baby-syndrome by a 40+ man! Even @ArvindKejriwal isn't shy To call @ rahulgandhi2020 a Bachcha insane")

❖ ('2015-12-15 01:19:48',
Some call @rahulgandhi2020 'Buddh, Some call
him 'Papp, Aren't you mighty embarrassed, you- @
SoniaGandhiG, making about him so much ado!")

❖ ('2015-12-15 01:24:45',
@rahulgandhi2020 showing his temper Against @
Plaid_Singh & now against @Narendramodi_PM is
like a miniature Fly humming, attacking Elephants')

❖ ('2015-12-15 01:33:14',
@narendramodi I venerate you, Sir, As Reincarnation of
India\'s Iron-Man! "Ek Bharat","Shreshth Bharat" swar
Gunjata Ghar-Ghar every Instant!')

❖ ('2015-12-15 01:37:20',
@narendramodi 4 this very reason, I wrote Novel
"REINCARNATION OF THE IRON-MAN" before
2014-Election, To carry this message for the Nation!')

❖ ('2015-12-15 01:48:12',
@narendramodi My Verse-Tweets Also form a chronicle
of events-- This"MODERN LITTLE MAHABHARAT"
treats The Nation\'s characters & temperament')

❖ ('2015-12-16 03:59:25',
@Swamy39 fire lit by @congressorg- To burn effigy of
@Narendramodi_PM Actually leaps to burn them who
barge On harming Truth--Holika-Dahan!')

❖ ('2015-12-16 04:07:50',
@StationCDRKelly @NASA @Space_Station Friendship
between arch rivals strives To flourish in #space--An
inspiration To keep Goodwill alive!')

❖ ('2015-12-16 04:13:39',
@narendramodi Ji, we are proud To have a PM like you
who is bent To serve the Nation day-&-night, a
stout Sentry of Freedom & #development!')

❖ ('2015-12-16 04:21:14',
@iamSRKFanLJ @narendramodi Then Try making a
Film on the book: "REINCARNATION OF THE IRON-
MAN" With,say @ramgopalverma20-how does that
look?')

❖ ('2015-12-16 04:27:27',
@NASA @Space_Station Such a Symbols of
International Cooperation they wear on their arms: it's
a Day To celebrate demise of Arm-Race dull!")

❖ ('2015-12-16 04:37:50',
@BJP4India @arunjaitley #Parliament- Logjam isn't
accidental,incidental; It's Preplanned strategy of
permanent Enemies of Democracy-2 stall.")

❖ ('2015-12-16 04:41:46',
@BJP4India @arunjaitley Clearly Simple efforts 2 make
#parliament Run wouldn't succeed;Opposition's tricky
Hurdles need a tricky settlement")

❖ ('2015-12-16 04:45:47',
Now @ArvindKejriwal has crossed All limits by calling
@Narendramodi_PM Coward and Psychopath, lost All
sense of decency & civility by CM')

❖ ('2015-12-16 04:49:19',
@Arvindkejriiwal has lost whatever Little sense he
had upstairs! This is just due 2 the eminent danger He
senses 2 be caught in his affairs!')

❖ ('2015-12-16 04:55:11',
A sly little fox calling dirty names To the Royal Lion, @
narendramodi, @ArvindKejriwal Threatening with no
shame! A laughable CM of #Delhi !')

❖ ('2015-12-16 04:58:47',
@rahulgandhi2020, @ArvindKejriwal & others
guilty of criminal activities Form gang 2 foolishly stall
Progress of India--this is most silly!')

❖ ('2015-12-16 05:05:28',
@Via_Satellite @japan & India shall, Cooperating
in such ventures in Space, Show the World how peaceful
Endeavors'd work, not arms-race!!")

❖ ('2015-12-16 05:11:13',
Child of 40+, @rahulgandhi2020, His wicked mother @
SoniaGandhiG, & @ArvindkejriiwaI holding the
country Hostage 4 their criminal activities!')

❖ ('2015-12-16 05:18:12',
I'm unabashed, unapologetic Admirer of @
Narendramodi, Able PM Who, in his visionary, heroic
Campaign 2 take India high up, faces obstacles")

❖ ('2015-12-16 09:29:59',
AN OPEN LETTER TO THE @RashtrapatiBhvn To @
PranavMukharji1, against the pandemonium Created by
@congressorg on purpose Simply to punish us')

❖ ('2015-12-16 09:32:36',
Respected Sir, @RashtrapatiBhvn, In front of your eyes
& ours, @SoniaGandhiG & @rahulgandhi2020
R playing a vicious drama 2 hide their 420.')

❖ ('2015-12-16 09:37:05',
They washed away the Summer-Session, And are doing
the same this #winter, By blatant and totally idiotic
disruption Of the #parliament, Sir!')

❖ ('2015-12-16 09:40:46',
I, @aksinh, living beyond 7 seas, But with #India in my
heart, like millions, Watch destructive acts & ways
Of @congressorg, on televisions.')

❖ ('2015-12-16 09:49:38',
Sir, you and we all, who Love our Country beyond Party-
Politics,should We helplessly just watch this hour Like
dumb lambs, butcher's food?")

❖ ('2015-12-16 09:54:45',
I am no enemy of @congressorg, And no political
affiliate of any party; Yet, I watch a drama unfold and
surge Everyday with a new turn dirty')

❖ ('2015-12-16 09:59:40',
First, it was "#PoliticalVendetta", To hide
#NationalHerald 420, then #Kerala, Assam--the Maa-
Beta Invent new excuse to disrupt #parliament')

❖ ('2015-12-16 10:04:18',
They think they r smart, hero! But they couldn't be
more foolish! They r going 2 become a big ZERO The
very next time people have a choice!")

❖ ('2015-12-16 10:15:24',
The purpose of this Open Letter Is to just ask you, @
RashtrapatiBhvn: Isn't there any recourse 2 put a fetter
2 such a destructive element?")

❖ ('2015-12-16 10:20:35',
A Nation's President, the highest Custodian of India's
#Constitution, Should be empowered to protect
Interest, Of, above all, the Nation!")

❖ ('2015-12-16 10:26:51',
Watching @congressorg destroy
#parliamentProceeding so blatantly Is tantamount 2 b
held hostage, a toy In hands (Panja) of vicious tyranny!')

❖ ('2015-12-16 10:31:32',
I, @aksinh, a citizen, implore you to save The country
from this tyranny; Pl. ask @congressorg to behave 4
Goodness-sake, be it an Oxymoron')

❖ ('2015-12-16 10:36:02',
@aksinh, writing in verse-tweets "Modern Little
Mahabharat" on Current Indian politics, bitter-sweet,
Like Dwapar Yuga\'s "Mahabharat" bygone')

❖ ('2015-12-16 10:47:49',
A poet sees & tells the Truth, Be it in Sanskrit
Shlokas or Digital Tweets; 1 sees villains ruth- Less
& Valiant Heroes of 2day & the yore!')

❖ ('2015-12-16 10:57:25',
It becomes clear how each Character, thus Fares on the
pages of history: whether Over the Bad, the Good turns
victorious, & the High spur.')

❖ ('2015-12-16 11:00:09',
In today's daily history being played On the
#Parliament's sacred temple, @congressorg is villain,
that said, You have to serve them sample-")

❖ ('2015-12-16 11:04:50',
A medicine to cure their wanton Disregard 2 people
& national interest, They mustn't get away with
their procession Like street-goons, pest!")

❖ ('2015-12-17 08:24:07',
#Google\'s Indian-Hero #AskSundar @aksinh is writing
using Verse-Tweets "Modern Little Mahabharat"-
wonders Of Indian politics, 2 offer treat!')

❖ ('2015-12-17 08:26:39',
@aksinh Hopes to graduate to world affairs Focusing
on Human Elements Globally-- Any advice how this
could fair On the world-scale socially?')

❖ ('2015-12-17 08:29:26',
#AskSundar @aksinh does to make His work apply 2
world as a whole: So after Dwapar's Mahabharat, 4 sake
Of humanity, it presents a new soul!")

❖ ('2015-12-18 01:55:40',
@NASA Breaking Barriers of distance (space-time) Man
steps into New Journey, Stretching Imagination's glance!
Victory 2 this Torch burning!")

❖ ('2015-12-18 02:06:18',
@historyofpluto @NASA We Define Planet as Natural
body orbiting Sun, & calling Pluto one decline
From, this is astronomical discrimination!')

❖ ('2015-12-18 02:22:43',
@japan @NASA @India We launch herds O'Satellites 4
GPS & such purposes; Then multiple Solar-Energy-
Birds Could fly 2 Save Environment's face")

❖ ('2015-12-18 03:27:46',
@RashtrapatiBhvn #ISRO is advancing By Leaps &
Bounds, writing in Space Saga of India's @HISTORY,
Victory; King Of the yore staking New Ace.")

❖ ('2015-12-18 14:43:32',
Today. @TimesNow, with @3DArnab's Coworker
anchoring a debate on #StartWorkNow, finally openly
snubs @congressorg's @brijeshkalappa's song")

❖ ('2015-12-18 14:48:48',
Every @congressorg spokesperson Sings & Dances
on tune of Maharani @SoniaGandhiG who controls her
son, @rahulgandhi2020, 2 from her Rajdhani')

❖ ('2015-12-18 14:58:18',
Rajdhani of @congressorg is called "Ten-Janpath"in
#Delhi, #India\'s #Capital, The Party #SummerSessions
stalled & #WinterSession, too 4 Null')

❖ ('2015-12-18 15:02:07',
Whether by #ParliamentRuckus, or Speaking over all
others, incessantly, Shamelessly, defending the #mother
& @congressorg unprecedentally,')

❖ ('2015-12-18 15:09:14',
@congressorg, from President down To VP, @
rahulgandhi2020 speak Over Speaker of House, like
clowns, Shouting with no logic or civil streak!!')

❖ ('2015-12-18 15:17:43',
@congressorg\'s top or foot- Soldiers have just 1
overriding Concern:How 2 save the dynasty\'s root;
Their "Kursi"--@BJP & Janata they sting.')

❖ ('2015-12-18 15:24:29',
@congressorg stalled two Valuable Sessions of
Parliament, bringing 2 standstill Democracy,
Disallowing BJP to table Any Legislation or Bill.')

❖ ('2015-12-18 15:29:32',
@congressorg surely wanted 2 avenge with @BJP4India
AS WELL AS PEOPLE at large, for they granted @bjp_ a
massive victory, as one could tell!')

❖ ('2015-12-18 15:33:48',
Blocking #GSTBill by @congressorg Was criminal,
resorting 2 all tactics. @PoliticsVedanta, then all sorts
Of nonsense, political injustice!')

❖ ('2015-12-18 15:41:26',
#StartWorkNow said the country whole, Disgusted
with #ParliamentLogjam 4 2 precious Sessions @
congressorg stole, Rather robbed, GR8est Harm')

❖ ('2015-12-18 15:44:30',
This is symptomatic on part Of @congressorg, its own
vendetta, Caring nothing 4 the country, sort Of putting
not India First, but Maa-Beta!!')

❖ ('2015-12-18 15:48:30',
@congressorg said for a show: They back #GST, but
with some Changes, they continued to crow; Their main
aim was to hold country for ransom!')

❖ ('2015-12-18 16:01:12',
@TMClachaine, SP, #bsp15, @NCPspeaks R 4 #GSTBill;
@cpimspeak, #cpi Oppose some clauses, 2 tweak;
Higher compensation @aiadmk wants to try.')

❖ ('2015-12-18 16:11:34',
@TimesNow narrated this history Of #GSTBill for
viewers' benefit; All along @GVLNRAO of #BJP Snubbed
by @congressorg, truly down in the pit!")

❖ ('2015-12-18 16:14:26',
This Modern Little Mahabharat Wouldn't be complete
without This narration on this sordid episode Of @
congressorg which tooth-and-nail fought")

❖ ('2015-12-18 16:22:58',
#CitizensRights of having #Parliament Work 4 benefit
of country, it seems Has been robbed;#government
Must break blockade, #India 2 redeem.')

❖ ('2015-12-18 16:27:53',
@congressorg & @SoniaGandhiG & @
rahulgandhi2020 must now rise Above petty politics, if
they wish not 2 b Buried In Graves, invite Demise.')

❖ ('2015-12-21 07:14:53',
@NASA Earth being bombarded by Electrons &
ions from the sun (Solar wind)--is well-known. The sky
Is the limit for signals becoming undone!')

❖ ('2015-12-21 07:27:15',
@Swamy39 Ji, @congressorg now Is shameless,
spineless, they Act as if it's their GR8 victory somehow:
@SoniaGandhiG @rahulgandhi2020're jay!")

❖ ('2015-12-21 07:32:44',
If @congressorg disrupts and blocks #Parliament, as it
has done before, #GandhisInCourt #GandhisInDock Are
IN for much bigger shock,for sure')

❖ ('2015-12-21 07:38:07',
Due to mindless hue and cry In the House, in the Well,
by @congressorg, & should they try This stupidity
again, they should be bade bye-bye!')

❖ ('2015-12-21 07:42:22',
The nation, the people of #India Should devise some
way: criminal Suit against @congressorg; #media
Ignoring them, banishing from our soil!')

❖ ('2015-12-21 08:54:57',
Due 2 childish disruption By @rahulgandhi2020, a
spoiled Unruly chap, #Parliament's function Stopped 4
2 full sessions, though #BJP toiled.")

❖ ('2015-12-21 08:59:08',
Just 2 stall #Parliament, 2 hide #NationalHerald
criminal involvement, @SoniaGandhiG desperately
tried 2 hold 4 hostage #India's Development")

❖ ('2015-12-21 09:04:02',
Even important bills such as the #JuvenileRapist getting
tried As an adult, #FinalNirbhayaPlea By her parents
failed: and @AshaDevi cried.')

❖ ('2015-12-21 09:09:18',
On the other hand, #Delhi CM @ArvindKejriwal &
@AamAadmiParty Called names to @Narendramodi_
PM In uncivilized word, & alleged @arunjaitley')

❖ ('2015-12-21 09:14:12',
@arunjaitley, rightly, has today Sued @ArvindKejriwal
and #AAP For malicious defamation, and pay
#AAPanarchy shall dearly for their 'PAP'!")

❖ ('2015-12-21 09:20:31',
@KirtiAzadMP of @BJP4India has held Grudge against
@arunjaitley in vain; Even @AmitShah, @bjp_Head
failed To infuse sense in his sick brain')

❖ ('2015-12-21 09:26:47',
And there is @bhupendrachaube, Forgetting common
journalism, who Unintelligenly had to repeatedly say:
'Why @KirtiAzadMP wasn't also sued?'")

❖ ('2015-12-21 09:32:16',
Even a layman in the nation Knows that internal party-
discipline Is different from public defamation By #AAP,
and no doubt @bjp_ shall win!')

❖ ('2015-12-23 20:58:11',
@ArvindkejriiwaI @DrKumarVishwas Oh my! Do
U remember trick U played On the innocent farmer,
making him die It was a murder in snare U laid!')

❖ ('2015-12-23 21:07:01',
@ArvindkejriiwaI @RamJethmalani5, 1 Questions your
motive & judgement: U call @laluprasadrjd &
@Kasab as "Ji" Who as guilty & killer went!!')

❖ ('2015-12-23 21:12:24',
@ArvindkejriiwaI @RamJethmalani5, U defend
criminals & murderer Terrorists & call
yourselves GR8est leaders alive? U should b ashamed,
Sir!')

❖ ('2015-12-23 21:16:31',
@ArvindkejriiwaI Do you remember @AnnaHazarae
& his Anti-Corruption \'Nara\' Where U shared
dais to declare That @laluprasadrjd ate "CHARA"?')

❖ ('2015-12-23 21:18:53',
@ArvindkejriiwaI How shamelessly now U oppose @
Narendramodi_PM to gain False publicity & self-
grandiose, how You even dare ask PM to resign!')

❖ ('2015-12-23 21:26:13',
@ArvindkejriiwaI U know NOT ABC Of governance,
service 2 people Who trusted U with electoral victory!
Delhi only got an arrogant empty skull')

❖ ('2015-12-23 21:38:53',
@ArvindKejriwal, if U don't want 2 go down in history
as most stunt- & arrogant nut who ruled #Delhi
Prant, Apologize PM for your ugly rant.")

❖ ('2015-12-23 21:43:38',
@Arvindkejriiwal, it\'s not surprising That U call
Kasab as "Ji"-- May be U have agencies supporting U in
#Pakistan & #USA with Black Money!?')

❖ ('2015-12-23 21:52:23',
@RamJethmalani5've U lost All sense of propriety, 4
being paid High fee, defending @ all costs Criminals-
Terrorists-as @ArvindKejriwal said?")

❖ ('2015-12-23 22:04:30',
@3DArnab in journalistic zeal Of bashing Hindus
with a groove To foreign negative pressure, feels @
RamJanmabhoomi work is #SecretMandirMove!')

❖ ('2015-12-23 22:12:43',
When'll second-hand Malice toward their innate culture
English-trained journalists' band Will shun, NOT attack
Hinduism as hungry vultures??")

❖ ('2015-12-23 22:16:25',
History is replete with examples Of open and hidden
Jayachands Who subverted Hindu culture, principles To
prove their intellectual strands')

❖ ('2015-12-23 22:24:05',
Habit of automatically attacking Hindu sentiments is
journalist's fashion, zest @ArnabGoswami why U keep
batting 4 foreign vested interests?")

❖ ('2015-12-23 22:26:50',
Cutting down your own roots Is showy and pseudo-
intellectual Fashion, and even Islamic terrorists Will
love your journalistic stand brutal.')

❖ ('2015-12-23 22:32:56',
U think U R being top-rated Journalist by causing
hurdles @ each step just Hindus ill-fated Take; & U
pretend 2 serve justice's cause subtle")

❖ ('2015-12-23 22:37:57',
Fanatic Muslims, down from Babar 2 2day's Islamic
organizations In country benefit from your spur,
Succeeding 2 serve only foreign nations!.")

❖ ('2015-12-23 22:40:36',
@ArnabGoswami_TN you may not Realize how much
harm to India You cause, even trampling just thought
And sentiments with the weapon of media!')

❖ ('2015-12-23 22:44:22',
@RealArnabHere U are actually being A hollow hello in
your eagerness To appear anti-Hindu, even for seeing
Events with tinted broken glasses')

❖ ('2015-12-26 10:07:20',
@Swamy39 Many CONGRATULATIONS, & Thank
You, 4 invoking the Court 4 exposing Fraudulent actions
By dynastic @congressorg's queen of a sort!")

❖ ('2015-12-26 10:14:01',
@ramalingamabsid @Swamy39 Indeed @sptvrock
(Sunanda Pushkar)-murder- Mystery is has a veil
behind the lead Of @ShashiTharoor, a crime utter!')

❖ ('2015-12-26 10:19:20',
@ramalingamabsid @Swamy39 Reason Why @
ShashiTharoor ISN'T questioned Is because of
@congressorg's protection: C him behind @
rahulgandhi2020!")

❖ ('2015-12-26 10:23:26',
@ramalingamabsid @Swamy39 @ShashiTharoor is a
sad example Of how an intellectual is intertwined With
crime, slavery; turn in2 a bad apple!')

❖ ('2015-12-26 10:27:42',
@AnandDaranand @Swamy39 many Hindu temples lost
their autonomy And assets by Christianity's uncanny
Conspiracy against them by @SoniaGandhiG")

❖ ('2015-12-26 10:29:34',
@AnandDaranand @Swamy39 There Should be a
nationwide movement To regain independence and fair
Treatment under federal and state governments!')

❖ ('2015-12-26 10:34:41',
@Swamy39 This is a GR8 chance 2 bring 2 fore the need
supreme For Chinese Govt. 2 take a stance Of peace, not
confrontation or evil schemes.')

❖ ('2015-12-26 10:40:43',
@AnandDaranand @Swamy39 @Narendramodi_PM
Plans for #development are bound To bear fruits, yet
some people become Impatient in the 1st round')

❖ ('2015-12-26 10:47:21',
@Swamy39 @Narendramodi_PM's Informal visit to
#Lahore, #Pakistan Delights peace-loving world; but it
seems It upset @HafizSaeedLive's clan!")

❖ ('2015-12-26 10:51:44',
@Swamy39 NaMo is a Supreme Statesman To have
extended hand of friendship To @nawazshrif and his
Pakistan-- Sail on, O Captain of the Ship!!')

❖ ('2015-12-26 10:56:36',
@Swamy39, @congressorg's old Guards ManishTewari
and @kctyagimprs Should now retire, if at the bold
Steps of @Narendramodi_PM they whimper!")

❖ ('2015-12-26 11:04:57',
No end of @ArvindKejruwal's Anarchist, Egoistic
behavior pattern: Now charging against @arunjaitley,
Now asking @Narendramodi_PM to resign!")

❖ ('2015-12-26 21:17:44',
#PayHikeForWhat, dear fellows, Occupying the
#Parliament? For your shouting matches? Nation owes
You little!U should rather have punishment!')

❖ ('2015-12-26 21:22:07',
@congressorg's @rahulgandhi2020, @MallikarjunINC
@nabigulamazad, You should all be fined heavily...
Blocking #parliemant! #PayHikeForWhat?")

❖ ('2015-12-26 21:25:40',
@congressorg has nothing better Than 2 hamper
country's #development By every means..they r trend-
setter For negative policy in #Government")

❖ ('2015-12-26 21:35:25',
Some call it #BirthdayDiplomacy, Some say it was
prearranged. @congressorg can't appreciate any GR8 @
bjp_-move, Even seeing the sea-changed?")

❖ ('2015-12-26 21:40:50',
@Narendramodi_PM stopover in Lahore Is humane
leadership at best; Let @HafizSaeedLive open venom's
door; & @congressorg in grave feel unrest")

❖ ('2015-12-26 21:47:21',
@ShatrughnaSinha & @KirtiAzadMP Pls.
reply 2 my Verse-Tweet.. Couldn't U express your
dissatisfaction 4 not getting by @bjp_ special treat?")

❖ ('2015-12-26 21:54:25',
@StationCDRKelly @NASA That Toe Is a small limb 4 a
Man, but a Giant Step for Mankind, indeed; and so Shall
Man win over all bodies defiant!')

❖ ('2015-12-28 16:13:08',
@Swamy39 For your "Followers" You should\'ve spelled
out TDK. And remember Mussolini, Fascist, a curse,
Who was hung up-side-down,all naked?')

❖ ('2015-12-28 16:18:04',
Today, it\'s a good time to narrate Discussions among
participants Of @AMISHDEVGAN\'s "#BigDebate,
BigStory", always with all sorts of rants!!')

❖ ('2015-12-28 16:33:56',
Today, rants were provided by Rashid Alvi & @ tariqanvar of @congressorg; @shrikantsharma of @ BJP4India did try To talk sense, less or more!')

❖ ('2015-12-28 16:39:50',
@AbhayDubey, a Sr. Journalist Was on the fence, yet defending @congressorg, as he did insist That all parties the same song & tune did sing!')

❖ ('2015-12-28 16:46:45',
@BillGates Aah! the bitter-sweet Feelings of what could have been... Now a Multi-Billionaire laments treat Missed in Time's Shifting Scene!")

❖ ('2015-12-28 16:53:03',
@BillGates How enchanting & poignant Is imagining as 2 what could've been... How about those billions with scant Air 2 breathe TODAY's gene?")

❖ ('2015-12-28 16:56:09',
@BillGates You have done a lot To improve a lot the lots of unfortunate Lots; yet indeed the task ought To be taken by many like @BillGates')

❖ ('2015-12-28 17:03:45',
@sanjaynirupam apologizes for Articles published in @ congressdarshan, @congressorg's magazine of the yore That criticizes party's top-guns")

❖ ('2015-12-28 17:10:52',
The article states in no uncertain Terms that Nehru,1st PM did cause Tibet-China & @KAshmir issues in vain! Now much passion he does arouse')

❖ ('2015-12-28 17:18:38',
If Sardar Vallabh BHai Patel Was chosen to be the 1st PM of India, History wouldn't have been forced to dwell So badly with such intermedia!")

❖ ('2015-12-28 17:27:32',
Nehru, Trying to be a Messenger Of Peace on World-
Stage, Shortsightedly, Damaged Country's Interests; he
erred. Sardar Patel acted bravely!!")

❖ ('2015-12-28 17:37:20',
@SoniaGandhiG current @POTUS Of @congressorg
is corrupt at heart! Battle between Hand &
the Lotus-- Between @congressorg & @
bjp_,sea-apart!')

❖ ('2015-12-28 17:41:58',
@SoniaGandhiG, the article dared 2 say, is daughter of
Fascist Officer; Her style shows it, too (Recall how she
fared @babaramdev4 earlier!)')

❖ ('2015-12-28 17:49:31',
@SoniaGandhiG, with help of her Chamacha-Ministers
& Delhi-police, Raided @babaramdev4's camp to
stir People out at midnight--a cowardice!")

❖ ('2015-12-28 17:52:48',
@SoniaGandhiG and her son-- @rahulgandhi2020
blocked #Parliament From functioning--& Country
should shun Their presence in the #Government!')

❖ ('2015-12-28 17:56:46',
The daughter of Fascist and her Silly son have no right
to be part Of #Government where they prosper By
corruption; let #Development Start!!')

❖ ('2015-12-30 17:10:06',
@NASA That's using sludge-hammer 2 kill a fly--at least
aim to learn a bit 2 peek into the Universe's True Nature
& Origin: learn Sanskrit!")

❖ ('2015-12-30 17:28:14',
@KirtiAzadMP Aye estranged MP of BJP, U have a funny
idea about fighting: U say "No Dushmany with Jaitley,"
Yet say & do most damning thing.')

❖ ('2015-12-30 17:31:54',
@KirtiAzadMP You seem to want A great deal of
attention, like a child: You & @ShatruganSinha
always chant Slogans against @BJP4India wild!!!')

❖ ('2015-12-30 17:38:15',
@KirtiAzadMP When'll you end Your venomous hisses
against #DDCA- Management so long ago, my friend? Do
you want a post? Itna halla kisliye?")

❖ ('2015-12-30 17:45:23',
@KirtiAzadMP Selfish motive wearing Garb of "Anti-
Corruption" U are! @ShatruganSinha & U can bring
@NitishKumar & @laluprasadrjd down in war')

❖ ('2015-12-31 14:02:20',
@HafizSaeedLive Where were u When 300+ INNOCENT
CHILDREN, WOMEN & MEN lost their lives, u do
Remember that, for U directed it from your den!')

❖ ('2015-12-31 14:10:14',
@HafizSaeedLive u r going straight 2 Dozakh 4 killing,
spitting venom Against, #Indians, that's yr fate In life
& death, u, humanity's scum")

❖ ('2015-12-31 14:17:15',
@HafizSaeedLive Your own countrymen Will give a
dog's death, as u preside Over murder & terror, u
chicken, Behind words of hatred as u hide.")

❖ ('2015-12-31 14:29:23',
@HafizSaeedLive After killing so many, lo! U express
condemnation 4 #MardanBlast, Sau-sau chuhe kha ke
bilaiya chali Hazz ko! Dice is cast!')

❖ ('2015-12-31 14:35:47',
@Swamy39 @impuni Do give hell 2 @SoniaGandhiG
& Buddhu, Sir! And Hell is the destination, 1 can
tell, For @HafizSaeedLive across the border!')

❖ ('2015-12-31 14:46:31',
@Swamy39 @impuni @rammadhavbjp Ke munh me
ghee-shakkar; he said: A day'll come when, culturally
India, #Pakistan #Bangladesh'll be reunited")

❖ ('2015-12-31 14:54:17',
@Swamy39 @impuni 1 day in continent, #Pakistan
#Bangladesh #Afghanistan Will be 1 with India, as in
ancient Times,2 make Bharatvarsh again!')

❖ ('2015-12-31 15:01:52',
@Swamy39 @impuni This is predicted By a Poet,
author of Modern Little Mahabharat, as parts are led To
unite to excel in the Village Global!')

❖ ('2015-12-31 15:11:49',
@Swamy39 @impuni @Narendramodi_PM Has
initiated with #Pakistan a new way Of friendship,
visiting @lNawazSharifl, PM To wish Happy Birthday!')

❖ ('2016-01-03 17:28:11',
@Swamy39 It's said, & very truly so, That the path
of idealism is arduous! For, otherwise, thugs'd go On
ideal paths as their first choices!")

❖ ('2016-01-03 17:38:36',
@NASA Glory to @NASA_Hubble! Beyond
Space&Time's bounds it sees! It's Third Eye of
Shiva, all-seeing & subtle, Modern Man's gift to
Rishis!")

❖ ('2016-01-03 17:52:53',
@Swamy39 This picture presents True Place of Swamy-
-among Judges Of Sanatan-Samaj--taking on relent-
Lessly evil-doers, in Court of Sages!')

❖ ('2016-01-03 18:06:28',
@3DArnab, like Pakistani PMs & @ISI, U seem not
2 learn the way 2 discipline debaters so they try 2 talk
1by1,not shout together in disarray')

❖ ('2016-01-03 18:13:41',
Only if U allowed each person 2 take turn in time-
rationed manner, Could your TV-viewers learn A bit of
debaters' views in @TimesNow banner!")

❖ ('2016-01-03 18:26:38',
@TimesNow organizes significant Debates, but they R
marred by Shouting matches: participants Scream all at
once; mostly, our (Na-)Pak Bhai')

❖ ('2016-01-03 18:41:13',
Clearly, Pakistan's consistent trend Is Aggression +
Denial! (we haven't yet Learned this?): Pak has, without
an end, This Open Policy pet!")

❖ ('2016-01-03 18:46:52',
#PathankotTerrrorAttack is just one More instance of
this policy of Pak! @ISI & JasheMuhammaed would
plan Any number of such terror attacks')

❖ ('2016-01-03 18:52:17',
@lNawazSharifl'd patently pretend Not 2 know about it;
even call within 30 seconds @Narendramodi_PM 2 send
Message, after committing the sin")

❖ ('2016-01-03 18:55:54',
It's part of the package, because Their religion allows
heinous crimes Like killing and lying without pause 4
advancing territory of @Islam!")

❖ ('2016-01-03 19:00:24',
Pak needs to be taught a tough Lesson that India is no
longer their Dominion and any thought or bluff Of this
type they should never dare!')

❖ ('2016-01-03 19:05:23',
Any number of friendly gestures India and @
Narendramodi_PM offer Will fall on Blind &
Mindless Parties in Pakistan, only India'll suffer!")

❖ ('2016-01-03 19:10:43',
What's the ultimate solution 2 deal with a barbaric
neighbor? India must pay Pak back in its own coin:
Damage Pak's array of terror centers")

❖ ('2016-01-03 19:19:53',
Talks'll start, talks will stop... Mumbai and
#PathankotAttack... The series will probably still stop
Not, unless a lesson hits home 2 Pak!")

❖ ('2016-01-03 19:23:50',
Pak stupidity has no End, for the poor country has lost
Three big wars with India; and so, Pak will continue
enmity with India at all cost!')

❖ ('2016-01-03 19:29:02',
If, in the long run, India, Pakistan & Bangladesh
were to again become One-- That might be a respite for
Peace, Finishing all rogue elements')

❖ ('2016-01-04 21:52:06',
@BJP4India @FinMinIndia @mygovindia It's time
results of #development projects Started showing on
ground 4 critical media & 4 best effects")

❖ ('2016-01-04 22:05:30',
@BJP4India @FinMinIndia @mygovindia For example,
take #Gangaa Clean-up! Planing & Cleaning
"Prakriya" Should begin as Big & small Start-up!')

❖ ('2016-01-04 22:08:20',
@BJP4India @FinMinIndia @mygovindia Not letting
people suffer inflationary rate Is most important, 2,
before media Makes it topic of Fate!!')

❖ ('2016-01-04 22:22:35',
@BJP4India @FinMinIndia @mygovindia Good 2 hear
from your Ministries Abt #PathankotAttack; now the
Inertia Shouldn't govern a Fitting Reply")

❖ ('2016-01-04 22:29:51',
@BJP4India @FinMinIndia @mygovindia Pak'll deny
everything as b4; Is the pattern 2 continue?Or Hashia
Of History should spell better score?")

❖ ('2016-01-04 22:36:05',
@BJP4India @FinMinIndia @mygovindia Lying thru
teeth, aggression, is in bloody DNA of Pak, they dream
of terrorizing India, With impunity.')

❖ ('2016-01-04 22:40:58',
@BJP4India @FinMinIndia @mygovindia A hard blow
in their psyche & the pit Of their stomach Indian
media & Govt must serve, as a reply fit!')

❖ ('2016-01-09 22:00:45',
#PathanKotAirBaseAttack it is Another step #PakArmy
has, pity! Taken towards its own virtual demise In the
hands of world community!')

❖ ('2016-01-09 22:15:35',
@Narendramodi_PM is @ #Pathankot To assess
#Pakistani attack; @NawazSharif rides a double-boat:
Masquerading as friend & stabbing in back!')

❖ ('2016-01-09 22:33:52',
Terrorists aren't only those who kill Innocent people by
bombs & bullets, But also those who intently will
Block #Parliament, stop Progress")

❖ ('2016-01-09 22:46:25',
@congressorg says it's non-partisan Website 2 educate
communities- Ha!Ha! @SoniaGandhiG is just a con
Holding India's progress, under siege!")

❖ ('2016-01-09 22:59:08',
@arunjaitley rightly said it's just High-command @
SoniaGandhiG Who is blocking #GST in shear lust
O'power,@congressorg defeat's despondency")

❖ ('2016-01-09 23:06:43',
Now @SoniaGandhiG, in her Lust of power and
desperation, Goes 2 see @CMOJK's daughter To stir new
trouble in J&K, to further hurt our nation")

❖ ('2016-01-11 23:09:11',
@chacko_gilbert @Swamy39 @ethicalman3 After u
breathe last, Chacko, can 1 prove That u ever existed,
except 4 the memory People'd have of)

❖ ('2016-01-11 23:13:26',
@chacko_gilbert @Swamy39 @ethicalman3 There may
b other signs--yr story, Yr legacy, yr pictures--u c: Every
true Indian holds Ram's memory")

❖ ('2016-01-11 23:22:35',
@chacko_gilbert @Swamy39 @ethicalman3 Ram's
memory & legacy in epics by Valmiki, Tulsidas--
1000s of years ago b- 4 2 millennia after u die!")

❖ ('2016-01-11 23:26:24',
@Swamy39 @ethicalman3 loonies Are sworn enemies
of spirituality; So, as"Dinakar"in Russia said many
Years ago, they first attack religiosity')

❖ ('2016-01-11 23:31:08',
@laluprasadrjd u must b dreaming To bring #JungleRaj
back in Bihar-- It would b better u stopped schemeing
& just disappeared from scene far')

❖ ('2016-01-11 23:40:42',
@laluprasadrjd's & @MulayamSingh's Names'd
be immortal as the Rakshasas Who killed innocents 4
vote-bank politics: @SoniaGandhiG's men khas!")

❖ ('2016-01-11 23:43:16',
@laluprasadrjd Don't u feel ashamed To make such
announcements, to be The king of #JungleRaj untamed,
Taking #Bihar down & down in history?")

❖ ('2016-01-11 23:53:06',
@Arvindkejriiwal @aamir_khan #DelhiGovt Has no
money 2 pay 2 city-cleaners, But 2 sing glory of CM, a
man of stunt, Double salary he offers')

❖ ('2016-01-22 07:05:47',
@Arvindkejriiwal Bah! nutty, shameless CM Of
#DelhiHatesKejriwal, how cheap u are Selling yourself,
with a "setting" so lean, U\'ll go far!')

❖ ('2016-01-22 07:09:21',
@Arvindkejriiwal Now this explains Why you blame
your boss, PM, For your total failure that pains
#DelhiHatesKejriwal, our stupid joker CM!')

❖ ('2016-01-22 07:20:59',
@lNawazSharifl Snakes Pak has fostered Against India
w/- bullets & blasts-- Terrorists are biting you--
Pak must gird To end terror real fast')

❖ ('2016-01-22 07:31:05',
Innocent students dying in school In
#BachaKhanUniAttack, bullets in head, Wake up, @ISI,
Ultimate Fool, Dismantle terror camps b4 u r dead!')

❖ ('2016-01-22 07:42:34',
@BillGates Your compassionate outlook Is exemplary, as
is your social media- Liking, like @Narendramodi_PM
who took Mission for Clean India.')

❖ ('2016-01-22 07:54:26',
@Swamy39 Death of @sptvrock-Sunanda Cries of foul
play--is @ShashiTharoor To blame, @congressorg High-
Command Providing protective cover?')

❖ ('2016-01-22 08:00:20',
@BillGates You are a True Role-Model For the super-rich
caring for the down-trodden; How one wishes riches
didn't compel Neglecting poor men")

❖ ('2016-01-22 08:13:23',
@Swamy39 Hare-Krishna people were Destroyed
in USA by Christian-Zealots! Hindus should make
evangelists who dare To convert face same lot!')

❖ ('2016-01-22 08:21:40',
@Swamy39 Conversion is like Murdering the soul,
Gandhiji said! It robs of one's identity to strike At the
Root of Life, ruptures one's head")

❖ ('2016-01-22 08:31:42',
@Swamy39 Coercive/forced conversion Must be
internationally banned! This curse of Christianity/
Islam; @Narendramodi_PM Need resist thru UN!')

❖ ('2016-01-22 16:07:51',
@ShatruganSinha Dear Sir, may be You are, in your own
peculiar way, Trying to terrorize and harass @BJP By
saying things you shouldn't say!")

❖ ('2016-01-22 16:16:02',
@3DArnab Sorry 2 say you too Often wrap simple
things in artificial Complexity; then allow 4-5 people to
Shout simultaneously: ruckus dull !')

❖ ('2016-01-22 16:29:33',
@3DArnab Is proper debate In Indian media culture an
alien thing? Yo ve to exercise control, so @ any rate One
speak in turn, no shouting")

❖ ('2016-01-22 16:34:53',
@BJP4India @smritiirani You all Have to face
#communist evil design & @congressorg & @
ArvindKejriwal Scheming & butting for votebank
gain')

❖ ('2016-01-23 17:44:13',
@Arvindkejriiwal Yo ve no shame In admitting your
abject Failure..& fighting with & blame
Everyone else..you should retire, at any rate.")

11h11 hours ago
It's Time for Grand 'Samapan'
Of "BHARAT-PARVA," a Festival
Of Joyous Celebration of Cultural
Excellence of INDIA, our Incredible Nation!!!

11h11 hours ago
All Humanity-Loving Forces
Must Fight for Full Eradication
Of **#terrorattac**, Pooling Resources
Of Love, Peace, Harmony in Each Good Nation !!

11h11 hours ago
When **#ISIS** attacked **#Paris**,
@Narendramodi_PM'd decided
To Invite **@fhollande** as Chief Guest this
Year, Humanity-Lovers are Always Befriended

12h12 hours ago
Let Nation Rejoice
On Its 67th Republic Day, yet the best,
Hailing **@Narendramodi_PM**'s choice:
France's President **@fhollande** our Chief Guest!

12h12 hours ago
So Arrogant 4 being in Nehru-Gandhi
#dynastytrades, ruling the Country
4 over 6 Decades **@SoniaGandhiG**
Fails 2 face her Defeat thoroughly !

12h12 hours ago
@congressorg carried, blatantly,
(With **#CorruptionPerceptionIndex**-0)
A vast bag of Corruption, belligerently
Thinking it was Right to do so

12h12 hours ago
Instead of crying @politicalvendetta),
@SoniaGandhiG & **@rahulgandhi2020**
Could better learn philosophical Vedanta,
2 introspect well pretty!

12h12 hours ago
Now, naturally, to **@congressorg**
And Chief **@SoniaGandhiG** finds
This as a political vendetta of a sort,
By **@Narendramodi_PM**, an axe to grind

13h13 hours ago
#ArunachalTussle is on vigorously
As **@RashtrapatiBhvn** imposes rule
Due to a crisis in 2016 early—
CM **@NabamtukiCM** playing foul, or a fool.

16h16 hours ago
Vote-Bank Politics does instill
GR8 rush among politicians; a pure
Parody that would be laughable to the hilt
If it didn't pure tragedy pour

16h16 hours ago
#Hyderabad was visited by
@congressorg's **@rahulgandhi2020**,
#TMC's **@derekobrien**, who did try,
With **#AAPCheatsDelhi**, 2 skin politics unclean

16h16 hours ago
A few days ago, **#DalitLivesMatter**
Became hub of unrest among
#Dalit **#Hyderabad** students, to shatter
Their dreams, as one died suicide-stung!

16h16 hours ago
@Narendramodi_PM said it
Best, "Reasons and politics behind
The controversy might fit
Many forms, but Mother (India) lost a "Laal" in shine.

16h16 hours ago
Much loud hue and cry still looms
In some quarters of Indian society
On the old issue of Intolerance,
Be it manufactured, or squabble petty.

17h17 hours ago
So, let **@swarupananda1**
Worry whether Shani is a god or planet,
And **@KamalFarooqi** defend Islamic tradition—
Women's point is equality 2 get.

17h17 hours ago
It's not so much a matter
Of faith; but equality of genders-
A big issue turning heads altogether,
Shaking Indian patriarchy, for the better

17h17 hours ago
Struggle on part of women,
To get status equal to men,
Surfaces every now and then;
But **#RightToWorship**-movement never did such shape gain!

17h17 hours ago
In India, Demonstration by Activist
(Hindu Women in **#ShaniTemple**
And Muslim in **#hazibuli** Dargah) is
On, for **#RightToPray** --plain and simple!

17h17 hours ago
Like @**KirtiAzadMP** expelled
From @**bjp** , @**ArvindKejriwal**, u
Crave cheap media-publicity, spelled
Disaster for #**Delhi**, know nothing else 2 do

17h17 hours ago
Fighting against @**Narendramodi_PM**,
In Benaras in 2014 Election
(Now daily), u think u equal him!
But @**ArvindKejriwal**, u're not worth mention

17h17 hours ago
Big in DHARANA, @**ArvindKejriwal**,
U're a big 0 in 'Karana';
Your head should surely roll, fall;
Only to #**Delhi**-CM-Chair, your heart is Fanna.

20h20 hours ago
Even Muhammed Tugalaq who hails
In History as 'sir-phira (Head of State
With up-side-down head)' pales
To u @**ArvindKejriwal**, u demonstrate!

20h20 hours ago
With a boasting miles-long
U pledged to fight corruption,
But a fool more Corrupt, head-strong
On the #**Delhi**-throne never saw this nation!

20h20 hours ago
U care little about "SWACHHA-
BHARAT," and u willingly stall
Life in #**Delhi**--worse than a Bachcha
Totally spoiled u are Mr. @**ArvindKejriwal**?

<u>20h20 hours ago</u>
SO, in your wonderful Delhi-Raj,
The city would, for the 3rd time,
Become a garbage-dump--you stage
Nation's Capital with GR8 light-lime.

<u>20h20 hours ago</u>
So, with your fight against **#BJP**,
You paid no salary to Workers
Who clean up **#Delhi**...what a pity!
Pretending, for them, you've no purse!

<u>22h22 hours ago</u>
@ArvindKejriwal Here u go again:
#delhihateskejriwal 'cause u only
Know is discord, disdain, Against
@bjp_ Govt. be it the Center or **#Delhi**.

<u>23h23 hours ago</u>
@BillGates With your kind permission,
I'd love to send to you my Verse-Tweet
Book (and "REINCARNATION
OF IRON-MAN") to you, my humble treat!

<u>23h23 hours ago</u>
@BillGates To explain this, I write:
Literature, Satellite Communication,
(This is no PR, nor being erudite)
My love: Physics and Fiction.

<u>23h23 hours ago</u>
@BillGates If these structured treats
I send to you seem strange—
It's 'cause these verse-Tweets
In "Modern Little Mahabharat" I'd arrange.

23h23 hours ago
@BillGates Putting Feynman's famous
Lecture-Series in physics online for free-
Access by those interested in Physics
Is your sweet melody

23h23 hours ago
@BillGates Quite believably,
You are ALSO WORLD'S GREATEST
PHILANTHROPIC genius, so ably
Helping eradicate many diseases the world infest.

24h24 hours ago
@BillGates It is so nice
To know that being the world's richest
Man diminished not your humanity (a common vice)
But made you man's crest.

Jan 27
**@AnupamPkher @ShekharGupta
@SubhashGhai @ SubhashChandra**
May I request you to kindly help a Fan,
& Comment on my Attached book "Iron-Man.

Jan 27
**@aksinh @BarkhaDutt @rahulkanwal
@vikramchandra @SirPareshRawal**
May I request U to kindly scan
& Comment on my Attached book "Iron-Man...

Jan 27
**@3DArnab @sardesairajdeep
@vidhuvinodchopr @mbhandarkarFC**, a Fan,
May I request U to take a peep,
& Comment on my Attached book "Iron-Man..

Jan 27
@YuvaiTV @BJP4India @smritiirani
Can I humbly request you to launch my BOOK
"REINCARNATION OF THE
IRON-MAN" Of NEW INDIA a NOVEL LOOK?

Jan 25
@AnupamPkher @vidhuvinodchopr,
@SirPareshRawal, @ShriRaviShankar
Humble #Congratulation, Sons of India,
Who bring name to country for ever.

Jan 25
@narendramodi @fhollande India's
Hand of friendship & mutual cooperation
For all countries of the world--stage
Set for #Terror's eradication

Jan 25
@narendramodi @fhollande This must
Be a GR8 historic ride for France in India,
A new Chapter of Friendship and Trust,
Minus glaring Media.

Jan 25
@INTELSAT @Arianespace, it was the
#INTELSAT-7 only yesterday when we
Labored on; and now we've #Intelsat29e—
Technology flies Hi as we see

Jan 25
@NASA 4 1 one likely Explanation,
See "NEW DIRECTIONS IN ELEMENTARY
PARTICLES AND COSMOLOGY (2nd Edition)"
(http://amazon.com)--Easy!

Jan 25
@ArvindKejriwal AAP bahut bahut busy
Rahate hain--kitna kaam hai:
Koi nahi milane par khud ki parody
Aur Exposure karate hai, mere CM Bhai!

Jan 25
@narendramodi We truly Admire
Your regime--it would shine in INDIA's
History like ASHOKA's of Maurya-Empire,
Despite Opposition's -ve ideas

Jan 25
@NASA Thanx to **@NASA_Hubble**
4 such stunning pictures of our universe:
We live NOT in dreamy trifle bubble,
But amidst rich starry treasures

Jan 25
@Swamy39, Now **@SoniaGandhiG**
Wishes **#BJP** claimed no heritage
From them, so she could claim she
And **@rahulgandhi2020**'s offered them patronage!

Jan 25
@StationCDRKelly @NASA @Space_Station
Even after Trips 2 Moon & Mars,
Pictures of Earth as 1 Home 4 Humanity places it, and
U, above Stars.

Jan 23
@Arvindkejriiwal You've no shame
In admitting your abject
Failure..& fighting with & blame
Everyone else..you should retire, at any rate.

www.ingramcontent.com/pod-product-compliance
Lightning Source LLC
Chambersburg PA
CBHW051227050326
40689CB00007B/829

* 9 7 8 1 5 1 4 4 5 5 5 0 0 *